LIVING WITH BAD SURROUNDINGS

The Cultures and Practice of Violence Series

Series Editors:

Neil L. Whitehead, University of Wisconsin, Madison

Jo Ellen Fair, University of Wisconsin, Madison

Leigh Payne, University of Wisconsin, Madison

The study of violence has often focused on the political and economic conditions under which violence is generated, the suffering of victims, and the psychology of its interpersonal dynamics. Less familiar are the role of perpetrators, their motivations, and the social conditions under which they are able to operate. In the context of postcolonial state building and more latterly the collapse and implosion of society, community violence, state repression, and the phenomena of judicial inquiries in the aftermath of civil conflict, there is a need to better comprehend the role of those who actually do the work of violence—torturers, assassins, and terrorists—as much as the role of those who suffer its consequences.

When atrocity and murder take place, they feed the world of the iconic imagination that transcends reality and its rational articulation; but in doing so imagination can bring further violent realities into being. This series encourages authors who build on traditional disciplines and break out of their constraints and boundaries, incorporating media and performance studies and literary and cultural studies as much as anthropology, sociology, and history.

LIVING WITH
BAD
SURROUNDINGS

War, History, and Everyday Moments in Northern Uganda

Sverker Finnström

Duke University Press   Durham and London   2008

© 2008 Duke University Press

All rights reserved

Printed in the United States of America
on acid-free paper ∞

Designed by Heather Hensley

Typeset in Minion Pro by Keystone Typesetting

Library of Congress Cataloging-in-Publication
Data appear on the last printed page of this book.

Huts will be rebuilt, and compounds cleared
And the mango trees will blossom with fruits . . .

CAROLINE LAMWAKA, IN MEMORIAM

CONTENTS

ACKNOWLEDGMENTS

"An anthropologist has usually called on the assistance, imposed on the patience, and trespassed on the hospitality of many by the time his work reaches print, and the least he can do," notes Dyson-Hudson (1966: ix) in his classic on the pastoralist politics of northeastern Uganda, "is to make some acknowledgement of the fact."

I, too, am indebted to so many people, first and foremost my family. They are now deeply involved with Uganda and my research efforts, to me an illustration of the true nature of anthropology; that is, to bring worlds together. My parents, Kerstin and Orvar Finnström, visited me in Uganda. And together with my siblings with families—Åsa, Leif, Sara, Hanna, Torkel, Birgitta, and Fabian—they have wholeheartedly welcomed Ugandan friends to Sweden. Most important and every day, Helena Edin gives me strength and peace, in Sweden, Uganda, and everywhere. Without her support and love this book would have been completely impossible.

My journey into anthropology started at the Department of Cultural Anthropology and Ethnology, Uppsala University. Per Brandström introduced me to anthropology and showed me what it could be. He nurtured my doubts and encouraged me to try my own thoughts. I have also profited greatly from friends, colleagues, and comembers of the department's Living Beyond Conflict Seminar. I especially want to mention Hugh Beach, who has been so supportive in my efforts to step out into academia's wider world.

In Uganda, numerous people assisted me in various ways. The late Caroline Lamwaka introduced me to Ugandan realities. Throughout the years Anthony (Tonny) Odiya Labol and Jimmy Otim p'Ojok have been my true partners in research, my best guides, interlocutors, and mentors, and vigilant readers of messy manuscripts that eventually became this book. I also want to thank Lucie Aculu, Apio Lucy Susan, Flora Atimango, Doreen Akech, Komakech Charles Okot, Lucy Lapoti, Rosalba Oywa, Dan Odiya, Dennis Okwar, Lagwe, Winnie Lawoko, Opio Wilbert, John Muto-Ono p'Lapur, Oola Richard, James A. A. Otto and his colleagues at the Human Rights Focus, Ladit Levy A. Arweny, Ladit Yusuf Adek, Ladit Obwoya John and Helena, Ladit Ngomlo-koco, Ladit Hilary Ochara, and Ladit Abic. In expressing my genuine thanks and appreciation to all these dear friends, I include also their families. I want too to thank Fabius Okumu and colleagues at Gulu University. Olof Otika Finnström, Adoch Kerstin, and Nathan Petum are just three of many resilient young friends who grow up in the shadows of war, who constantly give me hope for the future. Fellow Swedes Gisela Holmén Yngrot and Svante Yngrot gave me a standing invitation to their quiet home in Kampala, something that I have made shameful use of during some of my travels to and from northern Uganda.

Michael Jackson's sensitive anthropology has been an inspiration for me, a source that never goes dry. His friendship and perceptive comments have been no less essential sources of encouragement. In my efforts to understand Ugandan realities, I have borrowed and processed his existential-phenomenological concepts of the quest for control and balance in quotidian life as guides throughout the book. Continuous conversations with Ron Atkinson have been very motivating, and his comments fast, astute, and generous. Tim Allen has been equally supportive, a crucial guide to Ugandan ethnography but also to that of the print world.

In seminar rooms and at local pubs in Uppsala, Lars Hagborg has always been an essential interlocutor in anthropology and beyond. Likewise Mikael Kurkiala is an important friend and colleague, in contemplating life but also in engaging anthropology.

My Ph.D. research (1997–2003) was financed by the Ph.D. Candidates' Fund of Uppsala University, the Department of Research Cooperation of the Swedish

International Development Cooperation Agency, the Swedish Council for Research in the Humanities and Social Sciences, Olof Palme's Memorial Trust for International Understanding and Mutual Security, Lars Hierta's Memorial Trust, and Helge Ax:son Johnson's Trust. In my postdoctoral work (2005–2006), I was again generously supported by the Department of Research Cooperation, Swedish International Development Cooperation Agency, with additional funding from the Pontus Wikner Memorial Grant for Philosophical Research, Uppsala University. Research in Uganda was endorsed by the Uganda National Council for Science and Technology. I thank all these agencies for putting trust in my ideas.

This book has grown out of a much rougher text, my Ph.D. dissertation (2003, Acta Universitatis Upsaliensis/Uppsala University). Also, it partly brings together, restructures, and updates arguments that have appeared in briefer versions elsewhere—in the journals *Critique of Anthropology*, *Anthropology Today*, *Africa*, and in the anthologies *No peace no war* and *Navigating youth, generating adulthood*. I am sincerely grateful to the publishers for the permission to revisit, rethink, and rework my texts. In doing so, Neil Whitehead's continual encouragement has been indispensable. Valerie Millholland, Miriam Angress, the reviewers, and everyone else at Duke have been equally important to me.

I alone am answerable for the stories, interpretations, and conclusions that follow. Still, I want to end with some final words of appreciation for those who contributed to this book. Whatever may be good about this work is due in large part to Helena, Tonny, Otim p'Ojok, Caroline, and all those friends and colleagues who shared their realities with me, inspired me, encouraged me, and patiently worked with me along the journey. Thank you, all.

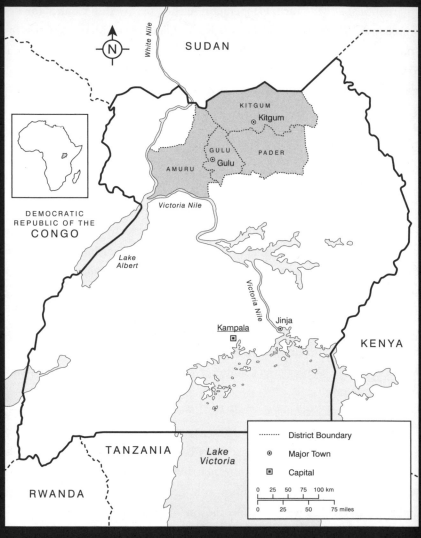

MAP 1 Districts in northern Uganda (Acholiland). Prepared by Jonatan Alvarsson.

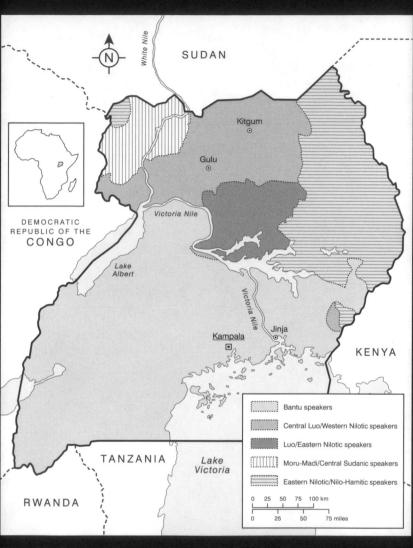

MAP 2 Ethnolinguistic groups in Uganda. Prepared by Jonatan Alvarsson.

WAR AND CULTURE IN UGANDA

BOO IS BITTER

Potentially every culture is all cultures.

PAUL FEYERABEND

One night in July 2000, around two in the morning, some noise woke Atek Mary as she was sleeping with her husband and baby child in their hut on the outskirts of Pagak camp for internally displaced persons and uprooted families in Acholiland, northern Uganda. It was totally dark outside. The light of a torch flashed around, then fixed on her face, blinding her. She realized that somebody had opened the small window of the hut. It must have been opened by force, as it usually was locked from inside. Scared and confused by the sudden flashlight and the noise, she still noticed that her husband, Olwor Reuben, and their baby son, Tekkwor, were asleep. Mary could hear some murmuring voices, and then, somebody pounding on the door. In a forceful voice, she was ordered to open the door. She refused to answer or open. The voice from outside repeated the order, and she could now detect several voices. At least three men were standing outside the hut.

Mary managed to wake her husband, only to hear again the agitated voices from outside demanding to have the door opened. Again, the harsh light from the torch flashed at them. Mary and

Reuben kept quiet and decided to refuse to open the door. Then the people outside threatened to throw a bomb into the window of the hut, if the door was not opened. The threat was repeated: "If you refuse now, we're going to hit you with a bomb!" Mary and Reuben again declined to answer the men outside, but they chose to raise an alarm, with the hope of alerting the soldiers in the nearby Ugandan army detachment. There was no response to the alarm. Then there was a sudden explosion. The blast threw Reuben against the back wall of the hut and threw both Mary and little Tekkwor aside. Mary and Reuben immediately lost consciousness.

After some time, impossible to know how long, Reuben regained consciousness. He realized that a grenade had gone off inside the hut. He felt a great pain, and his body was sticky with blood. One leg felt very heavy, and he could not turn around. Yet Reuben managed to crawl out of the hut, passing through the broken window, but he was weak and fell just outside. From there, he saw three men standing under the mango tree in the middle of the compound. Naked and confused, he escaped by crawling toward the nearby garden to hide.

Then the men must have disappeared as relatives rushed to the hut, alarmed by the heavy explosion. They broke down the door and found Mary, who was seriously injured. Tekkwor was also badly injured. However, the people could not find Reuben, and someone cried out, loudly, "Oh, they have killed Reuben." Hearing friendly voices announcing his alleged death, Reuben crawled with great pain back to the compound. The situation was assessed, and the injured were given some rudimentary first aid, but it was evident that they all needed to be transported to a hospital as soon as possible if they were to survive. In the meantime somebody managed to get a vehicle from Gulu town, and in the morning hours around seven o'clock Mary, Reuben, and Tekkwor were taken to St. Mary's Missionary Hospital just outside Gulu town. Their serious injuries forced them to remain in the hospital for several months.

In early December 2000, they were finally able to leave the hospital. Reuben still had splinters of metal in his body, and one of his legs was very seriously affected. He cannot walk long distances anymore, and he cannot dig in the gardens or do other heavy work. Both of Mary's legs were seriously injured, and one leg needed to be amputated. She is now walking with an artificial leg. Tekkwor had a big, nasty cut in the side of his body, around the hip, but besides the many scars and some shrapnel cuts, he seems to have survived without permanent internal injuries.

When the family returned to Pagak and the compound where Reuben's mother was still living, they received several threats from some young men. They also recalled a certain young man who had vaguely hinted a threat before the attack, that "something was about to happen." Reuben had been running a small business, and the men were expressing envy in a way that he felt was threatening. Reuben and Mary concluded that these young men belonged to the group who threw the bomb. Mary had even recognized the voice of one of the men during the attack, and thanks to her information, five men were arrested, though eventually released. It turned out that the men were *boo kec* bandits.

A security and juridical vacuum has followed the prolonged war in northern Uganda, and various bandits have seized the opportunity to harass, loot, and kill. *Boo* is a local spinach-like vegetable, while *kec* means bitter. The local epithet, then, indicates that boo kec bandits prefer to loot nice food such as meat at gunpoint, rather than to work in the gardens like honest people or live on poor man's food, that is, local vegetables. In Kitgum, east of Gulu, the same kind of wartime bandits are sometimes called *pit kumi*, "feeding the body."

Investigations proved that the boo kec bandits who tried to kill Reuben, Mary, and Tekkwor carried guns and grenades that were given to them by the commander of a Ugandan army detachment in another camp nearby. Some time before the violent attack on the family, seventy-five grenades had been found in the bush in a suspected rebel hideout. They were taken to Gulu town army barracks for registering, but some of them never reached the destination. Instead, a few grenades remained with the local army commander, and one was used in the attack on Reuben, Mary, and Tekkwor. When Reuben returned after his time at the hospital, there were persistent rumors that the bandits were still around, which increased Reuben's fear for his life. Reuben imagined that they wanted his money, which he had made in his small business, but he was also convinced that they wanted to kill him "straight away." In a similar night attack in a neighboring camp, a petty trader had been robbed and brutally killed. "Boo kec will always kill, because they do not want to be known," Reuben reasoned.

Boo kec and pit kumi are not rebels. Frequently they are connected with the Ugandan army, and many people in rural Acholiland fear bandits more than they fear rebels. "The rebels, at least, are open about their business, but if you encounter boo kec, never look them in the eyes," people frequently told me.

Reuben and Mary decided to move to the relative safety of Gulu town, leaving only Reuben's mother behind, as she refused to leave their rural place. After some serious discussions, Reuben and his friend Otim p'Ojok decided "not to push the case, since this would only invite more problems." The bandits were not charged, but could continue to harass people in the camp. The main suspect, however, left the area.

UNFINISHED REALITIES

This book explores the various ways Acholi people in northern Uganda struggle to establish control and balance in their daily lives in the midst of civil war, and how they construct meaning and understand the war as they live their humanity—always, however, in intersection with the wider global community. The Acholi homeland has been ravaged by war since 1986. The Uganda Peoples' Defence Forces (hereafter UPDF or the Ugandan army), commanded by General Yoweri Museveni, who is also the president of the country, is fighting the Lord's Resistance Army/Movement rebels.[1] Joseph Kony, a self-proclaimed general, fronts the Lord's Resistance Army/Movement, more commonly known simply as the Lord's Resistance Army (hereafter the LRA/M or simply the rebels).[2] In 2006, after several previous failures to find a settled solution, the semiautonomous government of Southern Sudan invited the fighting parties to new talks. In August the same year, the parties signed a historical but shaky cessation of hostilities agreement, mediated by the South Sudanese.

As guiding tools throughout the book, I will use the Acholi concepts of *piny marac* and *piny maber*, which I have chosen to translate as "bad surroundings" and "good surroundings" respectively. More specifically, *marac* refers to something that is very bad, *maber* to something good. *Piny* is usually translated by nouns like the "ground," "earth," "world," or more broadly the "surroundings of everyday life." *Piny* is part of the wider landscape; and landscape means existence, Cohen and Odhiambo (1989: 9) write. An old-time anthropologist like Evans-Pritchard (1965: 210) translated *piny* as "tribe," while Cohen and Odhiambo (1989: 31–35) elaborate and describe *piny* using terms like territory, people, country, and nation; for some people today it carries even the connotation of a "global motherland." As an adverb, *piny* indicates that something is on the ground (Savage 1955). This can be related to *ru-piny*, the word for dawn, "when the sun breaks through and drives away the cover of darkness and night," as p'Bitek (1971: 155) notes. Yet the daytime is also the period when humans face daily risks and sufferings as they expose themselves to their adversaries, and the ideal night, p'Bitek holds, is the time for rest and peace. "Even nature is at rest," p'Bitek (1971: 155) writes, adding that only antisocial beings such as witches are at work. In war-torn Uganda night is indeed ambivalent. The rebels, for example, most often attack during the dark hours, as did the bandits who assaulted Reuben, Mary, and Tekkwor.

An example may illustrate my orientations. Former rebel fighters testified to me that the rebel command sometimes claims that it wants to establish a new moral order, with the objective of breaking with the violent postcolonial history of Uganda (see also Behrend 1998a; 1999b). From the rebels' perspective, I suggest, the claim to a new moral order provides them with the legitimacy to abduct children to their ranks. The children, cynically speaking, are suitable targets to be initiated into this new order. The claim has also provided the rebels with the motivation to mutilate or even kill people, notably old men and women, who practice ancestral worship or otherwise promote the existing Acholi cosmological order.

Arthur, a former rebel religious functionary or a so-called controller, told me about the strategy of the early 1990s, when he was with the rebels. He was then about eighteen years old. At one point, Arthur had been engaged in destroying ancestor shrines in the Koch area, south of Gulu town. Elders and spirit mediums were also killed. However, some of the shrines in the area were so powerful, Arthur told me, that it was almost impossible to burn them down. In one case, his rebel unit tried for three days, but they finally sent for Joseph Kony, the rebel leader, who came and set the shrines on fire. "It was easily done for him," Arthur said about Kony. "He is a man with the spirit. He has it." Today many rural people have let the shrines fall into neglect and decay. Shrines were allowed to become dilapidated also in peacetime, eventually to be put in order when they were needed, notably when sacrifices were to be made (Malandra 1939). In these days of war and great unrest, however, people sometimes even actively destroy the shrines in an effort to avoid rebel reprisals. Others allow the bush to grow over and hide the shrines. On an existential level, I suggest, people in the war-torn region experience a lessened control over ontological security in everyday life (see Giddens 1991; Jackson 1998), and to destroy or hide the shrines is an immediate response to the difficult situation.

I also encountered efforts to resist the rebels' violent pattern of destruction. Ladit Abic and his family used to live in Patiko-Bongatira, a few miles outside

Gulu town (in Acholi, *ladit*, plural: *ludito*, is the address of respect given to elderly men, or men who are senior to you). Both rebels and Ugandan army personnel tend to frequent and pass through the area. In March 1995, the rebels abducted one son of the family. A second son was abducted in April 1998. So far, only the second son has returned. He escaped from the rebels in February 2000 but did not return to the family in Patiko-Bongatira, as he feared being abducted again. According to unconfirmed information that Abic has gathered, his other son is still alive, by now fully integrated into the rebel movement. This son was once wounded in battle but recovered, a person told Abic. Some persistent rumors, however, say that he died in battle.

The family's compound was a wonder of normality. I noted that the ancestral shrine was prominent in the compound, and indeed well kept, like the rest of the compound. A central feature of the shrine was a grinding stone, so much used over the years that it had a big hole in it. The stone, Abic told me, "represented the first granny of the clan." The compound also housed supplementary shrines for spirits not specific to the clan, but that have been erected when problems in everyday life, notably illness and health problems, are coped with. Impressed with the neat compound, which extended both in space and time, including both living and dead, I asked Abic if he did not fear that the rebels would disturb him. "That one, we leave it to God," he answered calmly. "In this world, everything is up to God."

To interpret Abic's stand as fatalistic misses an important point. Rather, as I will elaborate in this book, his stand can be understood in terms of lived and existential realism. "Realism," as the philosopher Merleau-Ponty (1964a: 32) has cautioned us, is a term perhaps too burdened under the yoke of various philosophical doctrines, but my only intention is to acknowledge, as Abic does when he reflects upon his predicament in life, that we are always tied to history and the wider world. For Abic and his family, in the context of war and increasing violence, which were seemingly senseless developments, it was most meaningful to keep the relationship with the spiritual and greater world active. To actively attend to these relations, which I suggest is about orientation in life, exemplifies the existential effort to cope with the difficult situation, ultimately in order to be able to govern it. Culturally, socially, and bodily informed practices, inescapably entangled, are the main means through which war and its effects are interpreted and acted upon, something that sustains the experience of war, making it and its multiple forms of violence routines among other routines in everyday life (e.g., Kleinman 2000). Parallel to this, however, informants expressed distress about the fixation of meaning to a limited set of cultural and ethnic stereotypes that propaganda of war and chauvinistic politics impose upon the local social realities and the national order of things.

This book paints a broad but specific ethnographical, sociopolitical, and historical background to the existential struggles of today in Acholiland. I will balance my reading of the literature on Uganda, in the first place, against my informants' stories of a colonial past followed by a postcolonial debacle with interrelated wars, and, following that, against their stories of politics, propaganda, and pragmatics of war, and the fact of their internal mass displacement. This is the organizational progress of the book, chapter by chapter, which I continue by investigating the role of rumors, religion, morality, and cosmology in times of war. Cosmology I want to define as everyday but infinite surroundings. With this broad focus, it will not be possible for me to present any conclusive or final answers to the questions that my study raises. This is partly a consequence of my understanding of culture as both a resource and a constraint in human activities. It is situational, neither total nor final, and more about existential orientation than anything else, and activated by "the drive to experience the world as meaningful," the most prominent of human universals (Hornborg 2001: 237). This is nothing new or original; rather, my stance adheres to the current and widespread anthropological understanding of culture. As Merleau-Ponty (1962: xix) puts it in his investigation of what he calls the existential structures, "Because we are in the world, we are *condemned to meaning*, and we cannot do or say anything without its acquiring a name in history."

The word "meaningful," as I want to use it, when applied to people's experience of the world, simply indicates that a phenomenon is situational and can be made comprehensible and comparable with other phenomena, and that people who live together articulate and mediate experiences and stories among one another in a patterning and systematic manner (Århem 1994: 19–24). To find common ground is a principal concern in cultural life everywhere in the world. One voice finds recognition in other voices, to paraphrase Das and Kleinman (2001: 5). This is not to say that the meaning is once and for all given. However, as illustrated by Ladit Abic's account, to keep the ancestral shrines in order in the midst of war can be a most meaningful activity. When I met him in 2006, he had finally left Patiko-Bongatira. The

Ugandan army appeared on almost a weekly basis to harass him and rob the few resources he and his wives had tried to raise, which made life next to impossible. "The surroundings are bad," as my Acholi friends so often phrased it. With this in mind, a general and complementary aim of this book is to stimulate understandings that acknowledge the great lived everyday complexity of a war zone, a complexity that nevertheless tends to be obscured by the black-and-white propaganda that war and armed conflict produce.

THE GROWING MILLET UNDER THE AFRICAN SUN

History, belonging, and politics are all issues of contention. It is indeed difficult to write about and intellectualize bitter conflicts. The causes and consequences of the war in northern Uganda, the reasons for it, and facts about it—they all differ, depending on whom you are listening to. There is no one version that is fully agreed upon by all parties involved. Perhaps this is a truism to many readers, but it is still important to emphasize because contemporary conflict analyses often tend to emphasize single causes for war in ways that are reductionist. Regarding war in Africa, ethnicity is most often invoked as one such single cause. Consequently, African realities are reduced to little more than the antithesis to the order of Western civilization, which on the other hand is taken for granted as modern and civilized (Allen 1999; Richards 1996). An otherwise well-researched report of the plight of young people in war-torn Acholiland is illustrative, in its sketchy description of the cause or even root of the conflict: "The current conflict in northern Uganda has its roots in ethnic mistrust between the Acholi people and the ethnic groups of central and southern Uganda as well as in the religious and spiritual beliefs of the Acholi people and the manipulation of these beliefs" (Women's Commission for Refugee Women and Children 2001: 81). The quotation mentions aspects that play a role in the conflict but are not necessarily its roots or even central cause. This reductionist image of the war and its causes, only too common in the understanding of conflicts in Africa, must be taken with great caution.

In most wars, propaganda and harsh words almost completely close the avenues of dialogue and mutual understanding. Turmoil and mistrust prevail, and almost every matter, even the more conventional aspects of anthropological research, can become very sensitive. During some periods, the rebels keep a low profile and their attacks are few, and consequently the Ugandan authorities relax, being cooperative and friendly even to the outside researcher. During other periods, the rebels are very active, and in the Ugandan counterinsurgency practices almost everyone can be regarded as an enemy collaborator, including the researcher. Sometimes the rebels create havoc; killings, rapes of women, and other forms of wanton violence have been rampant. Over the years, several thousands of children have been abducted and forced to join rebel ranks (see, e.g., Amnesty International 1997; 1999; Human Rights Watch 1997; 2003a).[3]

The war is indeed a global war even if fought on local grounds. For some two decades, it has rolled back and forth, like the changes from rainy season to dry season and back to rainy season. The massive influx of international humanitarian aid has ended up being deeply entangled with the realities on the ground. The U.S. government included the LRA/M on its post-9/11 list of global terrorist groups when the Ugandan government joined the global war on terror. Rebel leader Joseph Kony and four other commanders, one of whom has since died in action, are wanted by the International Criminal Court in The Hague.

During some periods the rebels are disciplined and seek local support, more like fish in the water, to recall Mao Zedong's famous dictum on the guerrilla fighters' absolute need of local support to survive. In such periods, the repressive measures of the Ugandan authorities increase (e.g., Human Rights Watch 1999). In January 2003, the magistrate's court in Gulu town reported that two boys aged fourteen and sixteen who returned home from rebel captivity were charged with treason, and that twenty-five more minors were being held in military custody without charges, under pressure to join the Ugandan army or face treason charges (Gulu Archdiocese 2003a; Human Rights Watch 2003b). The justice system became one of the first institutions to suffer from the war, and most cases of rebel as well as Ugandan military abuse of the civil population have not been addressed (African Rights 2000).

Against this background, it has been necessary for me sometimes to change dates and the names of places and people in order not to disclose my informants' identities. At times, other details are altered as well. Sadly, the situation does not allow me to acknowledge properly the great input of my interlocutors and coworkers in the field. The reader will note that I frequently refer to statements of rather anonymous "informants," something that is necessary in the effort to protect their identities. However, when Ugandan friends read some of my texts that I brought back to them, many soon located their stories in the texts, sometimes nodded in agreement with my interpretations, and even revised or elaborated upon them. In such moments anthropology felt like just the right thing to be doing. Where I had used pseudonyms, some insisted on having their real names and real places given in my writings, which they claimed gave authenticity to the stories in the book. As my Ugandan friend and coworker Anthony (Tonny) Odiya Labol argued with reference to an Acholi proverb, "The growing millet does not fear the sun" (*bel ka otwi pe lworo ceng*). More often than anthropologists tend to admit, informants want to be remembered for what they have said and contributed. Any secret agent will be disappointed, however, as this book does not present anything that is not common knowledge among most people in northern Uganda. Disclosing new information has not been my ambition. Anthropology, as I have chosen to practice it, is about painstakingly investigating and analyzing the common, general, mainstream, and even taken-for-granted stuff of everyday life in a particular context, rather than the seemingly subversive and revolutionary.

THINK ABOUT TOMORROW

In war-torn Acholiland, young men and women, whose situation was the main focus in my investigations, struggle to find balance in life, "a sense of agency in the face of disempowering circumstances" (Jackson 2002b: 15). Indeed, young people (and, of course, other people) live under conditions that they frequently described as "bad surroundings" (*piny marac*). This is true when armed fighting is intense, but it is also true in periods of lull, when the war, at least on the surface, seems to be far away. The attack on Reuben, Mary, and Tekkwor happened during a period of lull in the fighting. Maybe it was a period of no war, but certainly it was not a period of peace. At the same time, I was repeatedly struck by the younger generation's unconditional struggle for a comprehensible life in the midst of war and displacement. As these young people aimed to establish themselves as adult individuals in Uganda, they also struggled for some measure of security in their lives. Ultimately, on a larger, collective scale, they struggled for "good surroundings" (*piny maber*), for individual lives in balance with the greater scheme of things, persons, relatives, ancestors, and God. The young Acholi did not passively wait for future solutions; rather, in everyday life they built for a future despite displacement and social unrest. Good surroundings, Acholi held, are not primarily to accumulate wealth or riches but rather to live under endurable conditions, in which future wealth can be imagined, even planned for. Growing herds of cattle and young people who marry are the ultimate signs of good surroundings, older people would say. Democracy and the possibility of higher education is another, younger people would add.

It was my coworker Otim p'Ojok who introduced me to his clan brother and friend Reuben and his family in Pagak. As is the case with internal displacement all over Acholiland, the Pagak camp had grown rapidly around the local trading center, as the Ugandan army had forced rural people to assemble in camps, often at gunpoint. Reuben's connections to the land in Pagak, however, preceded the war. By the time of my visits, their home had become fully integrated into the surrounding displacement setting, and Reuben allowed some displaced people to stay on his private land. The family had managed to keep some agricultural areas just next to the house, making it an unusual compound in the many overcrowded camps in Acholiland. When I first visited the place, I immediately came to like it very much. It was a neat compound, centered on a family with their children and some elderly relatives. I encountered the typical Acholi hospitality in abundance, and I felt genuinely welcomed every time I came there. I made sure not to leave without arranging for my next visit.

Acholi say that the visitor brings satisfaction (*welo, kelo, yengo*) to the home—nice food that would otherwise have been kept for the future is prepared and shared. Maybe a chicken is slaughtered, or even a goat. Indeed, in Reuben's compound I was invited to share some of the nicest meals and discussions I ever had during my fieldwork. I was impressed by the young family's struggle for normality in midst of war. Reuben had raised by himself the wealth necessary to marry his two wives. Besides tilling the soil, he had started a small-scale business in the camp. On top of that, Reuben and a few friends in the camp had initiated a soccer club. The club had a wider agenda than just playing soccer. Rather, the football was the carrot in the recruitment of idle children to the club, which also practiced agriculture and promoted Acholi values. They had named their club Tam Pi Diki, "Think About Tomorrow."

DIRTY WAR AND BAD SURROUNDINGS

As I see it, the two concepts of good surroundings and bad surroundings are not absolute categories. Rather they represent quotidian moments along a lived and at times very uncertain continuum. Peaceful life can be infested with conflicts and frustrations, but in the peaceful order of things, problems are handled, strategies beyond mere survival are developed, life is continuously constituted and reconstituted. Uncertainty is handled.

The alleged absence of war and military violence does not equal peace. Rather, as a man in Kitgum told me in late 1999, "The silence of guns does not mean peace." Illustratively, some few days after our meeting, war resumed after a relative lull of almost a year in the fighting, when rebels launched new attacks. Intermissions in fighting gave people some hope for the future, but this hope faded repeatedly each time fighting resumed. Continued stress and existential uncertainty about the near future were central aspects of every-day life.

The fact that fighting resumes repeatedly after shorter or longer periods without serious battles, confirmed my informants' claim that that the war has not come to a closure. Even when rebels withdraw to their bases in Sudan and the Democratic Republic of Congo, the fact that they have withdrawn to base is also a fact of war. As long as rebel leader Joseph Kony is somewhere with his fighters, so experience told my informants, one could never really tell what will happen next. The only thing one can know for sure is that war is not over. Sudden lulls over the years have given the population breathing space but no peace in life, and no peace of mind. When I arrived for fieldwork in mid-2002, I had been away from Uganda for exactly two years, during which the rebels had kept a very low profile. If we follow the statistics of the so-called battle-related deaths, there was no war during these two years. Again, it was during this period that the home of Reuben, Mary, and Tekkwor was attacked by bandits connected to the Ugandan army. Rather than an isolated incident, the attack must be read as an event; that is, as a story among many similar stories that, when listened to, unfolds a violent pattern of dirty war in the most mundane everyday life. Ladit Abic's flight from Patiko-Bongatira after so many years there was another such event.

During my fieldwork in 2005, the Ugandan army was declaring the war over. Only a "few mopping-up operations" remained. They had said so many times before, but this time most foreign diplomats and Western observers bought into the government's description of the state of affairs. At the same time, the mortality rate in the camps reached unprecedented levels. About one thousand Ugandans died every week, the overwhelming majority of curable diseases and malnutrition (World Health Organization et al. 2005). Battle-related statistics can only be tentative, as it is almost impossible to establish battle-related or combat-related casualty rates (Allen 1999). Even more, what exactly is a battle-related death? As it often is in civil wars today, the majority of people will not die in direct military violence, but as a result of malnutrition and illness and in the aftermath of uprooting, displacement, and forced camp life (James 1996).

In questioning the commonly made distinction between low-intensity and high-intensity wars, Munck and de Silva (2000) label today's wars "postmodern insurgencies." Kaldor (1999a) writes about "new wars." Nordstrom (1992) calls them "dirty wars." I will follow Nordstrom, because to me "dirty war" sounds less detached, less academic, more close to the lived realities. In dirty wars, Nordstrom writes, "both states and guerrilla forces use the construction of terror and the absurd as a mechanism for gaining or maintaining sociopolitical control over a population." In such a warfare strategy, "civilians, rather than soldiers, are the tactical targets, and fear, brutality, and murder are the foundation on which control is constructed" (Nordstrom 1992: 261). She has also called this kind of war "terror warfare," which "focuses less on killing the physical body than on terrifying the population as a whole into, the military strategists hope, cowed acquiescence. Strategic murder, torture, community destruction, sexual abuse, and starvation become the prime weapons in the arsenal of terror warfare" (Nordstrom 2002: 275–276). The war is without any clear distinctions between combatants and noncombatants or easily defined frontlines (see also Fukui and Markakis 1994: 3; Munck 2000).

Without conclusively defining war or even peace, I hold that the Acholi have been living with war since 1986. War and "negative peace," the latter here understood as the temporary absence of acts of violence, are essentially the same. They form variables along a lived continuum. Acholi informants frequently said that they were living with "bad surroundings" (piny marac). The alternative, "good surroundings" (piny maber), is when "hunting will be successful, evil spirits will be deterred from entering their villages, sickness may be unknown among the inhabitants, women may not be barren, their children will enjoy health and happiness and their crops will be abundant," as the missionary Malandra (1939: 27) wrote, from a position influenced by the colonial effort of pacification. However, good surroundings are neither an absolute opposite to bad surroundings nor the glorious tradition of static harmony, long and forever lost. The late anthropologist and poet Okot p'Bitek nuances the colonial imagination of static and uncontested harmony among the Acholi, and of the bad as the essential opposite to the good. Good surroundings, he writes, are "when things are normal, the society thriving, *facing and overcoming crises*" (p'Bitek 1986: 27, emphasis added).

Following p'Bitek the poet, rather than Malandra the missionary, the idea of bad and good as ends along a lived continuum captures my informants' imagination and conceptualization of a good life, but still as imagined under living conditions best described as bad. Even if the surroundings are good, bad things will happen, and they have to be handled. Equally, in war, too, people face and overcome crises in everyday life. Yet even for those who cope, resist or join the conflict in one way or the other, the wider surroundings remain seriously bad. Again to quote p'Bitek (1986: 27), bad surroundings speak to the fact that "the whole thing is out of hand, that the entire apparatus of the culture cannot cope with the menace any more." In other words, the violent conflict is beyond immediate control. Sickness is abundant, children are malnourished, cattle are gone, crops fail, bad spirits roam the surroundings, and people are killed or die at an early age and in large numbers.

CONTROL AND BALANCE IN EVERYDAY LIFE

Life does go on in the midst of war. The description of the situation as one primarily of bad surroundings should not be interpreted as if the local population or its culture is doomed to ruin. Rather, as Jackson finds in his existential-phenomenological anthropology, there is still some use for the terms "control" and "balance." "Control," Jackson (1998: 18) writes, "connotes governance and adjustment between self and other rather than the maintenance of a fixed line, the imposition of one person's will, or the establishment of a rigid order. As such it involves both self-reflection *and* dialogue. It is a matter of balancing, of dynamic equilibrium." As Jackson suggests, control involves an existential search for balance in everyday life. He continues, "But by *balance* I do not mean static equilibrium, harmony, or homeostasis. I mean to imply an ongoing dialectic in which persons vie and strategize in order to avoid nullification as well as to achieve some sense of governing their own fate" (Jackson 1998: 18–19). When the surroundings are good, crises and problems of everyday life can be overcome.

Some time after returning to Sweden after my second period of fieldwork in 1999–2000, I received the sad news from Gulu about the attack on Reuben,

Mary, and Tekkwor. "The incident has demoralised us very much," my friend Otim p'Ojok concluded in the faxed message that waited for me at the Department of Anthropology in Uppsala one morning when I arrived for work.

Their struggle continued. After some months in the hospital, the family decided to leave Pagak camp for Gulu town, to leave death threats for the relative security of an urban milieu. In January 2002, a new letter informed me that Otim p'Ojok and Reuben had started a small-scale but rather successful business in Gulu town. Some savings and the profit from the shop paid the hospital bills and continued to assist them in supporting their families. I cannot help recalling the name that these young men had once given the soccer club in Pagak camp. The soccer club could no longer function, but its name, "Think About Tomorrow," as I found out when I arrived in Uganda later on in 2002, was painted on the signpost of their small-scale town business. Sometimes, when a male customer in the store ended up buying only beers or the locally distilled liquor, these friendly shopkeepers would simply refuse to sell more alcohol and instead suggest that their customer save some money for soap and other necessities that the customer's family would need. Think about tomorrow, they carefully told their drunken customers.

BARRIERS AND BRIDGES

In essence, if there is such a thing, I am a European, non-African, or rather a foreigner, even a stranger, to Acholiland. *Muno*, as Acholi say. Obviously, my looks resembled those of the expatriate relief and aid workers, development volunteers on short-term or long-term assignments, or the journalists and foreign ambassadors who briefly visit war-torn Acholiland. In practice, I did my best to acknowledge the hospitality offered by my informants. I always ate their food, drank their water, wine, and beers. *Lawake*, Acholi call persons who do the opposite with a proud and bossy attitude. "Like a *muno* [foreigner] who refuses to eat what is offered; who doesn't mingle with locals," as an old man explained. I participated in my informants' reconciliation and cleansing rituals, and I went to their baptisms and funerals. I constantly and eagerly listened to my informants' stories. I especially remember one senior ex-rebel who talked without a single break for more than five hours, as I was seated in an uncomfortable chair doing my best to write down everything he was saying. It was totally fascinating, but my buttocks and my back ached and my writing arm was cramping when we finally decided to call it a day.

Fieldwork was divided into five phases. I arrived for the first time in 1997 and stayed for about three months. Then I came back for seven months of fieldwork in 1999. In March 2000, my parents, Kerstin and Orvar Finnström, visited me in the field for two intense weeks. It was a great experience for my parents and me, as well as for my Acholi friends. I returned to Uganda in 2002 for two more months. This time I traveled together with my fiancée, Helena Edin, who, just like my parents, has taken a keen interest in my strange choice to extend my academic career to a faraway and troubled place in Africa. In 2004, Tonny visited my family in Sweden as we continued our research, now far from the immediate realities in Uganda. Since then I have returned to Uganda in 2005 and 2006; in 2005 Helena joined me for my third Christmas in Gulu. In 2006, Otim p'Ojok visited Sweden. We toured Sweden as we visited friends and family, but we also revisited our Ugandan research material. It is good to have been able to share my Ugandan encounters with my family, and Swedish realities with two of my best Ugandan friends. Indeed, my family is now extended over continents and imagined borders, and I value the friendships that have been built up between Uganda and Sweden.

I remain, however, an outsider, a visitor, to Acholiland. I cannot claim any essential connection to Uganda. Abu-Lughod notes that her status as a "halfie" (of Palestinian origin on the paternal side, but raised in the United States; see Abu-Lughod 1986; 1993: 39) or "insider" (Abu-Lughod 1989: 270) was both a door opener and a constraint in her fieldwork among Bedouins in Egypt. She has written two finely tuned and most insightful ethnographies that have been of great inspiration to me. She acknowledges that ethnographic accounts written by insiders must be subjected to the same kind of scrutiny as those written by outsiders (Abu-Lughod 1989: 270). Yet on a theoretical and general level, I remain not fully convinced of the insider or halfie claim of methodological superiority, or about the promotion of anthropology "at home" in such terms, which is now and then emphasized in the project of legitimating anthropology in a postcolonial world (e.g., Sichone 2001). At the end of the day, regardless of our respective backgrounds, it is ethnographic fieldwork that puts anthropology on firm empirical ground.

FIELDWORK ENGAGEMENT

Engagement rather than simple empathy has guided me in the encounters with my interlocutors in Uganda. I hold that the divergent experiences of the anthropologist and of her or his assistants and informants can fruitfully be communicated through an intercultural understanding of the phenomena under study, in my case the armed conflict, and its many implications for everyday life. Such intersubjective communication can provide a framework for dealing with the uncertainties of research in war, without however reducing intersubjectivity, as Jackson importantly emphasizes, to a romantic idea, built on the researcher's naïveté, of shared experience and blended worldviews between anthropologist and informants, of "empathic understanding or fellow-feeling" (Jackson 1998: 4). Such naïveté, says Matthews (2002: 39), can take the form, for example, of the social scientist's explicit claim to be "reliving the experiences of the human beings who were being studied . . . as a way of grasping their unique significance for the human being in question." But rather than emphasizing the *sharing* and *blending* of experiences, as has been increasingly in vogue in the growing bulk of ethnography of war, violence, and fear, I aim to follow Jackson, who stresses the dimension of *interexperience* when it comes to intersubjectivity. Interexperience and intersubjectivity, he holds, are "the ways in which selfhood emerges and is negotiated in a field of interpersonal relations, as a mode of being in the world" (Jackson 1998: 28). Therefore, I refute any methodological claim to having *suffered with* my informants. As an anthropologist from Sweden, I remained at all times in a very privileged position, with my return ticket in my back pocket, so to speak. For me, social security was a journey away, in reach in a matter of less than twenty-four hours. For my Ugandan interlocutors, this was never the case. To claim anything else, I strongly feel, would decontextualize and belittle, perhaps even caricature, the sufferings, pains, and sorrows of my informants.

During my fieldwork in early 2000, rebels were occasionally sneaking into Gulu town during the hours of dark. The conflict again escalated. As was the case a few years earlier, shooting woke people up in the middle of the night. At that time, I was staying in a small room in a town compound, which, besides me, housed three families and three shops facing the street. Most mornings, when my coworker Tonny came to my place for a cup of coffee and some final planning of the coming day's work, he had already gathered information about rebel presence in the near surroundings of Gulu town, or about ambushes along the rural roads. We tried to gather as much information as possible before we allowed ourselves to travel with our small secondhand motorbike to the camps or elsewhere. From my end, I had tried to do the same, but most often less successfully than Tonny. Essentially, if we had heard shooting during the previous night, we tried to orient ourselves about it. During these coffee breaks, we constantly revised our programs and tried to refine our methods. The numerous skilled bicycle mechanics along rural roads became our main sources of information regarding rebel movements. Their customers had often traveled far, and the mechanics' stands became the natural points where information was shared.

As time went by, and as my stay in the war zone made dangers somewhat less surreal, it became important to handle my own anxiety in order to carry out fieldwork as planned. Heike Behrend, an anthropologist who completed her research in Gulu a few years before my arrival, writes that researchers can always rely on their methodology as "a favoured means of reducing anxiety" (Behrend 1999a: 8). Through discussions of how to go about collecting our data, or about the gaps that needed to be filled in our material, and through the extensive traveling we did together, Tonny and I became very close. His claim that I was his junior clan brother felt genuine and was important to me. And my ambition to include him in the scholarly intersubjectivity was genuine. After all, as Behrend (1999a: 8) puts it, "one is not taking the path alone."

To have a sense of control, fictive or real, eased my mind and I imagine also my Ugandan coworkers' minds. Hard work from early morning to late afternoon gave us less time for brooding about what could possibly happen if everything went totally wrong. Still, in the end the only thing to do was to put our destinies "in the hands of God," as Tonny put it. Or, as he sometimes also put it, "We cannot but follow the way of the world." Even though skeptical when it comes to God's involvement in my personal life, I neither agreed to nor contested his touch of fatalism, or better, lived realism against the background of the wider and indefinite world. Like many of my Ugandan friends, Tonny actively acknowledged that uncertainties, difficulties, and suffering are parts of life. "He is a philosopher and knows that in life the ill must be taken with the good," to borrow some words from Evans-Pritchard's masterpiece on the Azande in neighboring Sudan (1937: 87; see also Jackson 1989: 99).

The knowledge of Acholi cosmology that Tonny, Otim p'Ojok, and other Ugandan friends offered me, paired with my anthropological passion to orient myself toward this cosmology, was of a certain therapeutic value. They guided me to see the world as it revealed itself in ways unfamiliar to me. Some of my own worries were given a new and comprehensible context. As a sidetrack perhaps, this book attempts to illustrate that the sharing of divergent experiences between anthropologist and informants, this intercultural process of shared existential orientations, might bolster psychological endurance during fieldwork in violent settings. As a complement to the more conventional contextualization of the research focus in historical, cultural, and sociopolitical terms, the sharing of experiences also works as a tool of intersubjectivity in the endeavor to represent and demystify the other, the unknown.

This is perhaps not very new. It is only another application of the old anthropological emphasis on participant observation, which, nevertheless, needs to be reconstrued in the context of war and violent conflict. Of course, to remain a neutral and cool observer is impossible. Again, this is nothing new to the social sciences, but it should be acknowledged. Perhaps the issue of nonneutrality (or political bias) surfaces more dramatically in a politically volatile milieu than elsewhere. It was not possible for me to conduct much traditional anthropological fieldwork. To stay any longer with a single family and its extension, with the ambition to follow carefully conventional strategies of subsistence and social networking, or to do an extended case study, was not possible. To stay in any rural setting was not advisable. Instead, I rented a room in Gulu town, the district headquarters of Gulu district. The town has more than 140,000 inhabitants, an increase of at least 100,000 since the beginning of the war. I would not describe it as a big town, but even so, it is still packed with various social services and military facilities. It now also has a small university, and is thus a kind of regional center for northern Uganda.

The Swedish anthropologist Kaj Århem (1994) describes the data collection of anthropologists as "participant reflection" rather than "participant observation." As anthropologists, we do our best to participate in the works, questions, joys, and sorrows of our informants' everyday life. Then we take a few steps back, to be able to reflect upon what we have learnt and experienced, again to step forward and participate. This we do daily in the fieldwork encounter. But I was also able to step back more profoundly both in time and space, as I divided my fieldwork into phases, spending the periods in between in Sweden, reading, writing, and trying to figure out the next step. Of course, to divide the fieldwork into multiple phases was also a necessity, as funding for the complete project could be acquired only in phases. Methodologically, however, for me it was an advantage to be able to participate and then to step back and seriously reflect, bearing in mind Århem's concept of participant reflection. Ideally, in the anthropological enterprise the interlocutors are final judges, and, more, coworkers (even cowriters) in the final textual representation of their lived realities. Because I divided my fieldwork into several periods, I was able to travel to Uganda with proposals, working papers, preliminary texts, and articles in my luggage. Over the years, several Ugandan friends have read and scrutinized every page of this book. My coworkers Tonny Odiya-Labol and Otim p'Ojok even took the time to travel around with draft chapters to consult people and cross-check the stories as they eventually turned out on paper. Their suggestions and corrections have been invaluable.

CONVERSATIONS IN THE FIELD

The views, feelings, and stories mediated by informants are important sources of data for the anthropologist, and these mediations will logically bias the final ethnography. Perhaps more today than ever, this is positive. "In a world where the powerful military-industrial centers of things do most of the talking, it is altogether appropriate that the peripheries should have their turn through the work of anthropology. That those voices should be heard is a fundamental anthropological task," writes Fernandez (1985: 26). For this endeavor to be successful, he notes, anthropology must "emphasize the other as an 'I' talking and we ourselves as a 'you' listening."

To pause in fieldwork for intermissions in Sweden allowed me to step back and rethink the stories from the field and reorient myself, something that was important in the effort to establish a proper critical distance to the material that I collected or read in books. In conceptualizing this aspect of the research, the hermeneutical approach of the philosopher Paul Ricoeur (1991) has been an inspiration to me. He advocates the necessity of a distancing movement (or a movement of *distanciation*) in the intersubjective and interpretative endeavor, which opens up the possibility not only of scientifically following and recording the stories that are narrated, but also of critically representing or retelling these stories. Understanding, from this perspective, can be the non-systematic or sometimes uncontrollable, even nonmethodological, moment that combines with the methodological moment of explanation. Understanding "precedes, accompanies, concludes, and thus *envelops* explanation," Ricoeur (1991: 142) argues, and explanation, in turn, "*develops* understanding analytically." He elaborates: "Whereas explanation appeared to do violence to understanding taken as the immediate grasp of the intentions of others, it naturally serves to extend understanding taken as the competence to follow a narrative. For a narrative is seldom self-explanatory" (Ricoeur 1991: 142). In this sense of the word, explanation is an understanding developed through questions and answers. The former conditions the latter and vice versa. When matters are not immediately understood, explanation enables better understanding, which is a kind of reciprocal relation. A narrative contains a wider story, perhaps a punch line, some cautionary suggestions, or an existential query, that the narrator wants to mediate to his or her listeners. "Narration alone is inadequate" (*aboka lam*), declares an Acholi proverb. Say that somebody experienced something, and that she or he now wants to narrate the experience to others who were not present when it happened. But alas! Aboka lam! Narration alone is not enough. In the effort to bridge this gap, a reciprocal explanation must follow the narrative, Ricoeur suggests. The story remains to be negotiated through dialogue and contextualization. Meaning emerges in social situations, which include also the visiting anthropologist, and middle ways can hereby be accepted.

Again, participant reflection rather than participant observation has guided me in my anthropological endeavor. There is a place just outside Gulu town that I used to visit frequently. I have many friends there, but my favorite informant is an old man, Jackson Okech, who told me so many stories about life in Acholiland and the difficulties of unrest and war. During these sessions, most often we were seated under the shade of a mango tree in the center of Okech's compound. Some of these sessions were typical anthropological situations, I believe. We were relaxed, enjoyed a good time sharing a glass of *gulugulu*, the liquor that the neighborhood's women distil and sell, planning where to build my hut someday in the peaceful future, and talking about ancestors, clan systems, and other matters that concern elderly people and anthropologists. After one such session, in the late afternoon I walked back to my room in Gulu town. During the following night, some thirty heavily armed rebels arrived at the place I had left. They looted and abducted people. They roamed around for several hours but left when it still was dark.

In the days that followed immediately after, I was engaged elsewhere, but less than a week later, I walked back to Okech's place to get information about the attack but also to learn more about Acholi traditions and customs. The routines of everyday life had returned; war seemed far away. To conduct research in a setting where memories and experiences of war are vividly and continuously reactivated in everyday life can sometimes be quite unreal. For me, the external and temporary observer, stories and narratives of lived experiences could appear fictitious against the background of the nice breeze under the shade of a mango tree. A helicopter gunship bombing a forest some kilometers away added to the strange experience. Of course, it became crucial for me to recognize that it was not the stories that I listened to that were fictitious, but rather any conclusion that I as an anthropologist essentially shared the experiences and biographies these stories mediated. My job as an anthropologist is not to absorb the stories of my informants as mine, or to impose uncritically my stories upon them. It is about their familiarity with the world, not mine. Perhaps the contrasting feeling of the friendly breeze under the mango tree assisted me in acknowledging this important feature of the anthropological encounter as I have chosen to practice it.

I had been to Okech's place a few times when he told his fellow villagers the following story. "You see," he is reported to have said, "this young man who comes here to ask questions about our clan and the ancestral tree, he is seeking his roots. That is why he asks all these questions." He continued his story, "But that is not very strange. In the late 1960s, I was in London and I happened to meet a lovely English lady. Olobo [the Acholi version of Olof, one of my given names] is the fruit of our brief encounter, and that is why he is coming now, in search of his roots. I am his father." The old man laughed, and the villagers laughed with him. He then concluded his story. "Everyone can see this, as we resemble each other very much. You only have to compare our faces. Father and son, you see."

I do not know if Okech ever visited London, but it must be added that he became blind in 1987 after the Ugandan army, and immediately thereafter the rebels, detained and seriously beat him. The army alleged that he had eight children with the rebels, which was not the case, and tortured him. The rebels accused him of collaborating with the army, which again was not the case. I arrived at his place only some ten years later. We had never met before he lost his eyesight, so I do not know his grounds in maintaining that we resemble each other. Nevertheless, it is a nice story, and I liked the ways in which informants eagerly created and offered me symbolic kinship, often with a touch of humor, which brings me back to Abu-Lughod's insider claim. Regardless of her status as an insider or halfie, she concluded that her informants soon created a symbolic and historical relationship between themselves and England, one of the Western nations with perhaps the most developed imperialism in history, as the informants also welcomed Abu-Lughod's English husband to the field with open arms. During the course of the fieldwork enterprise, she notes, her family situation became more important to her informants than any essential halfie status (Abu-Lughod 1993). Similarly and in my case, I eventually came to feel a strong belonging to northern Uganda and the people who without hesitation welcomed me so warmly. The fact that my informants celebrated the visits of my parents and my fiancée added to my feeling of being at home in Sweden as well as in Uganda. Anthropological fieldwork, then, became quite a privileged practice.

TO STOP ON THE ROAD IN ORDER TO LISTEN AND TAKE NOTES

I never became fluent in Acholi, the local language. I cannot even engage in a serious conversation on the matters that my research deals with. This I regret, but it is a limit that I need to confess. However, I decided to work on what I found to be key concepts in the research, as they developed in the field. Several days could be dedicated to concepts that my coworkers and I found to be occurring frequently, such as the phrase "life has become difficult" (*kwo odoko tek*); or the concepts of bad surroundings (*piny marac*) and good surroundings (*piny maber*); interclan reconciliation (*mato oput*); ghostly vengeance (*cen*); deep sorrow (*cola*) that must be swallowed by consuming the bitter root (*oput*), which otherwise can lead to the paralyzing fear of death (*ojii too*); which is not the same as ordinary fear (*lworo*); and so forth. Anthropological intersubjectivity is more than only words, and I hold that translation between cultures, whatever this means, is possible, even when the language is a barrier.

When I left Gulu in July 2002, I caught a ride to Kampala with Herbert, a German acquaintance, in his air-conditioned, four-wheel-drive pickup. I was happy not to have to travel this time in over-speeding buses bearing illustrative names like Die Hard One or Die Hard Two. In the middle of nowhere, halfway to Kampala, Herbert stopped to have a cup of coffee and a hand-rolled cigarette, made with his expensive German tobacco. I do not smoke, but we shared the single cup of nice strong black coffee. Then an old man appeared from the bush. He carried a spear and some mushrooms that he had collected. We greeted him, but soon found out that he was both deaf and mute. We understood that he very much wanted a smoke. Herbert rolled him a cigarette, and the man sat down by the roadside and enjoyed his smoke with slow, deep inhalations. Even a nonsmoker like me could see that the old man indeed enjoyed the German tobacco. We smiled at each other. There were some few but long minutes of silent communication. Then the old man bid farewell to us and went back to the bush. For me, this exemplifies one important instance of anthropology. Jackson (1998: 208) ends his account of his anthropological project, "Stopped on a road in order to listen and take notes."

One day, not long after my arrival for my second fieldwork period in December 1999, Tonny and I had returned with our small motorbike from a week of safari in northeast Acholiland, and we had come across the wreck of an ambushed lorry, containing both destroyed armory and skeletons. This, Tonny had informed me, was a site of great unrest, with many unhappy spirits of the dead (called *cen* in Acholi). Tonny wanted me to have his mother Rufina Labol's perspective on the matter, as she is a retired healer (*awjaka*, plural: *ajwaki*) once well known over most of west Acholiland because of her ability to deal and negotiate with the greater, extrahuman world. "Oh, dear," Rufina confessed. "I didn't know that your research concerned these things also. Now I understand that your research will indeed be difficult." Still she took great satisfaction in the fact that I had now complemented my research interest with spiritual matters as well. Maybe once every week during fieldwork, Tonny and I would visit his old mother, who lives some twenty minutes by motorcycle from Gulu town. Now and then, we brought photos from our field endeavor, of shrines, rituals, and various gatherings that we had attended. I soon found it to be an excellent thing to let Mama Tonny comment on these photos. Her lifelong experience of the greater, cosmological context placed them in relief.

EVERY CULTURE AND ALL CULTURES

A quotation from the late philosopher Paul Feyerabend (1993: 272) opens this book. Toward the end of his life, he rearticulated his stand, claiming that "*every culture is potentially all cultures* and that special cultural features are changeable manifestations of *a single human nature*" (Feyerabend 1995: 152). His claim guides my orientations, though perhaps I would have preferred the term "human existence" to avoid the laden concept of human nature, or just existence (*piny*). As conditional to human existence, I place emphasis upon intersection, sociality, and intersubjectivity (see also Carrithers 1992; Willis and Howell 1989). I also invite the reader to be skeptical of the idea that some cultures in essence are more prone to war than others. Acholiland in northern

Uganda consists of the Amuru, Gulu, Kitgum, and Pader districts. An exception to the rest of Uganda, the northern region has been described as "prone to popular millenarian protest and external disruption" (Hansen and Twaddle 1994: 2). In my ambition to write against such a conclusion, I will work along two lines. First, as mentioned, I will delineate some of the specific colonial and postcolonial developments that have preceded the situation in Acholiland today. Second, I will make a serious effort to listen to the stories of my informants. These stories forcefully counter any idea of Acholi culture as particularly prone to war. "What is tragic is that such concepts as 'the culture of violence' and 'violence-prone area' seem to have served as a shorthand for international agencies to define away their own role in the dissolution of the country by attributing a form of dangerous subjectivity to the inhabitants of these regions," note Das and Kleinman (2000: 3–4) in the introduction to a comparative volume on violence. Perhaps I should add that I do not propose any romantic conclusion that cultural life in Acholiland is the manifestation of the contrary, that is, a culture of peace. Like most anthropologists, I suggest that it is futile to speak about cultures in such essentialist ways. Instead I think it is important to work against generalizations that fix meaning in time and space. "All reflection is situational, none can be total, and the essences which we determine are justified only by the experience they clarify and are thus always subject to revision," cautions McCleary (1964: xx) in introducing the English edition of Merleau-Ponty's *Signs*.

My book has its focus on young people growing up in a troubled area. Young people's stories, in public only too commonly sidestepped or reshaped, are comments on contemporary Ugandan society as such. Their stories can deepen the understanding of contemporary African societies in emerging global realities. The choice of focus is quite modest but still, I feel, most relevant. Basically, I want the voices of marginalized young people to be heard, and I will balance these voices with those of older people.[4]

Many of my informants, including the younger ones, were above the age of twenty. Still, often they would define themselves as youth. Sometimes my coworker Tonny would describe himself in these terms ("We youth believe..."), but on other occasions he would position himself as an elder ("We elders think..."). As he was only thirty-seven years old when we first met in 1997, was he already an elder? His three wives and twenty-three biological children would disqualify him as a youth, I imagine. Regarding myself, I turned thirty during my second period of fieldwork, a symbolically burdened birthday in Sweden, which is of necessity celebrated with a big party. From an anthropological perspective it is a mistake to conclude that a person cannot be young in one context, and an elder in another, hold one position in the first context, to shift in another as social relations are continuously produced, reproduced, and contested (Bucholtz 2002).

This and other existential orientations in everyday life, as well as seemingly contradictory disorientations and reorientations, will be illustrated continually in this book. In all its complexity, everyday life is lived in the world, or in what phenomenologists call the lifeworld, "that domain of everyday, immediate social existence and practical activity" (Jackson 1996: 7). The lifeworld is above all a social world. It is thus not simply a worldview statically reproduced. Cosmology, from this perspective, is an everyday process of social contest and human creativity (Kapferer 2002). Jackson elaborates on this lifeworld: "[It] is never a seamless, unitary domain in which social relations remain constant and the experience of self remains stable. Nor is it ever arcadian; it is a scene of turmoil, ambiguity, resistance, dissimulation, and struggle" (Jackson 1996: 27). War and social unrest, one could say, bring ambiguities of the lived situation to the surface. My informants unraveled such ambiguities in the effort to govern the lived surroundings. "I do not support the rebels, nor am I supporting the government," as an eighteen-year-old unmarried female student once told me. "I am just in a dilemma. I would like to support the rebels, but they are killing my people."

During a visit to Kampala in 1998, I proposed presenting some of my preliminary findings at the Swedish consulate (which has since developed into an embassy). I remember a Swedish diplomat's questioning the whole idea of doing anthropological research among the Acholi. At the meeting, we also talked about the religious dimension of the war. He strongly questioned the rebels' spirituality, which indeed is violent and destructive. For him, the religious dimension was proof of something tribalistic, even uncivilized and savage, and he dismissed the religious claims of the LRA/M rebels as "humbug," only proving the Acholi's "inability to take their responsibility" in the development of Uganda. "This is typical for Africa. Why should the people in southern Uganda take the responsibility for Acholis killing other Acholis?" he concluded, thereby attaching an ethnic stigma to most people in the conflict area, and also echoing the wider diplomatic community at the time.

I was rather upset when I left his office, and I went to the nearest place where I could have a cup of coffee and rewrite my notes of what he said, before I forgot his exact phrasings. I had just arrived in Kampala after some three months with my Acholi friends in Gulu, and my compatriot at the Swedish consulate made his comments while he was drinking coffee. He looked out the window when I talked. He never invited me to share some coffee with him, which would have been a most rude gesture of distance keeping in the eyes of my Acholi informants. As I just had disembarked from the Gulu bus, perhaps that added to my frustration. The diplomat was not alone among my country-men in harboring such essentialist views. In Gulu town, I met a Swedish journalist who had come to interview former child soldiers. "The African cannot separate myth and rumors from reality and facts," he concluded as we shared some beers.

These efforts to falsify the religiosity of the rebels, or even Acholi orienta-tions in life, miss an important point. By bluntly rejecting efforts to cope with the new, violent aspects of contingency and uncertainty enforced upon the lived surroundings, they also fail to mediate local understandings of the con-flict and local efforts toward reconciliation. In other words, ignoring the complex politics involved, they fail to acknowledge the emerging *meanings in use*, a kind of knowing by engagement regarding the religious dimension of the rebel movement in relation to Acholi cosmology. Rather than being an expression of humbug or hypocrisy, I would argue, such meanings emerge in sociocultural and political processes of interpretation and counterinterpreta-tion that include not only influential agents, like the rebel leader or the West-ern diplomat, but also the active participation of ordinary people with per-sonal experience of the war.

Okot p'Bitek, a son of Acholi, concludes in his book on Acholi and Luo religion that religious beliefs and practices are used to diagnose, explain, and interpret the individual causes of misfortune and illness. They also provide "means and ways of coping with the individual situations of anxiety and stress," and if this does not work, he writes, people may turn to a rather profane expression of skepticism, like the shrugging of the shoulders, *wi-lobo* in Acholi, "This is the way of the world" (p'Bitek 1971: 160; see also Evans-Pritchard 1956: 12–13; Lienhardt 1961: 55). This is not, as I have suggested, religious fatalism but lived realism. In an analysis of p'Bitek's writings, Heron shows that p'Bitek attacks "the futility of the whole exercise of metaphysical speculation which creates explanations of existence containing irreconcilable contradictions" (Heron 1976: 136–137). As is the case with most aspects of human existence, religion is a rather contradictory exercise. Like other orientations in life, it is a practice more than a doctrine, or phenomenological rather than theological, as Lienhardt (1961: 32) once held for the Dinka of southern Sudan.

Malinowski's (1948) famous conclusion on religion and magic comes to my mind. When the order of things cannot be controlled fully, he held, humans turn to ritual and magic to reduce uncertainty and anxiety. Radcliffe-Brown (1952) presented an alternative reading: religion and magic, he argued, function as the glue by which society maintains and manifests itself and its values. Audrey Richards, in a classic study of the Bemba of today's Zambia, combined the two perspectives. Rites, she held, help the individual in his or her "particular anxieties and difficulties," as well as helping, if more indirectly, to maintain "the confidence of the whole community and its sense of cohesion" (Richards 1939: 352). Lowie, another old-time anthropologist, criticized functionalism of treating cultures as closed, whole systems, and he found the functional explanation to be obvious but useless. "Whether these are truisms or statements of deeper significance," Lowie (1937: 236) wrote, "the propositions are too vague to interpret what we wish to have explained."

The focus of this book is on people's existential uncertainties, intellectual worries, political frustrations, and religious queries in a situation of armed conflict and great social unrest, or how people orient and seek meaning as they engage the world and live their humanity. I aim not to reproduce any explanatory functionalism but instead to adhere to Heron's (1976) note on the irreconcilable contradictions and the unfinished realities of everyday social life. To strike a balance between the countervailing needs of self and other constitutes the central dynamic of human action, argues Michael Jackson (e.g., 1998; 2002b) in his existential-phenomenological anthropology. As elsewhere, so also in Acholiland.

Chapter 1

ACHOLI WORLDS AND THE COLONIAL ENCOUNTER

THE PLACE OF MANY HIPPOS

There is a place in southwestern Acholiland called "the Place of Many Hippos" (*Paraa*). Here the river Nile is mighty, calm, and wide. Today it is part of a national park. As the name indicates, hippos are plentiful here. There is no bridge, but a ferry takes travelers over the river.

In 2000, I had an opportunity to visit the area with my parents. We stayed some days in the park on our way from Gulu to Kampala. I was driving a rental car with Tonny next to me. My parents were in the back seat. We were driving through landscapes well known to Tonny, who is an experienced hunter. His hunting skills made him the perfect guide to the riches of the wildlife of the area. The nights we spent at a luxurious tourist lodge at Paraa. A few years back, the lodge was carefully renovated, in the most colonial style, as I imagine it. The hotel personnel were all dressed in perfectly ironed khaki uniforms. A clan brother to Tonny, employed at the lodge, welcomed us as we arrived. They both come from Anaka, on the north border of the park. Old-fashioned boxes and big trunks were strategically placed just next to the reception, giving the impression that Ernest Hemingway or some historical dignitary had arrived just before us. Dark wooden details and brown, British-style armchairs around small tables dominated the corridors and the many lounges. Big fans in the ceiling rotated slowly. They were more for decoration than for any cooling effect. On the walls there were various images reproduced from nineteenth-century travelogues. Familiar scenes invited the tourist to consume exotica, such as the endless caravans of the European explorers, or the sportsman John Hanning Speke in a close encounter with elephants or perhaps a lion, or the many "ambushes" Henry Stanley's team endured as they traveled along the Congo River, or Stanley's famous encounter with Livingstone.

After checking in, I joined Tonny for a stroll through the many rooms and saloons. In silence and with great care he looked at the many images, one by one. He finally stopped in front of an image in a small frame. It showed the European traveler seated in his palanquin, carried by four Africans, his beloved dog running next to them as the equipage progressed through the bush. "This is very painful. Very painful indeed," was Tonny's only comment before we went to our room to unpack our luggage and enjoy a swim in the pool. Later, when I was back in Sweden, I spent some time reading the old travelogues dealing with Uganda. Samuel White Baker had visited the region, and his conclusions were harsh. "Human nature viewed in its crudest state as pictured amongst African savages is quite on a level with that of the brute, and not to be compared with the noble character of the dog," he wrote (1866: 174, vol. 1). His pet monkey was more civilized than the Africans, he repeatedly claimed.

CULTURE IN THE MAKING

This chapter introduces the Acholi people. Samuel White Baker and John Hanning Speke, friends and fellow explorers, were among the first Europeans to encounter the Acholi. They traveled to Africa in the mid-1850s, at a time when the explorative curiosity of European intellectuals was increasingly determined by the paradigm of the day, which was legitimated by the natural sciences and focused on the classification of humanity into mutually exclusive and hierarchically arranged races. In the effort to sketch the background to today's developments in northern Uganda, the chapter explores the interconnection of European imperialism and racist ideology.[1] Of course, no imperial or colonial administration was homogenous. Rather, they were the result of conflicting social, political, and economic interests among their many individual stakeholders. Still, I will delineate some dominant traits of imperialism and colonialism in northern Uganda and develop the argument proposed by anthropologists such as Allen (1988–1989; 1991; 1994; 2006b), Behrend (1999a), and Vincent (1999), that Acholi ethnic identity and other Ugandan ethnic identities were reified or codified because of colonialism. But I also want to develop the argument, advanced by historians such as Atkinson (e.g., 1978; 1994; 1999), that Acholi collective belonging cannot be said to be a mere colonial invention, imposed from above.

My wish to unfold aspects of the imperial heritage of Europe in Africa is not new, but it is still important. When the imperialists arrived in the area that was to become Uganda, they applied their assumptions concerning others un-critically and without much reflection, basing their conclusions on already defined ideological hypotheses. They even claimed that the encounter between colonizer and colonized was dialogic, that colonial rule was wanted by the Africans. Maps were drawn and tribal designations were included in their reports. History was written. Little room was left for the colonized subjects to voice their concerns or even to steer their ways through the historiography. As the imperialists imposed their truths and acted upon the people to be colonized, the latter often experienced a crisis of control in everyday life as well as over their own fate. It was "the appropriation of a past by conquest," to make a parallel with Guha's (1997: 3) analysis of colonial India. The imperial agents tended to understand themselves as determining the periphery, filling with meaning the alleged void that had been discovered, almost with the claim to have invented it, while at the same time neglecting the ways in which their counterparts on the periphery determined them and their imperial centers (Pratt 1992).

In a discussion of identity politics in postcolonial Uganda, Okuku (2002: 8) claims that " 'tribes' themselves have usually been modern constructions through the intervention of colonialism, which froze the play of identities." Regarding Uganda and its postcolonial problems, this is somehow an agreed truism in scholarly writing. More generally, Hobsbawm and Ranger (1983) famously concluded that traditions are invented. Their argument has been widely debated, and Ranger was inspired to revise the position, concluding instead that traditions must change to stay alive. Self-critically, he notes that "invention is too once-for-all an event," as if the invention thereafter can be patented (Ranger 1994: 23). Already in 1970, Taban lo Liyong, a Sudanese writer raised in Gulu, wrote, "To live, our traditions have to be topical; to be topical they must be used as part and parcel of our contemporary contentions and controversies" (Liyong 1970: x).

In the anthropological study of colonialism in India, Fox wrote a fascinating account of the Sikhs, in which he explicitly deals with culture as in a "constant state of becoming" (Fox 1985: 13). Still, the bias toward colonial times makes it difficult for me to accept that the idea of culture in the making really differs from the idea of the invention of culture, tradition, or ethnic identity. What about precolonial times? What about the manipulation of identities from below? And what about postcolonial manifestations of collective identity?

It is in the process of human communication that collective belonging is fostered. Ethnic belonging is basically about drawing boundaries, and differences and similarities are evoked as people orient themselves in the world. The social context will determine which measurement will be weighted against the other. With this emphasis, I follow the anthropological consensus that challenges the idea that social groups, ethnic or other, are or have been isolated from one another. My process and contextual approach makes it hazardous for me to say anything final on the possible essences of the various ethnic belongings that people worldwide produce and reproduce on a daily basis. Ethnic categories and labels are in some senses of the word inventions and therefore always have a certain degree of fixity about them. However, and more importantly, ethnic identity and culture are socially lived, and created and recreated in everyday life, making it irrelevant to divide the world into two, the premodern or traditional and the modern.

THEMES IN ACHOLI ETHNOGRAPHY

The Acholi people today generally consider themselves a distinct ethnic group. They call their language Acholi, or sometimes Luo. When today's Acholiland was made a contact zone between people living there and European agents who extended their travels to the area, the local people were most often labeled after the chiefdoms that the Western explorers encountered, such as Koch, Patiko, or Payira, to mention only a few. The Acholi (Acoli, Acooli) denomination is of contested origin, but the variants Shuuli, Sooli, and Shooli became broadly used at the time when Arab traders in slaves and ivory moved into the region in the 1850s (Atkinson 1978: 504–552; 1989: 37–39). Relying on firepower and local rivalries, these intruders into southern Sudan and northern Uganda soon "installed themselves with bands of armed retainers in fortified camps called *zeriba*, and proceeded 'to fuse trade with robbery' " as "native tribes were set against each other in a mindless, self-destructive struggle" (Markakis 1987: 29). The slave and ivory trade devastated the region. Europeans who arrived slightly later built their own fortified camps, and they referred to the local people as the Shooli (e.g., Baker 1866; 1874; Mounteney-Jephson 1890). In parallel to this outside label, the Acholi were sometimes called Gang or Gangi, meaning home or village in Acholi, a name given to the Acholi by their southern neighbors (Girling 1960: 1; p'Bitek 1971: 3–4).

Currently, the Acholi live mainly in Pader, Kitgum, Amuru, and Gulu districts, four of the northern districts in Uganda, of which two, Amuru and Kitgum, border Sudan. Acholi are also found in the southernmost part of Sudan. According to the 2002 national census, the population of Acholiland numbered 1,145,437. This makes up almost 5 percent of Uganda's total population of 24.4 million. The four districts however, constitute some 12 percent of the country's total area, or 27,871 square kilometers (Rwabwoogo 2002).

The districts of Pader and Kitgum correspond roughly to *Acholi mamalo* or the upper Acholi, that is, those who descended from the hills. Gulu and Amuru districts correspond to *Acholi mapiny* or the lower Acholi, as Acholi say. For short, they say *lumalo* (the ups) and *lupiny* (the downs) respectively. In addition to this, but "long time back," as Tonny's mother Rufina put it, Acholi who lived around Palabek and the Agoro hills in Kitgum district, as well as those on the Sudanese side of the border, were called *lugot* (from *got*, mountain).[2] The river Aswa, running from the southeast toward the northwest, has naturalized the administrative border between the east and the west (Leys 1967: 18). In the colonial context, the lower Acholi were categorized as the western Acholi, with administrative headquarters in Gulu town, while the upper Acholi were labeled the eastern Acholi, with the colonial administration centered in Kitgum town.

This order has been naturalized over the years. Today many of my informants, as well as missionaries, hold that the upper Acholi are "more traditional" (a positive statement) or "more backward" (a negative statement) than their "lower" brothers and sisters. *Acholi lugot* (Acholi of the mountains), my friend Otim p'Ojok suggested, refers to "people who are strong or hard as stone," even "brave." Otim p'Ojok, who grew up and lives on the Gulu side, continued with an illustration that also said something about the gender hierarchy of the Acholi moral world. "It is like Gulu men who fear the stubbornness of Kitgum women," he pictured it. Actual marriages transcend such divides in everyday life.

The Acholi ideology of social organization is oriented to patrilineal descent with decentralized and exogamous lineages or clans called *kaka* (Girling 1960: 18, chap. 8). These groupings, Allen (1994: 128–129) suggests, may perhaps better be portrayed as close relatives, as they also can refer to women who have married into the group and people related on one's maternal side, with whom marriage is forbidden. Atkinson (1994: 76, n. 2) notes that the Acholi do not represent any "classic, segmentary society" in line with the ethnographic model presented by Evans-Pritchard (1940) in his account of the political organization of the Nuer of southern Sudan. As Evans-Pritchard (1949: 57) himself observed, "All these terms are relative and are used in a more or less comprehensive sense according to the context." A strong matrifocality colors everyday life in Acholiland, as noted by Girling (1960: 50–51). As a young adult, my friend Tonny took two names—Odiya from his late father, and Labol from his beloved mother—in this way stressing both the patrilineage and matrifocality. Also recall Ladit Abic, the old man who carefully nurtured his ancestral shrines despite war and oppression. Central to the ancestral shrine of the family was an old grinding stone, which represented the first "granny" of the clan, as Abic put it. "In a sense all kinship is through the mother, even kinship with the father and hence with the paternal kin," wrote Evans-Pritchard about lived kinship and neighborliness in Nuer society (1951: 156; see also James 1990).

Before war arrived in northern Uganda in 1986, many Acholi families kept cattle. During the course of the war, however, most cattle have been looted or killed by the fighting forces, and the majority of people depend on relief handouts. Only 2 percent, or some few thousand head, of the prewar cattle remain (Weeks 2002: 35). Cattle have never been the main source of income or subsistence for the great majority of Acholi (p'Bitek 1971: 19; Atkinson 1994: 56–57), but the symbolic significance of this cultural loss should not be underestimated. Many Acholi, especially older people, regard cattle as the most prestigious form of wealth. The Acholi also keep goats, sheep, and pigs. They have managed to keep these animals to a higher degree than cattle during the period of war and great social unrest. Agriculture, however, is the primary activity of subsistence for most Acholi. Although war and life in displacement have limited or even deprived the majority of Acholi from growing their own food, millet and sorghum remain the staple crops of choice, prepared as a kind of porridge or dough, or sometimes as beer. These crops are central in the Acholi imagination of a good, healthy life. If "you are what you eat" is a valid dictum, many old Acholi would refer exactly to millet and sorghum as being at the heart of a proper upbringing, both bodily and morally (*odoko dano*, to become a person, as Acholi say). As p'Bitek has it in a widely acclaimed poem that is required secondary school reading in Uganda:

Do you know
Why the knees
Of millet-eaters
Are tough?
Tougher than the knees
Of the people who drink bananas!
Where do you think
The stone powder
From the grinding stones goes?
FROM P'BITEK'S *SONG OF LAWINO* (1966)

The Acholi are millet eaters, so the poem goes. This would make them tougher than peoples living in southern and central Uganda, among whom the green cooking banana (*matooke*) is a daily staple. I had read the long poem several times, but it was a young unmarried man in Gulu town, a teacher by profession, who eventually pointed out the verse to me. According to him, the poem illustrated the senior generation's promotion of ethnic sentiments at the cost of a national Ugandan future (see also Oruni 1994: 15).

To the extent they can, the Acholi also grow maize, sweet potatoes, sorghum, cassava, peas, beans, sesame, groundnuts, squash, and various vegetables, as well as other savanna crops, largely for consumption. Before the war, avocados, mangoes, pineapples, and other fruits were grown for commercial use. Today people grow fruits mostly for personal use, though sometimes they are grown for small-scale businesses. Tobacco, cotton, sugarcane, sunflowers, and rice are grown for trade and consumption, but these activities too have been heavily affected by the war. In the late 1990s, imported rice from Pakistan made the market price fall in Uganda, which makes it difficult for farmers to sell their rice harvests with any profit at all.

One strategy of coping with destruction and war in the rural areas is to cultivate crops that are not easily looted or that demand careful preparations before consumption, and are therefore less attractive to loot in the eyes of hit-and-run rebels. In one camp for displaced people, one young man suggested growing rice and cowpeas, crops that the rebels will hesitate to loot from the gardens. "They will find it too problematic," he concluded. As Jane Kony (1997) points out in a student essay, most farmers in the war-torn north sell their products to urban middle-men as soon as possible after harvest, to avoid the looting or destruction of the rural granaries by any of the fighting forces. Eventually, the short-term coping strategy of selling off harvests and then buying food will make people increasingly entangled with the wider market economy and its fluctuations, or even dependent on relief distributions.

THE GREATER SCHEME OF SCHOLARLY CLASSIFICATION

In historical, linguistic, and ethnographic literature the Acholi are commonly grouped together with the Chope, the Paluo, and the Alur as Central Luo because of linguistic affinity and assumed common historical origin (e.g., Atkinson 1994; p'Bitek 1971). Most Acholi have no problem in communicating with the Alur people who live west of the Acholi, or the Lango (Langi), neighbors to the south. In cultural and linguistic terms, the Lango are said to be "Luo-ised 'Nilo-Hamites'" (Southall quoted in p'Bitek 1971: 34; see also Butt 1952: 92).

Older ethnographic sources assign the Central Luo to the broader category of the Nilotes (e.g., Seligman and Seligman 1932; Butt 1952; Säfholm 1973). The Nilotic designation refers to the various social groupings of the geographical region of the Upper Nile Basin, suggesting that there are cultural traits shared by these various peoples. In Evans-Pritchard's (1950: 1) terms, the Nilotic peoples constitute a "common ethnic stock" or an "ethno-regional cluster" of peoples (see also Butt 1952: 1). The Upper Nile Basin is assumed to be the cradle of Nilotic peoples, from which migrations of the proto-Nilotes are said to have originated (e.g., Säfholm 1973). The term "Nilotic" is applied to a language family, in the study of African languages (Greenberg 1955). Both uses indicate that we are dealing with scholarly fabrications or metacategorizations rather than empirically relevant social groupings in everyday life.

From my fieldwork experience, I would say that today most Acholi people strongly identify themselves as Luo. As often as they defined themselves as Acholi speakers, informants would say that their native tongue was Luo. People would commonly use the designation Luo when we discussed their cultural belonging in the context of the wider history of migrations in the region (see also p'Bitek 1971). Some historians, nonetheless, question the Luo origin of the majority of Acholi (e.g., Atkinson 1994). In everyday life, my informants would refer to themselves as Ugandans just as often as they portrayed themselves as Acholi or Luo. It all depended on context. Often, young informants referred to themselves as Africans more than anything else. In the present situation, with war, social breakdown, ethnic tension, and political turmoil, these young men and women found inspiration and hope from pan-Africanist ideas.

COLONIAL TRUTHS

The colonial rulers regarded themselves as instrumental in the formation of an overall ethnic belonging among the many Acholi clans of aristocratic (*kal*) and common (*labong*) descent. With colonial assistance, so it is said, the Acholi came to realize themselves as belonging to a nation, or to use the term of those times, "tribe." The colonialists first fashioned the Gulu (1910) and Chua (1914) districts, which later merged in what was to be labeled the Acholi district. As Rennie Bere, an agent of the colonial administration, wrote in 1947:

> The urgent trend of modern administration has been to bring the clans together and to make the Acholi conscious of their unity as a single people, without destroying their individualistic background. To this end the districts of Gulu [today's Gulu and Amuru] and Chua [today's Kitgum and Pader] were amalgamated in 1937, when a unified Acholi district was formed with headquarters at Gulu: at the same time the Acholi Council, with seats not only for chiefs but for representatives of the people from all parts of the country, was brought into being. (Bere 1947: 8)

He then refers to an old Acholi proverb when he concludes his discussion of the colonial creation of Acholi ethnic identity and nationhood. The colonial authority made the Acholi understand the truth, as Bere claims, of their vernacular proverbs: "The Acholi are beginning to feel a new unity and to understand, in their tribal life and the relationship of the clans, the truth of their ancient proverb that one blade of grass is not, by itself, sufficient to thatch a house" (Bere 1947: 8). My friend Tonny was not satisfied with Bere's version of the proverb, instead presenting me with an alternative version: "One blade of grass is not by itself sufficient to cause leakage of the grass-thatched house." Our communal cooperation will remain strong even if one bad character sets out to destroy it, Otim p'Ojok explained. Also, he continued, the community will support individuals in their everyday sorrows and sufferings. My two friends' comments indeed gave a twist to the authoritarian truth of the colonialist.

Bere arrived for administrative service in Acholiland in 1930, and he worked with the Acholi periodically over some thirty years. His ambition to define the truth, I suggest, illustrates the colonial "concern for keeping the natives in the places they belong," as Dwyer (1972: 202) puts it in an analysis of colonial politics in Acholiland. This colonial concern figures strongly in the writings of the colonial administrators. J. R. P. Postlethwaite was a predecessor to Bere. In his memoirs, he notes that during his twenty-three years of colonial service in Uganda, which began in 1909, he was assigned to various regions of the protectorate, but predominantly to the north and the east (Postlethwaite 1947: 22, 24). When assigned to the east, Postlethwaite encountered the Iteso people. He recalls that he was "much struck by the vagueness of the boundary set to the active administration of this district in the north, a boundary which was in no sense tribal and a constant source of petty irritation, and we accordingly pushed out further afield, determined to embrace at any rate the whole of the Teso tribe" (Postlethwaite 1947: 44).

It is not in doubt that colonial practices were powerful instruments in the making of more rigid ethnic boundaries and divides in Uganda and elsewhere in Africa (e.g., Lonsdale 1994; Ranger 1994). The market economy of the colonialists was to restrict interethnic movements. In precolonial Uganda, salt extracted on the shores of Lake Albert found its way to other places, and so did iron hoes and spearheads produced in Bunyoro, while bark cloth made in Buganda found its way to Alur chiefs in the West Nile region. Acholi chiefs were sometimes dressed in bark cloth made in Bunyoro. The Lango exchanged cattle for iron tools manufactured by the Acholi (Jørgensen 1981: 34; p'Bitek 1971: 33). Many of these products, exchanged in trade networks that crisscrossed the region, could not compete with the cheap goods mass produced in British factories, which were made available in stores all over the Ugandan protectorate (Atkinson 1994: 6, 57–58, 101–102; Karugire 1996: 24–25; Mamdani 1984: 6–7; 1996: 145–146). In this way, colonialists seized the control over the market, and they narrowed the room for action that Africans had previously had in these matters. An important feature of noncolonial interregional alliance making and networking weakened (Karugire 1980: 128). Even if the colonial market economy in theory opened new avenues of possibilities, in practice these were severely limited. The colonial authorities outmaneuvered the great majority of African small-scale traders. The price of trading licenses and taxes were kept high enough so that immigrant Europeans and Indians with large businesses came to replace African petty traders. Manual ginning of cotton was outlawed in favor of large-scale mechanized ginneries (Mamdani 1976: 72–77, 165–166; 1984: 12; Jørgensen 1981: 157–158).

In a parallel process, the Catholic mission presented its Acholi converts with the *Baibul*, the local version of the Bible. The missionaries furthermore encouraged and facilitated education. People did not join such developments without critical reflection, however. They rather aimed to realize their own intentions and political ambitions. To illustrate: in Acholi the Christian church was soon named the "reading house" (*ot kwan*) and the priests were called "teachers" (*lupwony*, sing.: *lapwony*), a term now used to refer to rebel commanders. After being baptized with a Western name in the reading house, bright pupils were encouraged to proceed to higher education (p'Bitek 1973: 71).

The missionaries encouraged the production of various vernacular texts dealing with Acholi history and culture, in which Acholi writers played an important part along with the missionaries (Girling 1960: 203).[3] Consequently, a variety of localized Acholi myths and histories were systematized, standardized, printed, and widely distributed, with the potential of promoting a higher degree of cultural coherence throughout Acholiland. As stated in a recent missionary account that looks back on the evangelization among the Acholi:

> Much of their history was compiled by the Combini Missionary Fr Vincenzo Pellegrini and published under the title of *Acoli Macon*, which school pupils have used for many years. This booklet, the title of which literally means "The Old Acholi," records the oral history of the great Acholi tribe, whose gallantry has always been acknowledged by everyone. (Marchetti 1999: 18)

An amazing 45,000 copies of the booklet on "the old Acholi" had been printed by the end of the 1960s and distributed all over Acholiland (Allen 1996b: 474). During fieldwork, I now and then came across tattered photocopies of the locally produced accounts, which were still in circulation in the war-ravaged north. In one case, when I visited representatives of the Lamogi chiefdom to record its history, they simply read out to me from the local historian Okech's (1953) account of Acholi history, focusing on the Lamogi rebellion, an uprising that was crushed by the British in the early 1900s but which has become an icon of resistance and independence in the collective memory.

The process of defining and labeling social groupings as ethnic entities had contradictory consequences. Missionary competition created new divisions between Catholicism and Anglican Protestantism, although in Acholiland Catholicism took the dominant position.[4] Simultaneously, colonial scholarship encouraged systematic comparison between groups to a degree not done before. As noted by Vincent (1999: 112), the most evident example is Fortes and Evans-Pritchard's (1940) introduction to an anthropological volume on African political systems. African societies were basically categorized into two ideal types. The first has centralized authority, like kingdoms, and the other is characterized by decentralized authority, or rather, as the authors chose to put it, the *lack* of centralized authority and the *lack* of government (Fortes and Evans-Pritchard 1940: 5). Between these two categories and more so within them, comparison was made, based on the criteria established. Simultaneously, local elites and nationalists also tended to overlook the actual heterogeneity of social life and the complexity of ethnic interrelations. Sometimes the process of homogenization was clearly intentional, as in the early years of anticolonial national movements and pan-Africanism when cultural, social, historical plurality was merged in the name of a greater cause.

The word "lack" is of central importance here. Non-Bantu-speaking peoples of Uganda were defined in terms of what political institutions they were perceived to have lacked rather than in terms of how they organized their political life. Again a fixation of meaning is imposed. Alleged to be a void, unoccupied by meaning or cultured people, northern Uganda was to be filled with order and meaning. For example, the colonialists' inability to identify and recognize any indigenous sociopolitical organization is a most frequent theme in the imperial mapping of the Acholi. Postlethwaite, the pioneer colonial administrator of Acholiland, recalls the effort to include east Acholi in the Ugandan protectorate. "I became so discouraged by the absence of any real chiefs with definite, permanent tribal authority, that I found my mind turning for salvation to the old Buganda Agent policy of the Eastern Province of Uganda and, in fact, I actually installed one or two Banyoro as advisers to individual chiefs," Postlethwaite (1947: 56) writes in his memoirs. He explains his motivation: "I was, however, dealing with a tribe who had no system of ancient holdings, nothing that answered to the Bataka [patrilineal clan heads] of . . . Buganda" (Postlethwaite 1947: 65–66; quoted also in Girling 1960: 175).

In his widely acclaimed writings on the Victorian explorers of the Nile, the Australian author and journalist Alan Moorehead (1960) reproduces the only too common stand, in which the Buganda kingdom of central Uganda is the constant and normative point of reference. When John Hanning Speke and James Augustus Grant crossed the Nile and entered Acholiland on their way from Buganda to Khartoum, Moorehead (1960: 68) proposes, "the tribes grew increasingly more primitive; they were back in a region of naked, painted men who carried bows and arrows and who knew nothing of the arts and crafts of Buganda." In replacing conventional imperialist conclusions with an explicit Marxist-Leninist perspective, Rusch still reproduces the evolutionist perspective. He holds that the art and handicraft of the Baganda "were of an amazing beauty and perfection far beyond the level attained by neighbouring peoples" (Rusch 1975: 374). Also, as he goes on to claim, "religion in Buganda had attained a much higher standard of development than any religious belief in the neighbouring countries" and the Buganda state "had reached a much higher stage of development than the majority of African countries" (Rusch 1975: 390). Despite ideological differences in the European centers then, which indeed were a patchwork of colonial and postcolonial interests, the appropriation of local social worlds remained the dominant trait of imperial and colonial conquest in Uganda.

COLLABORATION AND CONTEST

Bere, the administrative successor to Postlethwaite in Acholiland, notes that the British administration was influential in the election of chiefs who were willing to cooperate with the colonial administration. Consequently, the tendency was for the proportion of government nominees to increase at the cost of hereditary chiefs of the precolonial chiefdoms. "Many of the traditional chiefs were dismissed, retrenched or retired, and others were transferred to fill vacancies caused by these removals: new chiefs were appointed irrespectively of clan or family," he writes (Bere 1955: 51). The colonial ambition to unite the Acholi was not for any united Acholi nation, but rather a strategy to better administer the protectorate. Again Bere's words: "In the first place must be put the fact that an inherited capacity to 'make rain' and to carry out other traditional functions did not necessarily also ensure possession of those qualities which make a sound administrator, tax collector or magistrate" (Bere 1955: 51). On the eve of colonial rule, Acholiland was organized into more than sixty chiefdoms, ruled by chiefs of aristocratic descent (*kal*). When they were installed in their office, the chiefs were anointed with oil made from the shea butter tree. Even today, the hereditary successors of these precolonial chiefs are called oiled chiefs (*rwodi moo*, sing.: *rwot moo*). However, the majority of the chiefs appointed by the British were commoners (*labong*), as Girling (1960: 200–201) notes. With the usual colonial confidence, Bere (1955: 50) maintains that the ordinary Acholi readily accepted these new chiefs.

Other scholars, notably Dwyer (1972), have pointed out that a good number of local leaders and loosely organized intellectuals, as well as ordinary people I imagine, did indeed offer active resistance to what they regarded as the disruption of their indigenous modes for political representation. Just as ethnic codification was a primary means through which the colonial power of indirect rule tried to keep its control, so ethnic belonging was to become one of the main ways of protesting against the very same control. In other words, the colonial politics of ethnification was also an avenue of anticolonialism (Mamdani 1995b; 1996; Okuku 2002). The colonial conquest appropriated colonized societies and perhaps more important the past of these societies, but the colonized subjects "reconstructed their past for purposes opposed to those of their rulers and made it the ground for marking out their differences in cultural and political terms" (Guha 1997: 3).

To articulate their various interests in the colonial discourse, of course, the colonial subjects were dependent on their ability to write, read, and speak English. They also needed knowledge of the colonial system in order to collaborate with or challenge it. Formal education, which in northern Uganda was for many years monopolized by the missionaries, provided them with this. Education was, however, double-edged. As Mudoola (1993: 75) adds, colonial education domesticated its subjects, at least in part. Ordinary people in Acholiland took critical notice of the process of domestication (Karugire 1980: 149–150). Chiefs who were acknowledged, even put into office, by the colonial administration, obtained new designations in popular talk. The Acholi native council was referred to as the work of the Europeans or foreigners (*tic pa muno*) and its leaders called the elders of the government (*ludito pa gamente*) or chiefs of the pen (*rwodi kalam*), which effectively differentiated them from those chiefdom leaders who were ritually anointed with shea butter oil (*rwodi moo*).

Old ethnographic sources stress that the ability to make rain was a central characteristic of the chiefs in the noncolonial context (e.g., Butt 1952: 89–90; Grove 1919: 172–173; Seligman and Seligman 1932: 130–131), while the colonial administrator Bere (1955: 51) held that chiefs who could make rain were not always suitable in the colonial administration. In retrospect, it can be added that the reverse also applied. Chiefs who could write were not always good at making rain, or at performing the various other tasks required by their Acholi subjects, such as sending suitable representatives to mediate in conflicts. The administrative Acholi courts set up by the colonial authority, with chiefs appointed by the same colonial authority, did not assume some neutral administrative function only. In practice, as Acholi individuals were assigned to run the courts, some came to incorporate imperial attitudes, which were further disseminated and imposed on the subjects under colonial administration. Around 1950 the anthropologist Girling attended one of these courts, watching how it meted out beatings, fines, and imprisonments. "You see we must rule by fear," its divisional chief attested to the anthropologist. As the chief continued to legitimate his work, his words echoed the colonial image of Africans in general: "The people are lazy, they do not realise what good things the Government is doing for them. How can we Acholi progress unless we grow cotton, pay our taxes and dig latrines, as the Government wants us to do?" (quoted in Girling 1960: 198).

In many early travelogues, Payira was acknowledged as the most influential Acholi chiefdom, in part because it was by far the largest of the precolonial chiefdoms, and partly because of its close relation with the Bunyoro-Kitara kingdom to the south, which has remained over the years. In the effort to cope with intruding British expeditions and their increasing demands, the Payira sought allies. They met with the Koch chiefdom to "bend spears" with each other (Anywar 1948: 75–76). This is not only a profound ritual of reconciliation between chiefdoms. In contrast to the more commonly conducted inter-clan reconciliation (*mato oput*), which is performed to settle local homicides and the like, the bending-of-spears ritual (*gomo tong*) evokes, manifests, and remakes greater political alliances among peoples in northern Uganda. In the case that Anywar (1948) presents, the manifestation of political alliances was performed in the wake of colonialism, in defense of independence, but it must be assumed that it was not the first time that spears were bent in northern Uganda.[5]

With time, it turned out that the Payira chiefdom was the most successful and influential in collaborating and cooperating with the European colonialists, despite initial skepticism among the Payira leadership. Eventually the Payira chief, Rwot Awich, decided to set up a compound in Gulu town, supplementary to his chiefly court compound (Dwyer 1972: 172). Gulu town housed the provincial headquarters of the colonial administration, and was formally established in 1910 to replace Nimule in today's Sudan. Padibe, Paicho, and Patiko were other influential chiefdoms recognized by the colonial authorities. These chiefdoms all emphasized their historical links to the Bunyoro-Kitara kingdom, to the immediate south of Acholiland, a fact that was symbolically important in their efforts to legitimate their positions on the greater political scene in northern Uganda.

When the Payira chief fell into disfavor with the colonialists, chiefs of these other chiefdoms, notably the Padibe, seized the opportunity to collaborate more closely with the British (Anywar 1948: 77). In the colonial effort to pacify the Acholi, Awich was imprisoned twice and once sent into exile to Kampala. Still today, the deportation of the Payira chief is very vivid in the collective memory of the Acholi. Contrary to the colonial intention, I imagine, the deportations seem to have strengthened the esteem in which he is held in the collective memory. Few Acholi would agree today with Bere's (1946: 78) claim that Awich "must be counted a failure" only because "he missed his chance" to surrender and subject himself fully to the colonial authority.

"Oh, I am alone. I am one person only," Chief Awich allegedly declared when he arrived at the prison in Kampala, as informants sometimes let me know. *Kololo* was the Acholi expression he used in expressing his solitude, I was told. To be forced to live in solitude, a total restriction of ordinary social life, disoriented and disconnected from family and relatives, is very distressing, my informants held. The social solitude made the punishment even worse. In 1919, the Payira chief finally returned from his exile. As an irony of history, perhaps, the area where the chief spent his time in solitude and imprisonment has today developed into a fashionable and fancy Kampala suburb called Kololo. There, Western diplomats and officials live in heavily gated residences.

Imperial ideologies and the colonial drawing of ethnic borders, as well as the inclusion of Acholi on the global scene—for example, the Acholi young men who joined the colonial army and traveled overseas to fight in both world wars—encouraged intellectuals and political leaders to reformulate the structures of leadership. The aim was to be better able to face and take control over new challenges, as Uganda developed from a colonial protectorate into an independent state. The idea of a paramount Acholi leader was promoted, and several terms were suggested for the position, notably *rwot Acholi* (chief or king of the Acholi), *lawir rwodi* (the head of the chiefs), *rwot madit* (the big chief), and *laloyo maber* (the winner is good). One old informant suggested to me that these terms came into existence in direct response to the Buganda kingdom's increasing demands for self-determination in the independence process (see also Leys 1967: 19; Onyango-Odongo 1993: 9). Simultaneously, a struggle over the paramount status erupted between the Payira and the Padibe. Emerging party politics on the eve of independence added to the struggle. Uganda's largest party, the Uganda National Congress (UNC) with Milton Obote as its national leader, committed itself to the Payira's claim to Acholi paramountcy (Gertzel 1974).[6]

The term most commonly heard nowadays for a unified cultural Acholi leadership is *rwot Acholi*, the chief of the Acholi, or, as some informants prefer to put it, the king of Acholi. However, not all Acholi accept the idea of a paramount office. Today the Payira promote their chief as the paramount Acholi cultural leader. In this effort, the important link between the Payira and the Bunyoro kingdom is once more emphasized. For example, in 1999, when the new chief of the Payira, Onen Acana II, was anointed and ritually installed, official representatives of the Bunyoro kingdom were honored guests. The guests played a central role in the anointment ritual, as they had done also in the past when chiefs of the Payira were anointed and installed. Yet, as Säfholm (1973: 59) notes, "The chief of Payera could be more accurately described as the leading Acholi chief, than the chief of all the Acholi." And indeed, representatives from some other chiefdoms accepted Chief Acana under the assumption that the paramount chair would revolve between the chiefdoms. As the Ugandan constitution dictates, these chiefly offices are titular only, without any administrative, legislative, or executive powers.

In emphasizing its leading status, the Payira leadership made its seat in the old headquarters of the colonial administration and tax authority in Gulu town, one of two identical houses strategically located on a small hill facing the town. Until recently, the sister building housed the leader of the Lamogi, another influential and historically important chiefdom as well as one of Payira's closest allies. In Gulu town, exemplifying the wittiness that subaltern criticism of the established order often displays, people critical of the Payira chief as paramount of all Acholi did not fail to point out to me the irony in the fact that Payira and Lamogi took possession of the colonial buildings.

MAPS, MYTHS, AND STORYTELLING

In Acholiland, the imperial explorers could not find any close equivalence to the centralized kingdoms of Buganda and Bunyoro, nations that they traveled through on their way from the coast via Lake Victoria, before proceeding northward along the Nile. "There are no sultans here of any consequence, each village appointing its own chief," wrote John Hanning Speke (1863: 575). The colonial demand for such "sultans" made ethnic boundaries more rigid than before, and this demand eventually inspired Acholi intellectuals to fashion a paramount office of the Acholi. I hesitate, however, to conclude that an Acholi tradition or custom was hereby invented. Rather, it was lived and made manifest in particular social situations. The making and remaking of meaning follows the changing conditions of everyday life. Culture, in this perspective, is in a constant state of becoming, repeatedly made, contested, remade, and again contested. "Culture always 'is,'" writes Fox (1985: 13, 138) on identity formations in colonial India, "but it has always just become so."

When it comes to non-Western settings, history reaches farther back than anthropologists often tend to admit. Even today, there is a tendency to conclude that history only starts when it is written down. In the context of Uganda, the textualization of history was initiated in the colonial era, but the real history cannot be limited to that of colonial presence. Regarding colonial India, Guha (1997: 75) convincingly deconstructs this Eurocentric no-state-equals-no-history perspective, and I see no reason why his argument should not be valid also for the African context. The colonial mapping, designation, and ruling of "tribes," as well as formal education and missionary work, made ethnic and cultural boundaries more rigid in explicit and formalized contexts such as politics and education, or in writing and on maps. Ugandan "tribes" were inscribed in the dominant historiography. On the other hand, I find it equally important to note that the Acholi and Acholiland are not colonial inventions only, and that colonial boundary-making by no means froze the play of collective identities.

Much anthropological work on ethnicity and collective identity emphasizes the importance of the boundary between ethnic groups rather than the cultural content of the specific ethnic groups. "The critical focus of investigation

. . . becomes the ethnic *boundary* that defines the group, not the cultural stuff that it encloses," as Barth (1969: 15) notes in his seminal work on ethnicity. But while Barth emphasizes the boundary as a complex phenomenon of human exchange and interaction, colonial scholarship tended to draw ethnic borders rather uncritically.

As I see it, the challenge is to highlight the importance in everyday life of the "cultural stuff" while recognizing that cultural orientations in life are never deterministic or final. I want to illustrate with a myth about the ancestors of the Alur of the West Nile region and the Acholi, two peoples living on each side of the Nile, who split. Two brothers are said to have quarreled and they decided to part from each other. The river figures as a prominent feature in the myth. One brother crossed the river, while the other remained behind. Indeed, as the Catholic missionary J. Pasquale Crazzolara (1950: 60) noted some fifty years ago, "Every Acooli or Aluur can tell you the story of the weary search for a spear and the ripping of a child's belly to recover a swallowed bead." The myth was narrated to me on several occasions. This version I collected from Kitgum:

> A long time ago there was a family: a man with two sons. They were of Luo origin, and they came from Ethiopia via Sudan to Uganda. The man came to a place of no return [that is, he was about to die of old age]. He summoned his two sons, Labongo and Gipir, and handed over the ancestral spear to Labongo, the eldest son. The old man told Labongo to hand over the spear to his eldest son in the future. Then the father died, and the two brothers moved further south, to present Acholiland, east of the river Nile. One day, it was misty, very misty. The visibility was less than one meter. That very morning the wife of Labongo went out to look for firewood. She heard some movement in the garden, something huge was moving there. She raised an alarm, and Gipir, the younger brother of Labongo, came running, asking what was going on. Was there any danger? An elephant was approaching. Gipir rushed into Labongo's hut and grabbed the nearest spear, and he threw it at the elephant. But it happened to be Labongo's ancestral spear. Then the mist disappeared, and the elephant was gone. Gipir tried to explain the situation to Labongo, but Labongo became very, very angry with his brother. "You must get the ancestral spear back! You must go now!" Labongo ordered Gipir.

Gipir pleaded, but in vain. So he set off on safari, entering a dense forest, and for many months nothing was heard from him. Deep in the forest he found an old woman. "My son, what has brought you here?" she asked. Gipir told her about the wounded elephant and the lost spear. He had sore feet, his sandals were worn out, and he was totally exhausted. The old woman nursed him for one month. Then she told him of a place in the forest where elephants bring spears. Gipir went there with the woman, who managed to get the lost spear back for him. The old woman prepared food for Gipir's safari back home and she also gave him some beads. They were so beautiful that no one had seen the like. It took Gipir several months before he arrived at his home in Acholi. On arrival, he blew his horn and children came to greet him, but he just passed by them and went straight to Labongo, all worked up with anger and annoyance. He stuck the spear in the ground in front of his brother. Then he sat down, tired. Everyone came to greet him, and in the tumult, the beads fell out of his purse. One of Labongo's daughters picked up a bead and happened to swallow it. Gipir grabbed the girl and turned to Labongo. "My brother, she has swallowed one of my beads, and I want it back immediately." Now it was Labongo's turn to plead with his brother, but again the plea was in vain. So Labongo lost his temper and grabbed his daughter, cut her stomach open and gave the bead back to Gipir. The girl died.

The brothers decided to part and performed a ritual to destroy their relationship and kinship ties. They went to a small river, one on each side, turning their backs to each other. Then they cursed the woman who had breast-fed them. After the curse, they went in opposite directions. Gipir eventually arrived at the Nile, a river so big that no one had seen the like elsewhere. He found a huge tree, which he worked on for several weeks. He managed to cut it down, and put a log across the river, as a bridge. Then he crossed the Nile. (Kitgum town, December 1999)

In the myth, Gipir is the ancestor of the Alur, Labongo of the Acholi.[7] Various structural elements or themes can easily be identified, but the myth is always colored or even altered by the narrator's unique choice of style and emphasis. To live, it must be topical and part and parcel of contemporary contentions and controversies, to recall Liyong's (1970: x) assertion. In commenting on a draft of this chapter, my friend Tonny objected firmly to the idea that Gipir would have used a log to cross the Nile, and so did some elderly men he sought support from. Instead Gipir used an ax (*latong*) to divide the water of the river, he said, something that is suggested also by versions common in the literature (e.g., Bere 1947: 1–2; Wild 1954; p'Bitek 1973: 26).

The versions of the story already in print include features well-known from biblical mythology. In these versions, Gipir's crossing of the divided Nile is the central feature. Gipir "subjected himself to an ordeal by water to prove that he was not in the wrong and marched into the Nile, calling upon God to help him; the water divided and he passed safely over to the west bank" (Bere 1947: 2; see also Wild 1954: 3). Moses' crossing of the Red Sea is the well-known biblical parallel—as narrated in Exodus 14.21: "And Moses stretched out his hand over the sea; and the Lord caused the sea to go back by a strong east wind all that night, and made the sea dry land, and the waters were divided." Initially, one is inclined to conclude that the river is the border of no return, both symbolic and physical, which the myth as presented in the colonial literature also suggests. Gipir drove his ax into the riverbed, Bere (1947: 2) writes, to be a sign that neither he nor his brother could cross the river again. They could meet again only as enemies.[8]

TO RESTORE LOST RELATIONSHIPS

Kopytoff (1987) notes that Africa is a "frontier continent." Kin-based quarrels, factional struggles, and group fission are prominent themes in the historical mythologies of African societies and their migrations. Kopytoff emphasizes the conflicting principles of equality (for example, brothers) and hierarchy (age and seniority), most often made manifest in conflicts over succession, in which "the losing claimant would withdraw with a group of close kinsmen, adherents, and retainers" (Kopytoff 1987: 24). In an ideal model of fission, the losing claimant is a younger brother.[9] Here I want to highlight another but related theme, in which kinship and relatedness are emphasized. The myth cannot of course be taken as the historical and factual background of the Acholi. Still, the various versions illustrate the way in which ethnic labels and ethnic boundaries are constantly made and remade according to changing political and historical contexts.

Oral traditions are lived social documents rather than historical documents in the strict sense. They motivate action in the present (Jackson 2002b: 294).

The Kitgum storyteller emphasized common belonging, even kinship. The central theme was about the brothers who cursed their mother after the little girl had been killed. In the colonial version, the myth almost takes a biblical turn, making the split rather definitive. As Moses crossed the Red Sea, so one of the brothers crosses the Nile. As in the Bible, God is an active agent in this version, as he divides the waters, or orders his earthly agent to do so. Indeed this version adheres to the colonial concern for bounded ethnic entities, the so-called tribes. In yet another version that I encountered, the beads are not given to the traveling brother by the old woman but offered to him by Arab traders as payment for the tusks of the elephant that disappeared with the spear in the first place (Donga and Arweny n.d.). As the myth continues to be relevant over time, historical events are included in the storytelling, and meaning is recreated.

The Kitgum storyteller framed the myth in the context of the present war, and it emphasized the possibility of interethnic coexistence, even reconciliation. As we sat under a mango tree in his compound, the storyteller was explicit about the myth's moral lesson that he wanted to mediate to me. After I had recorded the myth in my notebook, he immediately proceeded to explain carefully his version to me. "Only truth, justice, mercy, and forgiveness will bring peace to Acholiland. Bitterness and guilt will hold you as a captive," he explained after narrating the myth. "Peace," he furthermore held, must be built on the "restoration of lost relationships." Explanation here is an understanding developed through questions and answers, a kind of reciprocal explanation that enables a deepened understanding of the lived reality (Ricoeur 1991). Storytelling, in this perspective, is an intersubjective practice. "What the map cuts up, the story cuts across," notes de Certeau (1984: 129).

The context in which a myth is narrated, and not its structure alone, is of relevance to anthropological understanding and explanation. Following the version that I recorded in Kitgum, I suggest that the brothers' joint curse of their mother is a central feature of the coming split. By way of the curse, the separation was performed and the boundary drawn. The curse was the consensual act that had to follow the killing of the little girl, a serious crime. A small river figures in the version above, but the crossing of the Nile only comes in later. I therefore suggest that the ethnic boundary is not really the Nile or any other river, as suggested however by today's printed maps of the region, but the killing of the girl and, subsequently, the brothers' joint curse of their mother.

Yet such a curse could be reconciled ritually and the social barrier thus lifted, if only with great effort (see also Onyango-Odongo 1976: 60–65). My Ugandan friends narrated the myth to me on various occasions, always with emphasis on the historical break between the two brothers, and consequently of two peoples, but often the storytellers wanted more to emphasize to me the relatedness and cultural affinity between the Acholi and the Alur, their western neighbors.

The Kitgum storyteller's version of the myth can be understood as an existential expression of coping. The storyteller's reworking of the myth provides, at least potentially, "a tentative basis for interaction" (Jackson 1998: 108). The storyteller made an effort to mediate a sense of direction in the present, or a sense of a future, despite the fact that war makes the surroundings seriously bad. Such coping strategies are best left not analytically categorized in terms of traditional or modern, ethnic or political. Nor do they have any inbuilt meaning once and for all defined, regardless of context. Rather they illustrate "the dialectics of identity," which can be fruitfully analyzed "not in purely cultural or political terms but in terms of an existential struggle for choice, control, presence, and ontological security" (Jackson 1998: 154).

In evoking the idea of a lived quest for ontological security, in which meaning is intrinsically tied to changing existential situations, Jackson proposes that anthropologists pay attention to what informants do with their beliefs and traditions, or how meaning is lived, rather than what these beliefs and traditions may mean in any final sense.[10] In their personal lives, as with many young people, my friend Otim p'Ojok and his life companion Susan have indeed reconciled the split proposed by the spear-and-beads myth, a split made definite in the literature of colonial forecasters. Otim p'Ojok grew up north of Gulu, Acholiland. Susan, however, comes from Pakwach in Alurland. They have a son called Petum. Susan became pregnant with Petum though she was still unmarried and living in her family's house. Her predicament, as emphasized by Tonny, was of course not a curse (kwong or lam), rather the contrary. But as her Alur relatives maintained, the young couple's actions had infringed the customary course of intimate social relations. The Acholi call these kinds of infringements kiir. For the sake of the couple and their families, not least Susan's unmarried brothers, the act of kiir needed to be settled ritually. Otim p'Ojok, an Acholi, agreed to provide a goat for the Alur cleansing ritual. It was performed, and the young family now has a place of their own in Gulu town.

The myth of the spear and the beads emphasizes precolonial—or rather non-colonial—dimensions of belonging, such as kinship idioms and the curse. Its storytellers will adjust it to meet present concerns, adding a moral dimension to the arbitrations of meaning in everyday life. Yet it is also a historical document of cultural orientations in the region. Dwyer holds that the idea of a common Acholi identity ought to be traced to precolonial times. "Although the individual Acholi's first awareness was of his [or her] clan," Dwyer (1972: 12) writes, prior to colonization "there was recognition of the limits of Acholi territory, particularly by powerful political leaders." In 1976, this argument was further developed in a volume that was colored by the historical-materialist and anticolonial approach of that time. The volume, focusing on myths and possible routes of migration, was entitled *The central Lwo during the Aconya* (Onyango-Odongo and Webster 1976a). *Aconya* is a local word for precolonial times. Thus the title of the volume suggests that we should not highlight only colonial or postcolonial times when describing Acholi history and Acholi ethnic identity. This suggestion alone proves the volume to be relevant reading even today.

The argument is more recently elaborated and refined by Atkinson, one of the contributors to the *Aconya* volume. Atkinson's (e.g., 1994) objective, like Dwyer's, is to trace the origin of Acholi collective belonging to precolonial times. Quite accurately, he points out that "the colonial and post-colonial representations of ethnic identities in Uganda, however distorted or manipulative, have not been plucked from the air or created out of nothingness" (Atkinson 1994: 2). Based on oral histories, the detailed account then sets out to identify precolonial dimensions of belonging among the many Acholi chiefdoms. Interesting to note, Atkinson (1984; 1994) argues that the notion of the Acholi people as Luo descendants should be taken with caution (see also Onyango-Odongo and Webster 1976b). Rather, Acholi collective identity as we know it today was formed from the early eighteenth century onward, when droughts and other processes forced the different groups of peoples in the region that is today's Acholiland to intermingle and cooperate in larger political units than previously. In the process, chiefdoms and a common language developed. According to Atkinson's (1984; 1994: 97–102) conclusion, the groups that mingled were Moru-Madi (Central Sudanic speakers), Teso-Karamojong

(Eastern Nilotic or Nilo-Hamitic speakers), and Central Luo (Western Nilotic speakers). From the eighteenth century onward, Atkinson argues, today's Acholiland can be likened to an internal African frontier, in Kopytoff's (1987) sense of the term. Eventually a chiefly sociopolitical order with aristocratic clans emerged, influenced by Paluo immigrants from the northern part of the Bunyoro-Kitara kingdom. Within a few generations, Luo was to become the lingua franca of the region, though in a variety of dialects (Atkinson 1984: 112–117). This internal frontier process, Atkinson concludes, is the historical circumstance that molded Acholi ethnic identity as we know it today. Girling advances a similar argument. "Acholiland is situated at a meeting point of the three language families usually known in Britain as the Nilotic, Sudanic and Nilo-Hamitic" (Girling 1960: 54). Girling quotes Stuhlmann, who already in 1916 argued that Acholiland has functioned as a "contact zone" in the history of migrations in the region (see also Crazzolara 1950; 1954; cf. Pratt 1992).

The myth about the spear and the beads does not establish any distinctive precolonial Luo origin of the Acholi. Rather, the myth is evoked to serve contemporary claims of historical Luo origin. It emphasizes precolonial collective belongings to the region, always expressed, however, in a context of contemporary problems and dilemmas. As the myth was narrated the storyteller made his intentions explicit: despite war and ethnic divides, the hope remains that differences can be bridged. In the narrative process, the myth became one of many stories that "cross, breach and blur the boundaries that demarcate crucial political and ethical spaces" of everyday life (Jackson 2002b: 30, 25). Still, it must be assumed that the myth, like the language in which it originally was narrated, or Acholi collective identity for that matter, is not a colonial invention. The Acholi's "domains of belonging," to refer to Fernandez (1986: xii), predates the arrival of Europeans in Uganda. People in the region have always organized their social worlds, it must be assumed. Ethnicity is not only about communicating differences over imagined or real boundaries, but also about the communication of sameness and unity.

Even if colonial practices resulted in a relative fixation of ethnic borders, communication, exchange, and interdependence over borders still remain frequent today. During fieldwork, I often heard old people encourage the younger generation to marry over ethnic divides. Colonialism and the world economy increased global connectedness, and borders were made more fixed than before. Districts were created, ethnic boundaries made into geographic borders, and maps were drawn, to mention a few examples. Yet, to put words to a phenomenon, whether in English or any other colonial tongue, or even to put these words in print, does not mean that something has thus been invented. Contrary to a printed text, culture as lived and celebrated in society is not fixed, as meanings are situational and never definitive.

"The Acholi did not exist in precolonial times," argues Behrend (1999a: 14). At that time, she continues, "there was *no real* Acholi ethnic identity" but only localized clan identities (Behrend 1999a: 16, emphasis added). When the colonialists created the Acholi district, she concludes, they were "thus creating an ethnic group that had not existed before" (Behrend 1999a: 18). Colonial ruling strategies indeed reified social groupings, various chiefdoms and kingdoms in Uganda as *tribal* (see p'Bitek 1970a: 9–16). Still, I think we ought to question the idea of "the Acholi" as a colonial creation on the grounds that historical forebears of the Acholi also lived and socialized with one another before Europeans discovered their land and put a name to it in writing, or put borders on the map. I therefore hesitate to conclude that Acholi ethnic identity was a colonial invention only because it was *labeled* tribal, or because colonial agents were the first to *write down* the term "Acholi."[11]

My discussion will give the reader an idea of the debate on the history of the Acholi people. My primary aim has not been to establish the origin of the Acholi, or whether the Acholi people are proper Luo descendants or not. Just as Murdock's (1959: viii) mission to bring "order out of chaos in African linguistic classification" was rather illusory, equally misleading was the enterprise of colonialists, colonial scholars, and their postcolonial followers to find definite categories and subcategories of Ugandans with clear-cut historical origins. Still, I want to stress that collective belonging in Acholiland did not begin with colonialism, nor were meanings of Acholi social worlds fixed once and for all with colonialism. Even though few scholars would agree with such a categorical assertion, it nevertheless had a lasting consequence on much writing on ethnicity and politics in Uganda. Okuku's (2002: 8) hasty statement in an otherwise insightful paper, quoted above, that "tribes" are modern constructions, interventions of colonialism, which froze the play of identities, is one such example. Equally questionable is Behrend's (1999a: 16) conclusion that "no real Acholi ethnic identity" existed in precolonial times, or even that the violent intrusion of ivory traders in the region in the mid-nineteenth century "was such a watershed that any outline of what life was like before then must be largely speculative" (Allen 1988–1989: 48; cf. Atkinson 1999: 33).[12]

Obviously, historical particularities form ethnic identity. It is lived, imagined, and politically manipulated. The Acholi district emerged during the colonial epoch, and present-day Acholiland was a contact zone between different stakeholders, of whom the colonialists had the most forceful powers. But a focus on colonial dominance only tends to bracket off the colonial epoch from precolonial and postcolonial developments. The colonial epoch is then regarded as formative and its political processes somehow final. Colonialism created "tribes," so it is said, and ethnicity has sometimes come to be defined as a modern phenomenon only. Precolonial processes are not included when the history of non-Western peoples is written. And postcolonial processes are equally neglected when collective identity formation is discussed. Such a conclusion, I suggest, is unfortunately close to the idea of ethnic identities as static and cultures as texts. Sahlins, however, reminds us that the dialectic of similarity and difference is the normal mode of cultural production. "It is not unique to the contemporary globalizing world," he writes. "On the contrary," he concludes, "its precolonial and extracolonial occurrences help explain the colonial and postcolonial" (Sahlins 1999: 411).

PRELUDE TO WAR

The treachery of the negro is beyond belief; he has not a moral human instinct, and is below the brute. How is it possible to improve such abject animals? They are not worth the trouble, and they are only fit for slaves, to which position their race appears to have been condemned. (BAKER 1874: 315, VOL. 2; SEE ALSO 1866: 56, VOL. 1)

Samuel W. Baker traveled extensively in Central Africa. After returning from his first journey in the early 1860s, he was knighted. With this official recognition in his luggage, he again set off for Africa, now with a proclaimed mission to suppress the slave trade. Yet, as he navigated his way back deep into the African continent, he sometimes forgot to follow the official agenda for his travels. As we see in the quotation above from his personal journal, which he chose to include in his published report, he instead conformed to the racist ideas that dominated imperial Europe at that time. "Any warm expressions . . . must be excused as a natural consequence," wrote Baker (1874: 314, vol. 2), justifying himself.

The travelogues dealing with Uganda are a sad prelude to the violence being committed today in Acholiland. John Hanning Speke, who traveled through present-day Acholiland in northern Uganda in late 1862 on his way from

Zanzibar to Khartoum, was impressed by the hospitality that Acholi people showed him. Despite reportedly difficult times with famine and granaries run dry, he was served food and drink. Still, Speke found it a contradiction in terms that almost naked people displayed hospitality and generosity. "What politeness in the midst of such barbarism!!!" he concludes of the Acholi he encountered, a people whose bodily postures he had a few sentences before compared with monkeys (Speke 1863: 574). Some years later Samuel Baker established stations in Patiko and Pabbo in Acholiland. Even Baker was to attest to the hospitality he experienced in Acholiland, and he described Patiko as "my little paradise" (Baker 1874: 473, vol. 2; see also 1866: 308, vol. 2).

To establish their own imperial agenda, the Europeans initially acted on behalf of Egypt's imperial ambition. Following their initial explorative journeys, they incorporated Acholiland into the Equatorial Province that, as the name indicates, consisted of the Nile equatorial region. From 1878, Emin Pasha administered Equatoria on behalf of the Egyptian government. Emin was under the decree of Charles George Gordon, Baker's successor and the region's governor based in Khartoum. Acholiland remained for a long time a colonial backwater, serving as little more than a corridor from Gondokoro (the administrative headquarters of Equatoria, which was accessible by boat from Khartoum) to the Bunyoro and Buganda kingdoms (Gray 1951: 128). The region was a buffer zone, protecting British interests against those of the approaching Belgians and French. Back in Europe, British diplomats convinced their French colleagues to surrender any claim to this "unknown and desolate swamp in Central Africa" (quoted in Gray 1952a: 44).

Baker, Emin Pasha, Gordon, Speke, and Stanley made the area known to the Western public. Their travelogues were translated into several European languages and were widely read in many parts of Europe. Baker, for example, published *Ismailia* in 1874, and the next year a Swedish translation followed (Baker 1874; 1875).[13] Baker is still vivid today in the Acholi collective memory as the person who ended the Arabs' slave trade. Even more remembered is that he traveled with his young wife, Florence von Sass. One Acholi clan, then based around Patiko, north of Gulu town, Baker's main station in Acholiland, has even taken an epithet after Mrs. Baker, informants told me. Pale and beautiful as the moon, Acholi people thought her, as they gave her the name *Anyadwe*, the daughter of the moon. Sometimes they call themselves the moon clan (see also Girling 1960: 135; Gray 1952b).

Imperial annals describe Baker as "terrible in battle, scrupulously just, at all times kind and jovial in demeanour amongst friends; a born ruler over a savage people." The words are Johnston's, the special commissioner to the Ugandan protectorate from 1899 to 1901, and as late as 1951 they were quoted to validate Baker's contribution to the colonizing project (Johnston quoted in Gray 1951: 127). On location in Acholiland, the colonial authority in northern Uganda actively promoted the memory of Samuel and Florence Baker. The authorities eventually decided to rebuild the walls of Baker's fort in Patiko. Despite war and destruction, even today these walls are there, "thus providing a material focus for the tradition" (Girling 1960: 152).[14]

Baker was as violent as most of his fellow European colonial emissaries, also involved in the scramble for Africa. His second travelogue (1874) ends with a blunt effort to justify the imperial project as it was carried out in Africa. The end justified the means, Baker argued, perhaps to counter the increasing criticism he was hearing from antiracist intellectuals in the imperial centers (see Hochschild 1998; Lindqvist 1996; 1997). Large numbers of Africans died when they encountered these explorative expeditions, whose underlying objective was to locate and annex the source of the Nile and thereby all the riches that this river generates. In European mythology, the Nile basin was really the heart of Africa and a prize many felt worth claiming, even at some cost. In the initial colonial mapping, lakes were named after British royalty, and perhaps of even greater symbolic importance, but of enormous hardship to the many African porters, steamers were brought all the way from Khartoum to traffic the Ugandan lakes.[15]

To open up the space for trade was central to the European mission to Africa. The dynamics of European imperial expansion were an absolute precondition for the development of European industrialization itself (see, for example, Hornborg 2001). Industrialization in Europe created new patterns of exchange and production, with new products—the machine gun, for example, perhaps the single most essential tool in the colonizing project. But to sustain itself and its development, European industrialization needed to transcend its own limitations. This was done through technological development but, more important here, also through the search for new markets and new sources of raw material, even manpower. Escalating industrial production, located in or close to the imperial centers, could be catered to only by a continuous expansion of overseas trade. Racist ideologies offered timely legitimacy to the imperial dimension of this expansion and even legitimated the gross violence that eventually led to genocide in some of the imperial and industrial peripheries. Imperial and industrial growth in the centers was accumulative but more important, appropriative. Eventually, Uganda became a reservoir of cotton, coffee, tea, and other raw materials needed for the industrial revolution in the colonial center (Mamdani 1976: 48). To extract these raw materials, labor in the colonial periphery was desperately needed.

The market economy in northern Uganda was initiated on unequal premises. For example, ivory was to be brought en masse to the imperial centers. Baker (1874) estimated the profit at a minimum of 1,500 to 2,000 percent, transport costs included. As he noted, "A few beads, together with three or four gaudy-coloured cotton handkerchiefs, a zinc mirror, and a fourpenny butcher's knife, would purchase a tusk worth twenty or thirty pounds" (Baker 1874: 250, vol. 2). The incorporation of Uganda into the world market was legitimated in moral terms, as a welcome dimension of the civilizing project. It is worth quoting Speke's first travelogue of Central Africa. This time it was the peoples living by the southern shores of Lake Victoria who came under imperialist scrutiny:

> This country being full of sweet springs, accounts for the denseness of the population and numberless heads of cattle. To look upon its resources, one is struck with amazement at the waste of the world: if instead of this district being in hands of its present owners, it were ruled by a few scores of Europeans, what an entire revolution a few years would bring forth! An extensive market would be opened to the world, the present nakedness of the land would have a covering, and industry and commerce would clear the way for civilisation and enlightenment. (Speke 1864: 344)

In their "dreadful sloth," as Speke (1864: 344–345) described the Africans he met, they were, "both morally and physically, little better than brutes, and as yet there is no better prospect in store for them."

The European explorers also took it upon themselves to speak for the Africans. "The great cause," Speke (1864: 344) concluded, "is their want of a strong protecting government." In the imperial rhetoric, only the *wazungu*, or the "white or wise men" as Speke (1864: 358, 269) interpreted the name that he and his fellow Europeans were given, could provide this government (see also Girling 1960: 133).

Violence, intimidation, and military action were endemic to the imperial mission. Baker (1874: 252, vol. 1) had staked an exclusive claim, in his annexation regulations for northern Uganda and southern Sudan in 1871, for the ivory, "all ivory being the property and monopoly of the government." He represented this government, and he made sure to secure the asymmetrical relations of exchange on paper, thereby assuming full legitimacy. In this process, it happened that whole villages were destroyed when they failed to satisfy the demands of the imperial agents and their personnel regarding food and porters, or if they refused to pay the tax necessary for the support of Baker's troops (Gray 1951: 126). If Africans along the route were regarded as hostile, they were also defined as legitimate targets of military violence:

> The first steps in establishing the authority of a new government in a tribe hitherto savage and intractable were of necessity accompanied by *military operations. War is inseparable from annexation,* and *the law of force,* resorted to in *self-defence,* was absolutely indispensable to prove the superiority of the power that was eventually to govern. The end justified the means. (Baker 1874: 513, vol. 2, emphasis added)

These words conclude his account. Before this conclusion, however, Baker presents the reader with narratives of the law of force, and his military operations in alleged self-defense. The Bari people, living in Sudan, north of Acholi-land, were ravaged in their encounter with Baker and his team:

> On our return to the station, I took a snider [rifle], and practically explained to the rascals in the village on the knoll what long range meant, sending several bullets into the midst of a crowd that scattered them like chaff. I at once ordered Colonel Abd-el-Kader to take eighty men and some blue lights, and to destroy every village in the neighbourhood. The attack was made on the instant. The large village, about 700 yards distant, which I had raked with the fire of a few sniders, while Abd-el-Kader descended the slope to the attack, was soon a mass of rolling flames. In an hour's time volumes of smoke were raising in various directions. (Baker 1874: 321, vol. 2)

The war of annexation, to use Baker's words, or regime of terror, to use a more adequate description, was crucial in the colonial pursuit of raw products and new markets. As was the case with trade and missionary work, the violence of the imperialist expansion was legitimated morally, in terms of a civilizing project. The Africans were to be civilized through militarization. Again Baker's words:

> I believe that if it were possible to convert the greater portion of African savages into disciplined soldiers, it would be the most rapid stride towards their future civilization. The fact of obedience being enforced, and the necessity of order, industry, and discipline, together with clothing and cleanliness, is all that is absolutely required to bring a savage within the bounds of good management. A savage who has led a wild and uncontrolled life must first learn to obey authority before any great improvement can be expected. (Baker 1874: 302, vol. 1)

After his final departure for Europe, the troops that Baker trained and left behind in Acholiland turned to gross abuse and violation of the local people. Neither Gordon nor Emin Pasha, his successors, managed to reverse this development (Gray 1951; Atkinson 1978: 516–522). Eventually Baker was to revise his stand on the civilizing project in Uganda, basing his argument mainly on the poor commercial prospects. These poor prospects, Baker held, were a consequence of the Ugandan population's laziness and idle lifestyle, which encouraged them to refuse to work for the colonialists. For the sake of British taxpayers, Uganda was best left out of further colonization projects, Baker concluded as he retired from the debate (Girling 1960: 149).

The colonizing project, however, continued. The Ugandan protectorate was announced in 1894, and by 1898 it included Acholiland as well. Colonial control in the form of imposed taxes, confiscation of firearms, and forced recruitment of porters and labor became the order of the day. In 1911–1912, a growing number of local malcontents were brought together under Lamogi leadership in western Acholiland. But the British played their cards of divide and rule well, and "the Lamogi rebellion" was soon crushed (Adimola 1954). In colonial parlance the rebellious Lamogi, and the Acholi in general, were now finally "pacified."

The Acholi, organized without sultans of "any consequence" as Speke (1863: 575) claimed, came to suffer under the racist imperial authority they had to obey. In the words of Postlethwaite (1947: 71), the pioneer colonial administrator, Acholi took "to soldiering like ducks to water." Postlethwaite confirmed the conclusion made by E. T. N. Grove in one of the first systematic ethnographic descriptions of the Acholi. As Grove (1919: 163) misleadingly wrote, "War was the constant occupation of the Acholi before the Government took over their country and usually took the form of night raids on other villages." Sometimes, Grove added, "war was raised however on a more formal scale," but the reader is left in ignorance as to what he really meant with the word "war."

As the First World War started, Postlethwaite recruited the so-called Acholi warriors into the King's African Rifles. Missionary accounts supported the image of the Acholi as lacking proper leadership but still potentially suitable for military recruitment. "On the whole one would call them a fine race physically, but not warlike. Probably if they had a leader, they would make a fighting tribe," the Anglican missionary Albert B. Lloyd wrote in 1904 (reprinted in Lloyd 1948: 84). A few years later and in a somewhat harsher tone, Lloyd again regretted that no centralized authority seemed to exist to govern the "warlike instincts" of this potential "fighting race" (Lloyd 1907: 211). As the irony of history had it, the colonized subjects, rather than the oppressive colonialists, were labeled as warlike. Taussig's (1984: 495) classic description of the construction of colonial culture could not be more fitting—it is a "*colonial mirror* which reflects back onto the colonialists the barbarity of their own social relations, but as imputed to the savage or evil figures they wish to colonize."

Few scholars have made any serious effort to question the view that the Acholi were warlike. Rather, academic understandings continue to reinforce the stereotype of allegedly dominant traditions and fixed categories. Colonial and postcolonial Uganda experienced a division of labor along regional lines, confirming to the stereotype image of the Acholi. With time, Acholi society was to become the stereotypical other. It is as if Baker's suggestion about the conversion of "savages" into "soldiers" came true. In postcolonial writings, the Acholi have been described in terms of a "militarized ethnicity" (e.g., Mazrui 1976: 258–263), "military ethnocracy" (Mazrui 1975; Doom and Vlassenroot 1999: 8), "military democracy" (Amaza 1998: 213–214), or as "the country's military elite" (De Temmerman 2001: vii). In text, discourse is fixed by writing, and the social context, which evoked the text in the first place, tends to evaporate. As Ricoeur (1991: 113) has it, the "place" of the story transfers into a "nonplace" of the text. Culture in the making comes to equal the invention of cultures, even "tribes." The social reality is then masqueraded as homogenous rather than heterogeneous and contextual.

This of course has implications even today in Ugandan politics.

Chapter 2

NEOCOLONIAL LEGACIES AND EVOLVING WAR

POLITICAL HISTORIES

Politics, Karlström (2004) argues in an article on postwar rebuilding in Buganda, south-central Uganda, has been independent Uganda's constant curse. It is politics, in other words, that characterizes the country's postcolonial nightmare. The "moral rehabilitation" and "development eutopianism" that now take root, he explains, are not the expression of a utopian impossibility but a realizable ideal, workable in everyday life. Indeed, most people, Ugandans as well as outside observers, argue that things have been slowly developing for the better in Uganda since Museveni's takeover in 1986.[1] The postcolonial nightmare is finally over, so the widespread feeling goes, and Uganda is held to be a success story of economic liberalization, development, progress, and increasing political stability, celebrated for its fight against HIV/AIDS.

Ravaged by twenty years of war, the Acholi have not shared in any part of this story of success. And it is Acholi stories of being caught up in the war that inform my understanding of it. In this chapter, I do not attempt to present a strict chronology of events. Rather, I will intersperse the chronology of war with digressions that discuss postcolonial politics in Uganda. This will help show how people in the war zone perceive the complex politics of war, and how they experience some of the measures and political reforms introduced by the Ugandan government. I will balance this horizon of understanding against a perspective, far more common in writings on postcolonial Uganda, in which the war in the north has most often been portrayed as a peripheral exception to the country's claimed success. In the dominant narrative, if the war in the north is commented on at all, the crisis is held to be humanitarian rather than political, and the typical depiction has been a one-sided and sometimes exoticizing focus on the various Holy Spirit rebel movements, and thus on the religious, even pseudocultural, aspects of the war. Karlström, for example, summarizes the war as "a tragically suicidal popular uprising in northern Uganda" and "a mass movement of collective moral expiation and salvation" (2004: 598).

In 2002 I had a conversation with a representative of the Carter Center, which has been involved as a mediator in the region. His work in Uganda and Sudan had given him thorough insights into the armed conflicts in the region. I was about to end fieldwork, on my way back to Sweden, and we met in Kampala to exchange views on the war in northern Uganda. He asked for my opinion of what the war was all about, and I answered by stating that it is not primarily about ethnicity. "Why not?" he immediately countered. "Because that explanation is too simple," I tried to answer, suggesting that such an explanation would be reductionist. "But the simple explanations are the best, aren't they?" he again countered with confidence.

Despite my firm belief that an armed conflict like the one in northern Uganda seldom has any single cause, his straightforwardness made me feel uncertain, somewhat nervous. I was left with the feeling that my words failed me. The conversation went on, and by referring to chauvinistic statements of various senior politicians on both sides of the alleged ethnic divide, he put his case quite successfully. Of course, regional tensions have deepened during the years of war, a development often portrayed in terms of ethnic cleavages inherited from the past. In Uganda it became a colonial truism that a soldier is a northerner, a civil servant a southerner, and a merchant an Asian. It is difficult to argue against the forcefulness of such neat and essentialist conclusions, but my aim is to do exactly that. Schoenbrun writes: "Local voices retool the semantics of ethnicity by being specific. Their specificity defeats the manipulation of ethnicity, itself a nexus for power. Failing to hear subaltern voices, still newer forms of oppression may masquerade as 'ethnic,' and be promulgated as such by intellectuals" (Schoenbrun 1993: 48).

The self-proclaimed field marshal Idi Amin, Ugandan head of state from 1971 to 1979, preferred to recruit people from the West Nile region to the secret police and armed forces. More particularly, among the people of West Nile origin he favored individuals from his own ethnic group, the Kakwa. On the other hand, the security forces of Milton Obote, who presided over Uganda before Amin's military coup in 1971 and for a second period from 1980 to 1985, were dominated by Lango and Acholi. The late Obote was from Langoland, which borders the south and southeast of Acholiland. There is a history of rivalry and conflict between the Acholi and the Lango, but also a history of exchange and cooperation across ethnic boundaries (p'Bitek 1971: 32–37).

After Idi Amin's coup, as Hansen (1977: 92) writes, "Obote the individual swiftly became identified with the whole Lango group, and his regime with the Acholi as well." During the early years of his violent rule, Idi Amin ordered mass killings of Acholi army personnel as well as executions of prominent Acholi intellectuals and politicians, including the Anglican archbishop Janani Luwum. Today's scholarship on Uganda widely acknowledges that thousands of Acholi individuals died and that many more fled the country.[2] Amin and his associates also targeted Lango individuals. Yet, as Mazrui (1975: 117) correctly notes, "Had the vengeance of the coup been directed at the government of Obote as a whole, it would have had to be directed at people from almost every corner of Uganda." Indeed, Obote's ministers came from all over the country.

Especially after the fall of Amin in 1979, many projected the violence and other failures of his regime onto West Nilers in general. For that reason, most West Nilers who lived in Gulu town fled. Early on during Obote's second term in power, lasting from 1980 to 1985, soldiers in the new army, including Acholi individuals, took revenge on people living in the West Nile region (see, e.g., Crisp 1986; Gingyera-Pinycwa 1989: 55; Kasozi 1999: 176–177). Many fled "in fear of Acholi soldiers. They were bad; they tortured people, killing, so people had to run away. . . . They were using tit for tat," as one of Leopold's (2005: 56) West Nile informants explained. At the same time, pro-Amin insurgents launched attacks from Congo (then Zaire) and Sudan into the West Nile region of Uganda, adding to the violence there. Within a few years, some 300,000 people had fled to neighboring Sudan (Harrell-Bond 1986: 32, 42–47).

During the Amin years, a Muslim-Christian division also became manifest. The late Idi Amin originated from West Nile and was a descendant of the so-called Nubi Muslims recruited to the early colonial army, and he played on both of these belongings (Leopold 2006). In the eyes of many Ugandans, political and military powers are intimately connected with the social order of regional division, but Amin and his contemporaries only continued what had been initiated during the colonial years. Ethnic and religious differences, real and fictitious, polarized. Tit for tat.

The legacy of ethnic divisions along these lines has been prominently manifested in Ugandan postcolonial politics (Vincent 1999: 109–110). Uganda gained its independence in 1962, and the first government was a coalition of the Uganda People's Congress (UPC), chaired by Milton Obote, and Kabaka Yekka (The King Alone), a predominantly Bagandan party that promoted the indigenous royal institution. A third party, the Democratic Party, was in opposition. Obote was prime minister, while Edward Mutesa, the *kabaka* or king of Buganda, was installed as Uganda's ceremonial president. However, oppositional groups attempted to unseat Obote and the hostilities between the two coalition parties increased. In 1966, Obote abrogated the constitution, made himself president, and ordered the military, led by Idi Amin, to seize the *kabaka*'s palace in an effort to curb opposition.

In the following year Obote presented a new constitution. Then in 1969, as the president of a one-party state, he authored the Common Man's Charter, a nationalist manifesto also known as the Move to the Left. The charter was loaded with anticapitalist, antifeudal, antiimperial and antitribal rhetoric. It was distributed both in the English original and in various vernaculars, for example, Luo and Luganda (Aasland 1974; Gingyera-Pinycwa 1978: chap. 9; Glenthworth and Hancock 1973). But especially in Buganda, with the constitutional crisis of 1966 fresh in mind, the Move to the Left was regarded primarily as an expression of "Nilotic" ethnic chauvinism, imposed on the Baganda and other Bantu peoples of Uganda (Vincent 1999: 112–113). With reference to Obote's ethnic background from Lango in northern Uganda, influential Baganda leaders equated his political program with an alleged Nilotic nationalism that was anti-Baganda. Ethnic chauvinists on the other side of the divide, however, interpreted the Move to the Left as a welcome decolonization of the north. Colonial authority, in this latter perspective, had favored a feudal Bantu (Buganda) model of centralized sociopolitical organization. Many older informants in Acholiland remembered the Move to the Left with nostalgia. Amin, however, seized state power before the Move to the Left had any implications on the ground, and even many Baganda politicians who had witnessed Amin destroying the palace of their king welcomed the takeover (Mutibwa 1992: 81–86).

Neocolonial forces have contributed to the continuous ethnification and increased political violence in Uganda. For example, increasingly worried with the Move to the Left, British and Israeli interest groups were deeply involved in Idi Amin's takeover, and the British government was the first to recognize Amin as the new head of state. Global traders in weaponry, with direct links to powerful organizations such as the American CIA and various British security and communication companies, and eventually also their Soviet and Libyan counterparts, supplied Amin with arms and military technology after the international community's official denunciation of his regime (Furley 1989; Jørgensen 1981: 317–318; Mamdani 1984). Uganda was no exception to amoral gunrunning and imperialist disordering.

KAMPALA, 1981–1986: SHIFTING BATTLE ZONES

Like a foreign body in your eye—that is the situation [of] the Acholi people.

(ACHOLI CLAN ELDER, GULU TOWN, DECEMBER 1997)

We are told by Museveni that the Lord's Resistance Army belongs to past governments. But the Lord's Resistance Army children are born under Museveni's rule.

(ACHOLI MIDDLE-AGED WOMAN, LONDON, JULY 1998)

In 1981, Yoweri Museveni and the National Resistance Movement/Army (NRM/A) launched a guerrilla war in central Uganda with the objective of replacing Milton Obote's second government (1980–1985), commonly referred to as Obote II. Museveni took to arms with the argument that the 1980 elections that brought Obote back to power were rigged. Mutibwa (1992) legitimates Museveni's armed struggle. There was an absolute need to revolutionize Ugandan politics in the aftermath of Amin's fall from power, he holds, because "the system" that brought Obote back to power had been "created" by the colonialists and "inherited at independence." It was then "perfected" by Obote in the 1960s and "matured" under Amin's rule (Mutibwa 1992: 155; see also Museveni 1992: 31).[3]

During the course of Museveni's war against Obote, Brigadier Bazilio Olara Okello and General Tito Okello Lutwa, two senior men in the Ugandan army, both from Acholiland, seized power in 1985. The coup was the result of ethnic tension and growing mistrust in the Ugandan army regarding the violent developments under Obote's leadership. The new, unstable government led by Tito Okello encouraged all armed groups in opposition to join the new government. Tito Okello "specifically and publicly invited Museveni and the NRM/A to cease hostilities and join in national reconciliation and nation-building" (Kiplagat 2002: 24). The former Kenyan president Daniel arap Moi facilitated Nairobi-held talks between Okello and Museveni, as well as other oppositional groups. Okello's invitation included pro-Amin insurgents, a gesture of great symbolic importance that insulted many people and became a source of mutual mistrust in the post-Obote turmoil. Museveni eventually signed a peace deal with Okello, but simultaneously decided to continue fighting. Ngoga (1998: 104) argues that Museveni's NRM/A "had little interest in peace negotiations for anything but tactical purposes, when it was in any event on the brink of victory." Kampala was captured by Museveni in early 1986, making the Okello government short-lived, lasting only from 1985 to 1986. Museveni restricted the space of action for political parties in favor of the no-party "Movement" system that he introduced, by some celebrated but described by his critics and political opponents as a virtual one-party state (see, e.g., Mugaju & Oloka-Onyango 2000). By the time Uganda reverted to a constitutional system with political parties in 2005, the long-established Movement had accumulated enormous military, numerical, and other advantages over other parties.

With Museveni's ascension to power, Uganda's succession of rulers from the north came to an end—Obote was from Langoland, Okello was an Acholi, and Amin was a Kakwa from the West Nile region. Museveni is from the south of the country (he is a Munyankole from the southwest). No account of postcolonial political history in Uganda fails to mention this neatness of ethnic divisions, pinned on the individuals who ended up as presidents. But too many analyses stop here.

In geographical terms, Museveni's insurgency was principally restricted to the so-called Luwero triangle in central Uganda, although the high command decided to open a second battlefront in the west of the country not long before Kampala was captured. The human suffering in Luwero was immense, and mainly attributed to Obote's government forces (see, e.g., Isis-WICCE 1998). Such conclusions accord with Museveni's own claims. "During the whole of the bush war, there were only four or five capital offences," Museveni (1997:

134) writes. His claim, it seems to me, has been widely and uncritically accepted by most observers, who were shocked by the gross violence committed by the Ugandan army in its counterinsurgency campaign against Museveni's guerrillas. During the peak periods of fighting, however, a day seldom passed that families in Acholiland did not also receive condolences from the Ugandan government for dear ones who had died in direct battle, ambushes, and landmine blasts in the counterinsurgency campaigns.

A quotation from Ngoga (1998) expresses a view common among scholars of war and armed conflict, where the end of war is erroneously equated with the capture of a capital, or the signing of a peace agreement. As Ngoga states, "On 26 January 1986, it [the NRM/A] captured Kampala and *the war was effectively over.*" He continues that the NRM/A was "one of the most effective guerrilla insurgencies in Africa, and the first to defeat an incumbent regime and replace it by a successful *post-insurgency government*" (Ngoga 1998: 104, both emphases added). Woodward writes that Museveni "had a remarkable army that had come from the bush to overthrow the existing regime in the capital by a popular guerrilla campaign, a rare success in Africa for all its internal wars" (Woodward 1991: 180). Hansen and Twaddle (1994: 2) argue that Museveni's takeover was a military success, "pacifying the greater part of Uganda and leaving only a small strip of land bordering the southern Sudan prone to millenarian protest and external disruption." Similar conclusions often find their way into comparative studies on postcolonial Africa. In one such study, Uganda is mentioned only briefly, where in very general terms the authors conclude that Uganda is one of the African countries "where a logic of violence has been replaced by a political process of negotiation and rebuilding" (Bayart et al. 1999: 5).

Instead of signifying the end of war, the 1986 capture of Kampala marked the starting point of several new conflicts in Uganda. Within two years of Museveni's takeover, some twenty-seven different rebel groups were reported to be resisting the new government (Bond and Vincent 2002: 354). In effect, the battle zone simply shifted location, from central Uganda toward the north and the country's other peripheries.

In eastern Uganda, the Uganda People's Army (UPA) opposed the new government with military means from 1987 to 1992 (de Berry 2000; Henriques 2002). When this insurgency eventually was quelled, remaining factions joined rebels in northern Uganda (Gingyera-Pinycwa 1992: 22). In the West Nile region, the Uganda National Rescue Front (UNRF), a rebel group formed after Amin's fall from power, settled with Museveni and the new government. Splinter groups, notably the West Nile Bank Front (WNBF) and the Uganda National Rescue Front Part II (UNRF II), however, continued the armed resistance (Leopold 2005; Ofcansky 2000; see also Harrell-Bond 1986). And while a large portion of the rebels in West Nile have surrendered to a recent amnesty, some have joined the rebels still active in Acholiland.

In southwestern Uganda, the Allied Democratic Forces (ADF) came into being, with bases located in the Democratic Republic of Congo. The ADF started its activities in 1995, and as is the case with the LRA/M, they soon resorted to recruitment by mass abductions. Also based in southwest Uganda, and in alliance with the ADF, is the National Army for the Liberation of Uganda, or NALU (see Lucima 2002; Prunier 2004). NALU has threatened to focus its attacks on Westerners, who are alleged supporters of the Ugandan government. Also in the southwest, the Interahamwe militia (Rwandan Hutu) have raided Ugandan settings from bases in the conflict-ridden Democratic Republic of Congo. In response, the Ugandan army has sometimes deployed deep into the Congo, adding to the complexity of armed conflict in the Great Lakes region. Diametrically opposite, in northeastern Uganda heavily armed Karamojong cattle raiders add to the security problems. And in mid-1999 in Lira district, south of Acholiland, clashes erupted between the Ugandan army and police and a new rebel group calling itself the Citizens' Army for Multiparty Politics (CAMP), but this movement was short-lived. Other defunct post–Obote II rebel movements that can be mentioned are the Ninth October Movement (NOM) and Force Obote Back Again (FOBA).

The government has persistently alleged the existence of a new rebel movement called the People's Redemption Army (PRA), with bases in the Congo and supposedly coordinated by defected high-ranking officers of the Ugandan army. Ugandan security organs have arrested a growing number of the government's political opponents and accused them of being behind this movement (Human Rights Watch 2003a). Now and then, media reports suggest that a number of these armed groups in opposition are coordinating with each other, mainly through meetings that take place in Sudan and Congo.

It is apparent that Museveni's government, ever since the seizure of power in 1986, has fallen short in its effort to establish nationwide order and security. When Museveni captured Kampala in 1986, many soldiers from the previous governments fled northward. From bases in Sudan, some of them regrouped and launched the Uganda People's Democratic Movement/Army (UPDM/A), called both *cilil* (go and gossip, let the government know, exaggerate the stories about our presence) and *olum olum* (people of the bush) by the Acholi population (see Branch 2005; Lamwaka 1998; Nyeko and Lucima 2002). Museveni's forces followed hard on the heels of the fleeing Obote and Okello soldiers toward northern Uganda, crossing the symbolically significant border of the Nile. They now faced the difficult task of turning a guerrilla movement into a regular army, with the capacity to counter the insurgencies that have emerged in various locations in Uganda. In northern Uganda, it turned out that the conduct of the Museveni's troops—allegedly a well-disciplined army, controlled and educated by its political wing—soon deteriorated. Killings, rape, and other forms of physical abuse aimed at noncombatants became the order of the day soon after the soldiers established themselves in Acholiland, which was foreign territory to them (Oywa 1995; Doom and Vlassenroot 1999; Otunnu Ogenga 2002; Pirouet 1991). Thousands of suspected rebels were taken into detention. Torture and maltreatment were common, and after some years Amnesty International (1992: 29–30) concluded that "there has been a consistent pattern of extrajudicial executions by soldiers since the NRM came to power."

THE LOOTED CATTLE

After years of war in central Uganda in the 1980s, many Acholi soldiers of the Obote and Okello governments found it difficult to adjust to a rural life back home. Behrend (1998a: 248) concludes that the arbitrators of the local moral world, notably the elders, failed to reconcile many of the former soldiers with rural life.[4] Rituals to demilitarize and reintegrate the soldiers were often not used, or did not seem to reverse the violent development when they were. Instead, many of the ex-soldiers chose to join rebel ranks when war reached northern Uganda. In due course the uprising found broad support among the inhabitants of Acholiland, who found their homes and belongings destroyed and cattle herds looted by soldiers of Museveni's army. The local rebels looted their share of cattle as well. As Museveni's insurgents had promised in central Uganda (see Amaza 1998: 89; Kabera and Muyanja 1994: 98), the rebels pledged to pay compensation to cattle owners as soon as the war was over. In almost every interview that I conducted, the issue of the lost cattle was raised, and the primary blame was put on Museveni's soldiers who, according to informants, sometimes even ferried cattle away on army lorries (see also Dolan 2000: 10–12). The same happened with sheets of iron, vehicles, refrigerators, and other items of value. One man retired from many years of work on the electric dams in Jinja saw the wealth he had invested in his rural house gradually taken away. Early on, the Ugandan army seized the house and used it as a commando center for several years, and when they left, even the frames for the windows and the doors were looted, leaving nothing of value.

In some cases, people filed complaints, which have resulted in counteraccusations from the Ugandan army. In a typical response, one senior officer holds that he has found it difficult to believe that his battalion seized any cattle illegally. Instead, as the commander maintains in his official response, "all animals were recovered from enemies' strong hold defences." He thus concludes that "the claimants must have been rebels or supporters of the rebels."[5] By filing official complaints in such matters, people run the risk of being labeled rebel collaborators. For example, in one instance, the army eventually admitted that it had taken 871 head of cattle, but the claimant was given to know that he would not be compensated, as he was accused of being a rebel collaborator. He was instead threatened with court-martial, after which he decided to drop the complaint for the time being. Yet, in 2006 more than 1,700 former cattle owners joined hands and sued the government, reports the *Daily Monitor* (September 5, 2006). Increasingly frustrated that most complaints so far had been in vain, even met with hostility, and that the little compensation that has been provided so far has been inadequate, even diverted, the group of cattle owners filed a joint suit at the High Court in Kampala.

People in the war-torn north have tended to see the army's looting of their cattle as a deliberate strategy. As one old man put it, "They remove the cattle to make the Acholi poor, to be able to control the Acholi." He claimed that he lost forty-six head of cattle at the hands of the National Resistance Army (NRA), Museveni's former guerrillas, who had become the new Ugandan army. Talking to me in 2000, the man concluded that the strategy has worked: "Even today, there is no development in Acholiland." My friend Otim p'Ojok aired a similar conclusion, common among young people in Gulu. "In the late 1980s, people had their cattle either stolen or grabbed by the NRA," he said. "This was for me another way of destroying the wealth of the Acholi people, of destroying the livelihood of the Acholi people." Before the war, he went on to explain, "cattle were sold so that somebody could pay for tuition, but this is now impossible. This has created poverty among the Acholi people. So many people are poor now. They are unable now to pay the school fees and tuition fees of their children." The rebels have given their perspective on the situation. "The NRA did to us what the Turk slave hunters did to us in the 19th century. They both treated us like animals, with contempt and open abuse; devastated our land, social infrastructure, decimated our culture and drove us out of our homes, into the bushes and hills" (Lord's Resistance Army/Movement 1996b.

Parallel to these developments during the initial years of war in northern Uganda, Karimojong pastoralists took advantage of the situation. After Amin's fall, some had plundered Moroto army barracks in Karamoja, after which they were very well-armed. Combined army and Karimojong looting led, within just a few years, to the loss of almost all the Acholi cattle. According to statistics for Gulu and Amuru districts, in 2001 around 3,000 head of cattle remained. This can be compared with the figure for 1983, which listed 123,375 head (Weeks 2002: 35). And even if another source that sets the number of cattle remaining in the two districts at some 11,000 head is accurate, this still represents only a fraction of the prewar figure (Rwabwoogo 2002: 28).

The destruction that followed Museveni's takeover affected all sectors of Acholi society to a degree never experienced before, and eventually elders and other influential members of Acholi society were instrumental in the increased recruitment of young people to rebel ranks. Many informants claimed, not only rhetorically, that a situation developed that was significantly worse than during the Amin era. The mass looting of cattle remains a very painful experience of the war, especially in the eyes of middle-aged and elderly Acholi. Tonny's situation is instructive. He has experienced postcolonial crises in Uganda since the days of Idi Amin, during which time his father passed away. When Amin decided to collect tax from all cattle owners in Uganda, Tonny— being the only son— had to leave school to raise money in order to take care of his late father's herd. He struggled hard and managed to keep the cows, but eventually he suffered the same fate as many fellow cattle owners in the mid- to late 1980s. The Ugandan army looted all his cattle.

Amin's forces, which were responsible for the killing of thousands of Acholi individuals, targeted mainly politicians, soldiers, and intellectuals. Unlike Museveni's army, claimed my informants when they compared their situation to that of the 1970s, Amin's soldiers never bothered to go deep into the rural areas to harass, loot, and kill ordinary people. The support for armed resistance increased as people experienced the unprecedented misconduct of the intruding troops. Others who did not explicitly support the uprising, according to a standard version that I often encountered, saw no alternative means of survival than to join the insurgency groups in one way or the other (see also Lord's Resistance Army/Movement 1997a; 1997c: 3). Joining the rebels was in many cases a direct response to the military brutality of the NRA (Brett 1995; Onyango-Odongo 1998). In their recruitment of young people, the various rebel groups frequently evoked the rhetoric of "join or die." Similar rhetoric was used in lobbying for rebel sympathies in eastern Uganda, where people encountering Museveni's army faced the same difficulties of violence and cattle looting (Henriques 2002: 209–210).

THE LEGACY OF THE PAST

Ever since Uganda's war reached the north in the mid-1980s, many Acholi have found it impossible to escape the past as expressed in the national memory. In Uganda, it is commonly held that the Acholi in the Ugandan army during the Obote II (1980–1985) and Okello (1985–1986) governments were particularly responsible for the atrocities committed in the counterinsurgency campaigns in central Uganda (see, e.g., Mutibwa 1992: 157). The animosity toward people from northern Uganda was a prominent motivation for some of Museveni's many child guerrillas, who numbered perhaps as many as 3,000 (Furley 1995: 37; see also Keitetsi 2003). Quoting the Uganda Human Rights Commission, an article in *The New Vision*, the Ugandan state-owned daily, notes that the majority of people in central Uganda perceived Museveni's war as a war against a regime of northerners, rather than the war for democracy that Museveni claimed it to be. Most witnesses from central Uganda "who testified before the Human Rights Commission described the UNLA [the post-Amin Ugandan army] soldiers as 'Acholis' yet many of these soldiers were from Buganda and the west" (*New Vision*, October 9, 2002; see also Allen 2006b: 199, n. 5). Another commentator claims that some of the most unruly functionaries of the Obote II government were not northerners at all but various local leaders who took advantage of the turmoil for their own political struggles in their respective home regions (Kasozi 1999: 151).

While he was a guerrilla leader, Museveni sometimes propagated Bantu commonality in an effort to strengthen local support in the immediate war zone. In doing so, he managed to build interethnic alliances, as well as rebuild old ones (Mamdani 1996: 208–209). At the same time, in Museveni's war propaganda, the enemy was alleged to be northerners in general and Acholi in particular (Okuku 2002: 22–23). The colonial stereotype of the Acholi as warriors was evoked in an effort to deepen fear and mistrust of Obote's government and its army (Nyeko and Lucima 2002: 20). This tendency was to continue after the seizure of Kampala in 1986. Official radio and newspaper propaganda of Museveni's newly established government initially held the north, and especially the Acholi people, responsible for Uganda's violent past (Behrend 1998b: 109; Pain 1997: 48; see also Parliament of Uganda 1997: 14).[6] When fighting against Museveni, the propaganda machinery of Obote's government, on the other side, evoked another ethnic stereotype and dismissed the NRM/A as Tutsi, Banyarwandan, or even Rwandan intruders, a theme that the LRA/M reproduces frequently in their written statements. Perhaps this propaganda of war in part turned into reality. As Mamdani (2001: 168) notes, "The more the repression of the Banyarwanda was stepped up, the more Banyarwanda soldiers joined Museveni and the NRA in the bush" (see also Brett 1994: 88; Otunnu Ogenga 1999a: 16–17). Many of these rose in rank among the NRA (Paul Kagame, who eventually became the president of post-genocide Rwanda, was one of many). And after Museveni's takeover, they joined the new government's counterinsurgency campaigns in northern and eastern Uganda (Otunnu Ogenga 1999b).

GULU, 1986: THE HOLY SPIRIT FORCES

In addition to the UPDM/A, the rebel force initiated by sympathizers of former President Okello popularly known as *olum olum* or *cilil*, the spirit medium Alice Abongowat Auma and her followers also took up arms. Alice Auma's Holy Spirit Movement (HSM) was initially formed as an egalitarian, gender-equal, nonviolent movement mainly concerned with healing and ritual cleansing. "They came to [Gulu] town without arms, for peaceful demonstrations, but they were shot at by the Ugandan army," a middle-aged female informant said as she recalled Alice Auma's entrance on the public stage. Eventually Alice Auma reorganized her movement into a military organization, the Holy Spirit Mobile Forces Movement (HSMF), with the objective of fighting Museveni's new government. Women fought alongside men, and the movement had a special women's desk, something that appealed to both young women and young men. When some influential male rebels questioned her role as a leader, the supreme commanding spirit who possessed Alice Auma declared that he had chosen a woman as a medium in the effort to end the oppression and subordination of women in Africa (Behrend 1999a: 79). Alice Auma eventually secured the role as leader of the rebel movement.

Alice Auma was known popularly as Alice Lakwena, and below I will follow the accepted practice. Alice Lakwena means Alice the messenger, and ever since, *lakwena* has become the most common Acholi name given to a rebel in the most general sense.[7] Various spirits spoke through Alice Lakwena, but she claimed to be a prophet rather than a messenger or spirit medium only (Allen 1991: 375). In producing a person like Alice Lakwena, it is often suggested, opposition in northern Uganda was now at "its most bizarre" (Woodward 1991: 181). Ugandan government officials dismissed Alice Lakwena as "a lunatic prostitute of Gulu Town turned witch" (quoted in Behrend 1991: 162). Western journalists, for their part, echoed the official standpoint. For example, Catherine Bond concluded that Alice Lakwena was "a voodoo priestess and a former prostitute" while Catherine Watson summarized the war as one between Museveni and "the primitive challenge" (both quoted in Omara-Otunnu 1992: 457–458). Similarly and more recently, De Temmerman (2001: 51) has written of the "savage world" where Joseph Kony, the leader of the LRA/M rebels and an alleged relative of Alice Lakwena, is the absolute ruler.

Alice Lakwena's movement clashed with the National Resistance Army, but also with the UPDM/A rebels. As war evolved, inhabitants in Acholiland came to differentiate between two parallel and intertwined aspects of violent insurgency—the initial and politically motivated UPDM/A and the spiritually motivated violence that emerged slightly later, with Alice Lakwena's and Joseph Kony's Holy Spirit Forces. The first dimension of violent insurgency was called "the Army of the Earth" (*mony me ngom*) and the second "the Army of Heaven" (*mony me polo*). Alice Lakwena soon became a popular leader who gained important support from her fellow Acholi, not least young men and women. She preached a universal message of redemption, love, and unity beyond earthly ethnic differences, and her movement gained considerable support not only in Acholiland but beyond, as the movement expanded geographically. Yet Allen (1991), Behrend (1998b; 1999a), Kayunga (2000), and others suggest that Alice Lakwena's inevitable failure was due to weakening support as the movement pressed farther south, toward Jinja and the source of the Nile. They then became northern invaders in southern Uganda. Over time, the initially gender-equal movement also came to conform to more conventional African gender hierarchies. Women took on the role of preparing food and otherwise served the combat units (Behrend 1999a: 54–55). In addition to this, as the moment expanded geographically, several of the female spirits possessing Alice Lakwena were increasingly marginalized when new male spirits entered the scene.

An informant and former member of Alice Lakwena's core group, then a young man, emphasized another dimension in the increasing fragmentation of the movement. He told me that the developing divide was along educational lines. As the movement spread outside Acholiland, toward the south via the east, he observed highly educated people joining in great numbers, and eventually a split developed between the initial members of the movement with little or no formal education and those with formal education who took positions in the high command. In November 1987, Alice Lakwena's forces were defeated outside Iganga, east of Jinja town near the source of the Nile, about one hundred kilometers east of Kampala. Alice Lakwena managed to escape to Kenya, where she remained until her death in January 2007.

After the defeat of Alice Lakwena's forces, her father, Severino Lukoya, launched another Holy Spirit rebel movement back in Acholiland. In contrast to Alice Lakwena, Severino Lukoya emphasized a rather exclusive and localized spirituality (see Behrend 1999a: 177; 1999b: 26–30). He did not gain the same broad interethnic popularity as his daughter had, and in August 1989 he finally surrendered to the government army.

The failure of Alice Lakwena's, Severino Lukoya's, and other, more local uprisings did not mark the end of armed resistance in northern Uganda. The rebel leader Joseph Kony, also an Acholi by birth, and an alleged second cousin to Alice Lakwena, has been fighting Museveni's government army ever since its arrival in the north. Initially, Kony was with the UPDM/A insurgents, before he created the LRA/M. For some time, Severino Lukoya was directly under Joseph Kony's command. When Lukoya eventually surrendered to the new government, a portion of Lukoya's soldiers remained in the bush and were absorbed into Kony's movement, as had happened also with fighters who defected from Alice Lakwena and the UPDM/A.[8] Kony, for his part, claims that he simply came to the assistance of the people who had now been deserted by their elders, families, and leaders. This claim is supported by many of my young informants, who deny that spiritual cleansing was the primary motive for joining Alice Lakwena's or Joseph Kony's insurgencies. Behrend (1999a) has shown that Alice Lakwena offered a kind of purification from the deeds committed in the recent past in central Uganda, something that was attractive to many soldiers of the fallen government. Ward (1995), a church historian, suggests that northern Uganda faced a crisis in religious leadership and a collapse of institutional church life. In the aftermath of the arrival of Museveni's National Resistance Army in northern Uganda, the Anglican bishop of northern Uganda left for exile in Nairobi, while his deputy left for Kampala. The Catholic Church, on the other side, closed its major national seminary located just outside Gulu town. It was in this situation of religious uncertainty, Ward proposes, that Alice Lakwena received increased support.

Still, most of my informants, who were teenagers at the time when Alice Lakwena was leading her insurgency, held that people joined Alice Lakwena, and later on Joseph Kony, because, as one young man claimed, they were there as "means of fighting" when there was "no one else to join." The Ugandan historian Omara-Otunnu proposes a similar conclusion. "Lakwena was merely a vehicle through which social discontent in the north of Uganda found expression," he writes. "She was able to gain tenacious followers who were prepared to risk their lives against all odds because a cross-section of marginalised inhabitants recognised her as a symbol of both their plight and their aspirations" (Omara-Otunnu 1992: 458).

ETHNIC STEREOTYPING IN THE POSTCOLONY

It is evident that the Acholi are popularly associated with Uganda's postcolonial violence. A photo and accompanying caption in an insider's account of Idi Amin's violent government is perhaps innocent but still instructive. The picture shows Amin dancing together with a group of Acholi dancers; the caption reads: "Amin dances the Otole, a traditional Acholi warrior dance. It was a suitable prelude to the killing three weeks later of two of his ministers" (Kyemba 1977: 212). In the photo, the two ministers soon to be assassinated are seen dancing with Amin.[9] Nevertheless, their tragic deaths have nothing to do with Acholi dances.

From their personal experience, many of my informants claimed that any Ugandan language not immediately understood by Luganda speakers in the capital is dismissed as Acholi or Luo. Sometimes when my informants travel south and fail to speak proper Luganda, or have a typical non-Luganda accent to their English, they run the risk of being nicknamed *konnies* after the LRA/M leader Joseph Kony (Kony is pronounced *konj* in Acholi). For example, this happened to Tonny when he traveled to Jinja in southeastern Uganda to represent Gulu in a dart championship. During the course of the tournament, he became increasingly uncomfortable with his competitors' frequent references to him as a konnie only because he shared language and ethnic belonging with rebel leader Joseph Kony.

Sometimes people need not even engage in a conversation; ethnic differences are communicated anyway. The stereotypical other is there to be found wherever he or she is expected to be found. One evening in September 2005, Otim p'Ojok and I were invited to share some drinks with a European diplomat working with the United Nations. So we joined him at the Acholi Inn, a fancy Gulu hotel. The loudspeakers in the background played American pop songs. Eventually the music changed into a tune by the famous Acholi musician Ogwang Clippa. The European diplomat immediately assumed that the management now wanted us to leave, because they now played this Acholi "war song." Otim p'Ojok tried to correct him, explaining that the song was about family planning and the problem of HIV and AIDS, actually a very informative song. But the diplomat insisted this was a "warrior song." *Abyssinian Chronicles*, the acclaimed novel of Ugandan writer Isegawa, is also illustrative. In the novel, which takes place mainly in Kampala during the Amin years, the author gives voice to Serenity, one of the main characters. "Serenity was shocked by the ugliness of tribal strife. All the soldiers he saw were tall, dark sons of northern Uganda" (Isegawa 2000: 120). In the novel, tall people in uniform, the alleged promoters of ethnic violence, are identified as from northern Uganda.

To associate cultural manifestations—such as the *otole* dance, Ogwang Clippa's songs, or the physical appearance of unknown individuals in uniform —with the idea that some cultures are more violent than others, was common already during the colonial period. This is one aspect of the everyday communication of ethnic differences. With an outlook colored by the race paradigm and its focus on primordial and immutable qualities of human types, early colonial observers claimed that the Acholi and other peoples of northern Uganda were martial. Still today it is common for people in Kampala and beyond to regard people from northern Uganda as backward and martial, and in the Ugandan context, sometimes the very epitome of primitiveness (Dolan 2002a: 63–64; Leopold 2005: 9).

"The Acholi in the armed forces have been the largest single group, going upward to one-third of the soldiers," Mazrui (1975: 113) writes. He too links the alleged dominance of the Acholi in Uganda's postcolonial armed forces to the European colonizers' idea of the Acholi as a "martial community," a suitable target for recruitment to armed services such as the King's African Rifles (Mazrui 1976). Because of this recruitment, Mazrui adds, the collective consciousness of the Acholi developed, and they "were later to be regarded as a particularly martial community" (Mazrui 1976: 260). Eventually the Acholi found solidarity in their "militarized ethnicity" (Mazrui 1976: 258) or, as he puts it elsewhere, in their "military ethnocracy" (Mazrui 1975; see also Hansen 1977: 76). In other words, with the Acholi as "the military aristocracy of the North," Uganda was divided along "primordial lines" (Mazrui 1975: 49, 40). According to this suggestion, the militarized Acholi ethnic identity was a creation of colonial policies that controlled and confined the colonized subjects to bounded areas such as the Acholi district. Mazrui argues: "What matters from the point of view of the colonial genesis of 'tribalism' is the simple fact that a broad new Acholi political consciousness became superimposed over the narrower parochialisms of the sub-units of the Acholi" (Mazrui 1976: 261). Mazrui highlights important consequences of the colonial practices of divide and rule and recruitment to the armed forces, but his emphasis on colonialism limits the understanding of ethnic identification as processual and always in the making. I also question his conclusion that the Acholi as a collective became militaristic. His narrow focus on colonial processes in the militarization of the Acholi is problematic, as it implicitly reduces local actors to passive objects of imposed change. Stereotypes of dominant traditions and fixed categories become the shorthand that mask other, more complex social realities.

Account after account recapitulates the view that the Acholi have a militarized ethnic identity. For example, the late Amaza, an insider in Museveni's nonparty Movement, describes Acholi society as a "military democracy" (Amaza 1998: 213–214), while Doom and Vlassenroot (1999: 9) conclude that the "post-Amin army, UNLA, was predominately Acholi-controlled (although the political leadership had different roots)." They do not expand on the issue of whether the majority of officers were Acholi; neither do they elaborate on the background of the political leaders mentioned. Even if a majority of the soldiers in the army were of Acholi origin, this does not mean that the Acholi necessarily controlled the army. Karugire adds a more historical nuance to the stereotypical picture:

The bulk of the protectorate's armed services were recruited from Northern Uganda, particularly from Acholi, Lango and West Nile, in that order of numerical representation. This became the established order throughout the colonial period and, as we shall see, for a long period afterwards. And it was not long before the colonial government invented a rationalisation for building this ethnically unbalanced army which rationalisation is directly contradicted by our history: the people of Northern Uganda were the "martial tribes" of the protectorate and, since the African soldiers required in a colonial army they were those of "strong physique, stamina, speed of reaction and upright bearing" the answer was tailor made: recruit from Northern Uganda. (Karugire 1996: 33)

Karugire continues his argument by pointing to the examples of the precolonial Buganda and Bunyoro kingdoms in central Uganda:

Buganda had attained her commanding position in the interlacustrine region because of her military prowess and her well regulated political control of her fighting men. Bunyoro had fought the Egyptian expansionists, and then the British and her local allies for some two decades, largely because of her sophisticated military organization. The other kingdoms, to a lesser degree to be sure, had built up their fighting capacities, and this is what had enabled them to control relatively larger populations than any that existed in any of the northern communities. (Karugire 1996: 33–34)

At the time of the colonial conquest, the Buganda kingdom could easily mobilize the most superior and best-organized army in the region, supplemented with equally well-organized naval forces on Lake Victoria, which made it possible for the Baganda to dominate and control the region (Reid 2002). The largest military threat to Buganda's dominance before the British conquest was the Bunyoro-Kitara kingdom to its north. Earlier, the Bunyoro-Kitara kingdom had been militarily more powerful than the Buganda kingdom. Nevertheless, to the colonial administration, it was not the Baganda or the Banyoro but northern peoples, such as the Acholi, who became labeled "warlike." In Mamdani's (1984: 10) words, "The colonial view that northerners were 'martial' peoples was simply racist hogwash; the simple truth was that northern peasants were put in uniform to crush the resistance of the southern peasantry."

Today Acholi intellectuals forcefully deny the thesis of their culture as warlike. Instead, by comparing colonial statistics of recruitment to the armed services with that of higher education, they argue that Acholi parents promoted education and white-collar careers rather than military careers for their children (e.g., Onyango-Odongo 1998). In an early ethnographic source and with reference to the Sudanese side of the colonial border, Captain R. C. R. Whalley makes a similar observation. "The average Sudan Acholi has a great craving for education," he writes. "At the various village schools one sees fully grown men, women, boys, girls, and children in regular attendance, and they can all, or the very large proportion, read and write their own language" (quoted in Seligman and Seligman 1932: 114). Seligman and Seligman confirmed Whalley's observation, and noted that the Acholi showed "a desire for and pride in reading and writing altogether fresh to us" (Seligman and Seligman 1932: 113–114). Indeed, this and other developments, in the agricultural sector, for example, or in the production of a written vernacular and local textbooks on culture and history, have been parallel to the recruitment of young Acholi men to the armed forces. Yet such developments are neglected in the reductionist historiography that focuses on the alleged militarized ethnic identity of the Acholi.

My informants of course questioned the idea of the Acholi as collectively to be blamed for most of the violence in Uganda, in particular during the counterinsurgency campaign against Museveni and his guerrillas in central Uganda. They point out, for example, that none of the members of Obote's security council during the 1980s was of Acholi origin. "I am not saying that Acholi soldiers were completely blameless, but they were under the command of officers who were not necessarily Acholi," Onyango-Odongo, one of my elderly informants, wrote in a *Daily Monitor* article (December 10, 1997). He continued, "But it appears that NRA soldiers were repeatedly told that the Acholi were the enemies, so when the NRA arrived in Acholiland, they first behaved well, but soon begun to destroy Acholiland systematically" (see also Gersony 1997: 10). During my fieldwork, I encountered some young men, frustrated by the collective blame put upon the Acholi, who painstakingly collected data and statistics to challenge the image of the Acholi as violent and militaristic. One of them pointed out that of the four battalions sent against Museveni's guerrillas, commanders from Acholiland led two. No Acholi was overall commander in the Ugandan army at the time. He concluded that "the Luwero Triangle is used by the government to discredit the Acholi, internationally, nationally and locally." A young male student more directly blamed Museveni for the many killings. "We Acholi are blamed for the deaths in Luwero," he said. "But it was Museveni's decision to start a bush war in Luwero that killed the people of Luwero." Referring to a common East African saying, he concluded that the grass will always suffer when two elephants fight. In commenting on a draft paper of mine, the late Caroline Lamwaka, a journalist and friend from Uganda, sent a letter (June 8, 1999) in which she questioned the widespread idea of collective guilt:

> The Acholi never started the war in Luwero, neither did the Acholi civilians and Elders organise themselves and bless the atrocities. Although a good number of the top commanders in the UNLA [the Ugandan army] were Acholi, there were also many from other ethnic groups. The real blame should have gone to the government of the day, that is Obote 2, and partially shared by Museveni himself who started the war. Individual commanders, including the Acholi soldiers, could then be blamed individually. (Lamwaka, personal communication, June 8, 1999)

If we are to consider the popular Ugandan picture to which so many Acholi informants objected, ethnic antagonisms between the south and the north had been promoted in the armed conflict in central Uganda during the first half of the 1980s. This can partly be blamed on the then army command of Obote's government. According to the Ugandan scholar Omara-Otunnu (1987: 162–163), soldiers of Acholi origin were caught in the middle. When Museveni and his guerrillas opened a second front in western Uganda, the Ugandan army sent reinforcements, the majority of whom were Acholi, to counter them. Omara-Otunnu acknowledges that the majority of the soldiers in the then army were of Acholi origin, but he rhetorically asks why front-line fighters were drawn almost exclusively from Acholiland. "The perception among the men from Acholi was that they were being sent so that they would be killed," Omara-Otunnu (1987: 163) concludes. The divide, imagined or real, between Acholi and other ethnic groups of Uganda was to deepen as war shifted from central to northern Uganda in 1986.

Acholi elders, or Acholi politicians for that matter, did not come together to bless the war or the atrocities committed in the counterinsurgency against

Museveni's guerrillas. Following this argument, so often put forward by my informants, we must also be skeptical about the collective blame placed upon this one ethnic group, the Acholi. This does not mean, again as many informants indicated, that it should not be acknowledged that Acholi individuals can indeed be held responsible for war crimes.

THE 1990S: TOWARD A REGIONAL CONFLICT COMPLEX

Museveni's National Resistance Army and the main faction of the UPDM/A insurgents ("the Army of the Earth") jointly signed a peace agreement in June 1988. The peace process, however, became infected with violence, frustration, and uncertainty. Lamwaka writes:

> The government's counter-insurgency campaign increasingly threatened the lives and livelihoods of people in Acholiland and allegations of atrocities resurfaced. The government's stated aim was to "annihilate the rebels." Part of the strategy was to deny them access to food—by destroying civilian food stocks and domestic animals—and other resourses that could strengthen them politically, economically and militarily. In October 1988, the government began mass evacuation of civilians from war zones without providing adequately for their basic care. (Lamwaka 2002: 32–33)

She concludes that the time that followed immediately after the peace agreement actually came to cement war, especially in the rural areas. "Thus, in the months following the peace agreement, the war's impact on civilians became more severe and widespread" (Lamwaka 2002: 33). The violent process of cementing war all over Acholiland has continued over the years, and many insurgents decided to remain in the bush, joining with Joseph Kony's LRA/M.

In the early 1990s, the government in Khartoum began to support the LRA/M with logistics and military equipment, and for many years the LRA/M had its base camps in southern Sudan, located close to military installations of the army of the government in Khartoum. Former rebels observe that the LRA/M camps, located on the frontier in the war in southern Sudan, which ended only in 2005, functioned as a buffer between the central Sudanese army and the south Sudanese rebels of the Sudan People's Liberation Movement/Army (SPLM/A). In return for this support, the LRA/M fought alongside the Sudanese army and its allied groups against the south Sudanese rebels. Child combatants, abducted in the thousands, were used in the front line by the LRA/M, both when fighting in Sudan and in northern Uganda. In the complex and often shifting terrain of regional proxy war, the Ugandan government for its part long supported various rebel groups in southern Sudan and eastern Congo.

In late 1999 the U.S.-based Carter Center facilitated the signing of an agreement between Uganda and Sudan to restore diplomatic relations, which had been severed in 1995 over the disagreement regarding Uganda's alleged support for the SPLM/A rebels in southern Sudan and the Khartoum government's countersupport for the LRA/M rebels. Paradoxically the Carter Center came to exclude the LRA/M rebels from the negotiating process and the final agreement, which obviously angered them but pleased the Ugandan government. Some Khartoum support for the LRA/M continued at least to the 2005 peace agreement in south Sudan and perhaps since, though handled more secretly now than before (Gulu Archdiocese 2003c; Human Rights Watch 2003a). The 2005 peace agreement established the semiautonomous government of Southern Sudan.

Neighboring Congo has also been part of this regional war complex, with important links between seemingly localized conflicts and the outside world. This was made especially clear in September 2005, when an important contingent of LRA/M established a base in the remote Garamba national park in Congo, headed by one of the most senior LRA/M commanders, Vincent Otti, and eventually including Joseph Kony. Long before that, for many years the Ugandan army systematically looted eastern Congo under the pretext to be dealing with Ugandan insurgents based there, especially the Allied Democratic Forces (Pruiner 2004).

During the early years of the twenty-first century, international efforts to improve the frosty diplomatic relations between Uganda, Sudan, and Congo opened new avenues to peace but simultaneously condensed the violent alliances in the region. After the 2005 peace deal in southern Sudan ended active hostilities there, Ugandan support for the south Sudanese became public. The common enemy became global terrorism and the LRA/M, and in 2005 the International Criminal Court in The Hague issued warrants for the arrest of the rebel leadership (see Allen 2006b).

The rhythm of the war in northern Uganda has always been an uneven one. During most of 1999, there was a lull in the fighting in northern Uganda. Most rebel units had withdrawn to their bases in southern Sudan. Only pockets of rebels remained, though the notorious *boo kec* bandits continued their activities. The intermission gave people new hope, although they still worried about the future as long as the conflict remained unresolved. For Tonny and me it opened the possibility to travel to remote places in rural areas. We visited ancestor sites, the rebuilt ruins of Samuel Baker's fort, numerous displacement camps, and tombs of Acholi chiefs. We even went to a cattle auction in Agoro, the most northern part of Acholiland, bordering Sudan. Dinka from Sudan came to sell cattle, and Acholi were selling radios, clothes, and other items. Radios were exchanged for cattle. And in contrast to previous auctions, the visiting Dinka had left their guns in a nearby Ugandan army garrison. Most of them, however, wore their rebel uniforms.

The Dinka visitors claimed that they had walked for some twenty days with cattle that they had taken from the enemy. In this case, "the enemy" were people who found themselves caught in the middle of Sudan's civil war. Since they were not explicitly favoring the Sudanese rebels, they had been accused of supporting the government in Khartoum, and were thus turned into legitimate targets in militarily motivated looting. This pattern is certainly not unique to political violence in Sudan or Uganda. One central dilemma of living with war, according to my informants, is repeatedly to find oneself labeled "supporter of the enemy." In a recorded speech from May 2000, for example, rebel leader Joseph Kony claims that his forces kill fellow Acholi not because they are Acholi, but because they are government supporters.

On the journey back from the auction in Agoro, Tonny and I passed the wreck of a lorry carrying a destroyed antiaircraft gun that was left by the side of the road. We later learned that it once belonged to the south Sudanese rebels. Approximately a year before our visit, there had been a period of heavy fighting in Sudan and the Sudanese rebels were pushed south by the army of the central government. As they had done many times before, the Sudanese rebels decided to regroup their forces on Ugandan territory. They entered Uganda through Kitgum district (northeast Acholi) and eventually went back to Sudan via Amuru district (northwest Acholi). They hoped thereby to be in a position to counterattack the Sudanese army from the rear.

During their effort to regroup in northern Uganda, the Sudanese rebels were ambushed by the LRA/M. This ambush was not like the arbitrary killings that Ugandan and international media most often write about when it comes

FIGURES 1–2
Ambushed lorry in
Madi-Opei, Kitgum district.
Photos by author.

to the war in northern Uganda. Rather, and as people we spoke to maintained, the destroyed lorry stood as a symbol of internationally orchestrated violence on a local scene. Ugandan rebels with bases in Sudan had attacked Sudanese rebels on mission in Uganda. The wreckage provided a concrete example demonstrating that northern Uganda was deeply entangled in the larger regional war complex.

The memory of the ambush was still vivid among people in Kitgum district when we visited the scene more than one year later. The fighting had been fierce, and some forty people had died. Bodies were abandoned to rot in the sun. For several months the smell in the area was unbearable, we were told. Even a year later, skeletons and parts of skeletons were still scattered on the ground. Initially I imagined the place to be like any historical war site. The sun was hot, a dry spell had made the surrounding bush parched and barren, and the burnt lorry had rusted. Shells, cases of fired ammunition, and pieces of weapons were spread in and around the lorry wreck. Everything was silent, and the LRA/M had not been in the area for several months. I felt uncomfortable walking among the remains of unburied men and women. I knew that the unburied should not be left in the bush, according to Acholi beliefs. A temporary burial is requested until relatives or others can gather and conduct a proper one. Some grass could be placed on the body, a gesture accompanied by a verbal declaration of innocence—"I was not the one who killed you." This is expected to calm the spirit of the deceased, but could hardly have been accomplished at the scene of the ambush. Survivors had fled, and when the Ugandan army arrived with reinforcements, the LRA/M had withdrawn. The army then sealed the area during the time it took for the bodies to decompose, with most bodies simply thrown a few meters into the bush. This approach to the battle scene was not unprecedented, as other instances exist of the Ugandan army purposely leaving dead bodies behind, as warnings so that potential rebel supporters will appreciate the danger in opposing the government (see also Amnesty International 1992). Roads are frequently closed, and the explanation given is most often that "rebel presence" has been reported from the area.

CIVILIANS, COMBATANTS, AND DIRTY WAR

When we were visiting the scene of the ambushed lorry, I noticed that Tonny shared my unease. He wanted us to leave as soon as possible. He was annoyed when I picked up a rusty shell, told me to drop it and immediately prepare to take off. I hurried to take some photos, and went back to the motorbike. Some miles further south we passed a group of Sudanese rebels. Their army jeep had broken down, and some of them were resting in the shade under a tree, their weaponry offloaded on the roadside. Two of them were working on the dead engine. We felt uncomfortable but continued without trouble, and we also slipped through the final roadblocks of the Ugandan army—one of us being a *muno* (European)—on the road to Kitgum town. The relative calm at the time made the Ugandan soldiers relaxed. The Sudanese rebels could pass freely as well, but vehicles carrying local people were stopped, as we noted, and most often the travelers were forced to offload their luggage to facilitate the Ugandan army's search for guns and rebel collaborators among the civilians.

"Civilian" is indeed a very broad and diffuse category of noncombatant people living in the midst of armed conflict. Armed conflicts and civil wars of today have blurred the distinction between "civilians" and "combatants" made on paper, and between the armed and the unarmed. Obviously, civilians frequently find themselves being targets and participants in the politics of war. Comparative research suggests that 80 to 90 percent of war casualties at the end of the twentieth century is civilian and unarmed; only the remaining 10 to 20 percent consists of military personnel. Around the beginning of this century, according to many estimates, these figures were reversed (Allen 1999: 21; Kaldor 1999b: 126; Nordstrom 1999: 155, 170). I do, however, imagine that wars fought in the name of colonization in Africa and elsewhere were bloodier when it comes to civilian casualties than available statistics suggest (see, e.g., Hochschild 1998). In today's dirty wars, in which both state armies and rebels use terror in the effort to control the population, there are rarely clear distinctions between combatants and noncombatants or easily defined frontlines, and noncombatants are often the tactical targets of harassment and deadly violence.

Before the peace talks brokered by the semiautonomous government of Southern Sudan in 2006, all the peace initiatives held over the years had failed (see Lucima 2002). When an important peace agreement failed in 1994, each side blamed the other for the failure. Senior rebels lost confidence in elders and cultural leaders as impartial arbitrators. Most remembered in Acholiland, however, is President Museveni's sudden and untimely declaration of a one-week ultimatum to the rebels to surrender with all their arms, which prompted most rebels immediately to take off into the bush. The LRA/M had already established contact with the Khartoum government, and they easily established permanent bases in southern Sudan. Over the years that followed, the rebels came increasingly to regard elders and civilians alike as supporters of the Ugandan government. As an Acholi elder involved in various peace talk initiatives observed, simply by being an ordinary civilian (in the simplest sense, an unarmed noncombatant) a person tended to be classified by the rebels as someone "supporting the enemy of the rebels."

Local efforts to dialogue in the early 2000s stalled. The Ugandan army repeatedly attacked the venues of the talks, even arrested acknowledged peace emissaries (Gulu Archdiocese 2001; 2002). It is common knowledge that so-called rebel collaborators have been imprisoned on treason charges, adding to the rebels' mistrust. During the peace talks held in 2006 in Juba, the capital of semiautonomous Southern Sudan, the rebels demanded that people detained in various detention centers for their alleged collaboration with them should be released immediately.

Throughout the 1990s, the rebels continued to create havoc and abduct people. Because of this, potential rebel supporters and government critics were alienated. But to separate cause from effect is not always an easy task. Many Acholi also lack confidence in the Ugandan army, given its passivity as supposed protectors and the frequent misconduct that prevails. Rape and fatal shootings by Ugandan soldiers at marketplaces and local discos as well as night robberies and thuggery have increased over the late 1990s and early 2000s (see Human Rights Watch 2003a). The Ugandan media increasingly reports about these cases, but a commonly expressed feeling in northern Uganda is that little is done on the ground to reverse the trend. On the contrary, in the process of relocating people to the camps by force, the Ugandan military has occasionally burned houses and granaries in the rural areas, and the use of helicopter gunships in their counterinsurgency strategies has resulted in increased numbers of people killed, both children abducted into rebel ranks and among the noncombatant rural population (see, e.g., Gulu Archdiocese 2003b).

Violence committed against the civilian population can also be related to local government officials establishing home guard troops and local defense units in the rural areas in the early 1990s. Even up to the present day, rural youth and children as young as ten are recruited into local defense, particularly former rebels, who seldom find meaningful positions or assignments in civil society after their return from the bush. Instead of a life of uncertainty and idleness in displacement camps, where primary schooling is inadequate if it functions at all, recruits into local defense groups are offered a uniform, a weapon, and a small salary. Still, not all recruits are volunteers. Some are recruited by force. In either case, local defense personnel operate in close cooperation with the Ugandan army and they are expected to engage the rebels, which they do. In rural Acholiland, local defense units have frequently found themselves in the forward position in armed confrontation, thus making them the first fighting force that encounters rebels, whether this has been an explicit strategy of the Ugandan army or not. In a tragic irony, while the Ugandan authorities do not recruit minors to the national army, something that is clearly prohibited in the Ugandan constitution, they have evidently been willing to recruit minors to the civilian armed defense forces that are sent to the front lines (Dolan 2002b; Human Rights Watch 2003b).

The local home guard troops in the early 1990s were poorly equipped. A compulsory order from the government's local representatives urged all men to carry pangas, spears, or bows and arrows, while every woman was obliged to carry at least a knife. Around Gulu municipality, roadblocks were set up, and people who ignored the order were not allowed to pass. Sometimes the market in Gulu town was closed, and people were forced to join demonstrations and chant slogans against the rebels (see also O'Kadameri 2002: 36). As suggested by Richards (2000), people in such home guard units or forced demonstrations are turned into legitimate targets of rebel military violence. Indeed, in northern Uganda the rebels have repeatedly blamed the government for dividing people by inducing them to fight with bows, arrows, and spears. When encountering home guards, the rebels therefore do not hesitate to kill them, and some of the most spectacular violence has been committed against individuals whom the rebels associate with the government. For example, in 1991 the rebels maimed at least twenty-nine men and twenty-six women, whose ears, lips, arms, and legs were cut off in a symbolic but most physical effort to silence them (People's Voice for Peace et al. 1999: 36). In the early 2000s, the rebels again took up this violent practice (Gulu Archdiocese 2003b: 5–6). Even villagers who happen to have a spear or only a knife in the hut are now and then accused of having joined the government (see also Behrend 1998b: 117; Gersony 1997: 31). To handle the tricky situation, as informants let me know, they generally do not keep such items of everyday use at home but hide them in the nearby bush. "Life has become difficult" (*kwo odoko tek*), as they commonly concluded.

FIGURE 3 *Kwo odoko tek* (life has become difficult). Shop in Anaka camp, Amuru district. Photo by author.

GULU, 2000: POLITICAL REFORMS AND THE MIDNIGHT KNOCK

In early 2000, President Museveni signed a blanket amnesty passed by the Ugandan parliament. It has since been renewed several times, most recently in 2006 as new peace talks were brokered by the South Sudanese. At the time when the amnesty was introduced and signed, however, Museveni claimed that he did not believe in it. "We should apply the law of Moses; an eye for an eye, a tooth for a tooth, to bring discipline to society," he instead suggested (quoted in *The New Vision*, January 21, 2000). As additional manifestations of his reluctance in relation to the whole issue, he did not sign the new law within the thirty days stipulated by the Ugandan constitution, and it was to take more than one year before the first office was set up in northern Uganda, making implementation of the law extremely slow.

According to the amnesty law, any rebel who "renounces and abandons involvement in the war or armed rebellion" can surrender to the amnesty. Individuals who are "collaborating with the perpetrators of the war or armed rebellion" or "assisting or aiding the conduct or prosecution of the war or armed rebellion" can also take advantage of the amnesty (Republic of Uganda 2000). The issue of the so-called collaborators is a source of continuous mistrust in northern Uganda. Local representatives of the government frequently brand individuals who are supporting the political opposition as collaborators, while President Museveni often label them "terrorist backers" (e.g., Museveni 2006) or "friends of the terrorists" (quoted in Branch 2005: 3). In a public meeting in Gulu town in February 2000, Walter Ochora, a powerful politician of the ruling Movement system and the chairperson of the local government council at the district level, claimed that only rebels could take advantage of the amnesty. The government, he claimed in the meeting following the amnesty law, should continue to hunt for the "bad collaborators," who would face treason charges.

Museveni introduced the local councils (LCs) during the war in central Uganda. Originally called resistance councils (RCs), they were renamed in the 1995 Ugandan constitution. This constitution also formally introduced the ruling nonparty Movement system, and made definitive restrictions on the scope of action for political parties. In the 1980s and early 1990s, the local councils were subordinated to the National Resistance Council, led by Museveni and his former guerrilla officers. The councils, or committees, were originally integrated and fused with the Movement and the local government structures, and were set up to function at village (LC1), parish (LC2), subcounty (LC3), county or municipality (LC4), and district (LC5) levels. According to a Movement ideologist, the LC5 "is the parliament of the district level" that is "fully equipped to run the affairs of the district" (Kabwegyere 2000a: 103). Similarly, and according to the Ugandan constitution, the LC5 has "the highest political authority within its area of jurisdiction," while its chairperson is the "political head of the district" who is to "co-ordinate and monitor Government functions as between the district and the Government" (Republic of Uganda 1995: 120–125). According to the constitution, the local councils are to be subordinated to the parliament.

The function of these local councils has been subject to some scholarly debate. Karlström, who researched them in Buganda in the mid-1990s, concludes that they revolutionized politics there. The system "has provided Ugandans with their first significant experience of democratic governance at the local level" (Karlström 1996: 498–499). In contrast to my informants from Acholiland, his were genuinely skeptical about political parties. "Political parties," as one of Karlström's (1996: 495) informants put it, "make each man the enemy of his fellow man. They just kill each other." As a genuine alternative to this, perhaps, the local councils of the Movement system have worked quite well in Buganda. It must also be understood that people there lived with a violent war during the first half of the 1980s. For them, Museveni's takeover brought peace. The war however continued, but in other regions, giving the people in south-central Uganda the space necessary for the development of local democracy.

With reference to Buganda, Karlström (1996: 499) concludes that "this pyramidal system of indirect representation is eminently assimilable to the Ganda model of legitimate authority as constructed from the bottom up and founded on nested solidarities." The local councilors are regarded neither as belonging to nor dominated by the state (Karlström 1999: 112). Mentioning northern Uganda only briefly, he refers to Ottemoeller, whose explanation is stereotypically superficial. The unarmed political opposition to Museveni and the Movement in the 1996 presidential elections, Ottemoeller (1998: 102) writes, was "not a significant political force outside of several ethnically de-fined constituencies in northern Uganda (the 'Nilotic' ethnicities of the Lango, Acholi, and Iteso), which hold Museveni and the NRM in deep enmity for having disposed the government of their favourite son, Milton Obote." But in what way can Milton Obote be said to be a favorite son of the Acholi as a group? If the constituencies in northern Uganda are ethnically defined, which Ugandan constituencies are not? After all, it was a general of Acholi origin, Tito Okello, who in 1985 ousted Obote, of Lango origin, shortly before Museveni seized state power.

My informants based their skepticism about the ruling Movement on the fact that for them, in the shadows of war and in contrast to the south-central Ugandan case delineated by Karlström, this system has come to represent political oppression and petty harassment, which has only increased over the years. In Acholiland, therefore, people I met did not regard the LC system as an equivalent to culturally informed leadership practices. The local councils have "chiefs of the pen" (*rwodi kalam*), Tonny explained to me in 2000, imposed from above today as they were during the colonial days. In the eyes of my informants, after years of war the local councils had become intimately associ-ated with the ruling Movement government, again imposed from above (see also Human Rights Watch 1999: 3; Okuku 2002: 26). I should hasten to add that local government councilors in the north have had the ability to air criticism of the Ugandan army's conduct. For example, rural local councilors have publicly raised objections to the Ugandan army's silent and often hidden recruitment of underprivileged young men, even minors, to its paramilitary groups, and the 2006 elections brought some prominent government critics in the LC system. It is common, however, that they remain silent in fear of army reprisals (e.g., Human Rights Watch 2005: 28). Even so, in rural areas I more often encountered people who expressed suspicion that the local government councils were working as Ugandan army intelligence, and in several cases I found that the local government councilors indeed had contributed to an environment hostile to advocates of political pluralism and to known government critics. Sadly, in the rural areas, and especially so in the congested camps, people alleged to be collaborators often find themselves deserted by friends and relatives who fear harassment from Ugandan authorities and the army. Okuku's harsh conclusion seems to be sadly accurate for the war-torn north. "Once in power," he notes, "the RCS [now LCS] became instruments of control rather than popular participation" (Okuku 2002: 26; see also Human Rights Watch 1999: 54–59, 135; Mamdani 1995a; Oloka-Onyango 2000: 41). The rebels, for their part, find it fully legitimate to target functionaries of the local government councils.

With these words about the local council system introduced by Museveni in mind, I want to return to the public amnesty meeting in February 2000 and the speech of Walter Ochora, the then chairperson of the Gulu LC5, the political head of Gulu district. As he publicly claimed that "bad collaborators" could not take advantage of the amnesty, he even mentioned a few individuals by name, and some individuals were eventually arrested. At least one individual was kept in custody for more than a year, only to be released without trial but with the orders to physically report to Kampala on a weekly basis.

Most of my informants were distressed by his speech, given at a meeting in which senior Ugandan army commanders, local religious leaders, and a representative of Save the Children flanked him. The religious leaders were not allowed to talk at the meeting, and the Save the Children representative grasped little of the speech, as it was given in the local language. The whole event fueled local discontent regarding the government's measures to end the war as well as the involvement of the international community. People concluded that the politician wanted to get rid of his political opponents and outspoken critics. The dilemma, as informants put it, is to openly criticize the government without being regarded as a rebel collaborator. "If you say that you are pro multiparty," Tonny noted, "you are straight away called Kony." Museveni's Uganda has a history of amnesties offered to various rebel groups (see Lucima 2002). However, as is the case with the present amnesty law, the previous amnesties have most often been accompanied by explicit orders to the "bandits," "hyenas," "murderers," "thugs," "criminals," and "terrorists," as Museveni frequently brands the armed opposition, to surrender unconditionally (e.g., Woodward 1991: 182).

In everyday life people express their mistrust in what they regard as a government imposed from outside, despite seemingly generous amnesties offered to the rebels in the bush. War has literally entered people's bedrooms, and even in the most small-scale disputes, alleged opponents of the government are occasionally accused of being rebel collaborators. In the late 1990s my friend Tonny had campaigned for the opposition politician Norbert Mao. In early 2000 Tonny got involved in a quarrel with his neighbor over competing beer-brewing businesses. His antagonist was the chairperson at the village level (LC1) in the local council system. Tonny's antagonist tipped off the military, presenting it with a letter headed with the official local council logo and accompanied by all the necessary stamps. Tonny was described in the letter as a "notorious man with a gun" who had "the intention to kill Uganda army personnel on patrol." In the middle of the night that followed, the military smashed Tonny's door and some twenty soldiers entered his home. The soldiers beat two of Tonny's wives and destroyed some property. They conducted a thorough search of the home before they departed with Tonny, who was taken into custody. By walking in their army boots over the very bed in which Tonny and his wife had been sleeping a few minutes before, they violated the most private sphere of their life.

Tonny was released in the morning, however, and no formal charges were made against him. No weapons were recovered during the night search. Eventually the quarrel between Tonny and the local council chairperson was resolved through mediation by the council at the subcounty level (LC3). This was the second time that the military had come to harass Tonny, and the fourth time they had come for a violent night search in the local neighborhood. In Tonny's view, the local council representative exploited his official contacts with the Ugandan army to harass political opponents and business competitors. If anything, Tonny emphasized with reference to the fact that he was a Ugandan citizen and protected by the law, the quarrel should have been taken to the police but not to the army. "The LC1 chairman is using the military for his own means," Tonny concluded. Like most people in Acholiland, he questioned the soldiers' violent method of conducting searches and their doing so in the middle of the night. Ultimately, to the extent that this is to be the chief experience people have of the army on the ground, the Ugandan government will be seen as offering only harassment to the people. As Wole Soyinka (2004: 2), the Nigerian Nobel laureate, generalizes from personal experience, this is "governance through a forced diet of fear, most especially on the African continent—in common parlance, the fear of 'the midnight knock.'" In Acholiland, life has become difficult indeed.

Chapter 3

REBEL MANIFESTOS IN CONTEXT

DISCONNECTED REALITIES

"As it is now," the young man said as he looked at me, "the bush is almost better than home." He was unmarried and a representative to the National Youth Council. Young people are vulnerable all the time, he claimed when we met in early 2000. In our conversation we had come to talk about the many mass arrests in Gulu and the army's arbitrary search for rebel collaborators.

Despite the gross and counterproductive violence committed by the LRA/M rebels, there has, nevertheless, for many years been an increasing frustration among noncombatants, and especially among young adults, over the fact that the political issues the rebels have tried to address are left without commentary on the public arena. Given its experience of being silenced, young adults claimed, the LRA/M's continuous struggle to articulate politically viable statements made sense. In this chapter, therefore, I reflect on the image of the LRA/M as it is presented in what I will call the official discourse. I will describe this discourse and also delineate the counterargument to it, or what the LRA/M rebels write in their manifestos. Throughout, I investigate how these two different representations, which for heuristic reasons I will present as rather neat counterdiscourses, relate to the opinions and experiences of my young adult noncombatant informants. Again, I hesitate to define their stories in terms of anything that is essentially modern or traditional. Rather, young people feel increasingly marginalized and alienated from developments in the rest of Uganda as well as in the wider world.

The official discourse too marginalizes and alienates them. A number of influential stakeholders, notably media, international human rights organizations, and the Ugandan government, define this discourse. These stakeholders have disseminated, from the local level in northern Uganda to worldwide media networks, a discourse that has tended to overshadow completely other aspects of the social reality. In other words, the official discourse is dominant. It defines and structures the ways in which the world, or parts of it, are to be talked about and understood. By such means this discourse proposes, even imposes, a fixation of meaning. To illustrate my point, the LRA/M's notorious mass abduction of minors into the fighting ranks has become a dominant issue (e.g., Amnesty International 1997; Human Rights Watch 1997), drowning out the rebels' efforts to launch any political agenda.

Although conceptions in war are often colored by black-and-white propaganda, there can seldom be any final answers of good and evil. Still there is an irreducible contradiction here that needs to be recognized. Over the years the armed struggle of the LRA/M has taken on a most violent logic of its own. The war has become an end in itself, it seems to me, with violence reinforcing further violence, which contradicts the political aims for which the LRA/M claims to be fighting. This development too alienates young people. Consequently, as noted by Branch (2005: 7), most observers, including academics, have dismissed the LRA/M on moral grounds and thereafter also disqualified the movement as resolutely nonpolitical. But as I see it, the challenge is to acknowledge that the LRA/M manifestos, despite the group's violent military tactics on the ground, pinpoint issues relevant to most people in Acholiland. Also, as Aretxaga notes for the Irish Republican Army (IRA) and the conflict in Northern Ireland, for a state to recognize insurgents is to recognize a legitimate player in the arena of international politics. "The British refusal to characterize the conflict in Northern Ireland as a war, despite the continuous presence of an inordinate number of military troops, aims at erasing the IRA as a political subject," Aretxaga (1997: 85) writes. She concludes that the British government refused to acknowledge that the IRA had a political voice, thus excluding them "from the sphere of legitimate discourse" (Aretxaga 1997: 172).

In other words, rather than concluding that the LRA/M's political state-ments are expressions of hypocrisy disconnected from Ugandan realities, I want to highlight *meanings in use*, or how these statements relate to local realities, and how they are socially embedded, of relevance to my informants as they orient themselves in the world. This social embeddedness—a kind of knowing by engagement—includes not only the most influential agents, such as the rebel leader or the Ugandan president, but more importantly, the inter-pretations and counterinterpretations of ordinary people with everyday expe-rience of the war. I will also argue that the war in northern Uganda ex-emplifies, increasingly so over the years, how international policies such as economic liberalization and structural adjustment implemented during the 1990s have promoted conditions conducive to political violence in Uganda's marginalized regions and among its marginalized peoples. "People act in the world in terms of the social beings they are," Sahlins (1999: 412) points out, "and it should not be forgotten that from their quotidian point of view it is the global system that is peripheral, not them." To challenge the official discourse can be unsettling, especially as this discourse in the Ugandan case very much focuses on the welfare of children. But the ambiguities of the lived surround-ings, communicated to me through my informants' stories, will always disrupt and threaten the neatness of the propaganda of war and its fixed meanings.

"WE HAVE GONE BACKWARDS"

As much as it may be the expression of a deepening of ethnic divides, the war in Uganda is increasingly about the marginalization of the war-torn north from the rest of Uganda and its developments. "What the opposition groups in the north and east of the country have in common is not ethnic identity or cultural traditions," the Ugandan historian Omara-Otunnu (1995: 230) writes, "but a history of being only peripherally included in the economic structures and processes of the country" (see also Omara-Otunnu 1987; 1992; Leopold 1999).

The marginalization or exclusion of peripheral areas in Uganda is not new in the country's politics. On the eve of independence in 1962, the division between south-central Uganda and its peripheries was a central issue in na-tional politics (Leys 1967; Gertzel 1974). Mamdani (1984) and Vincent (1999), among others, trace the division of central and peripheral Uganda to colonial times. Colonial divisions of labor emerged, in which the north became an important labor resource for the developing south and its plantations and industries. Simultaneously, most of the colonial social services like higher education and hospitals were concentrated in central Uganda (Mamdani 1976; Mutibwa 1992; Okuku 2002). Ever since independence, and perhaps especially so in the early years of independence, efforts have been made to reverse this uneven development. Secondary schools, for example, can now be found almost everywhere in the country. However, as Southall reports for the West Nile region, teachers and educational leaders "feel abandoned and are greatly distressed by the undeniable deterioration of staff, salaries and facilities as a whole. They speak bravely of development in public, but in private they say with profound sadness 'We have gone backwards.'" The conclusion is harsh: "Social development is dominated by the collapse of the health and education budgets of the central government" (Southall 1998: 259).

On a regular basis during my fieldwork, young concerned Ugandans arranged public meetings in Gulu. Various issues, set by the organizers in advance, were discussed, and sometimes they have even been broadcast on the local FM radio. The young organizers, who were often students, called their meetings *kabake*, a "hot debate." I was also told that it could be "a place where people sit together to try out a solution to a problem." An illness with no apparent cure could be such a problem. Issues addressed have included the problem of education, African identity, and the influence of Western morals. One meeting was to deal explicitly with the war. Representatives of the Ugandan government and some high-ranking army officials had been specially invited, but they all failed to show up.[1] Toward the end of the meeting, an eighteen-year-old woman spoke up:

> Everyone is coming here, and of course, everyone wants peace. Me, even me, I want peace. We all want peace, but can we define what peace is? I was only one year [old] when this thing started. I cannot right now even define what peace is. I don't know what peace means. . . . And, of course, if we don't know what peace is, it will just remain a dream which never will come true. (Gulu town, July 2002)

Being mostly young, few of my informants had lived through the promising era of nation building and early independence. For earlier generations who grew up with peace, young informants told me, the possibilities had always been there. Now it was different. Opportunities in life were restricted, as war has always been the main reference in life. "In the sixties, there were jobs," my friend Otim p'Ojok asserted. "But today even the elders admit, really, there are no jobs for the youngsters." As the young woman quoted above pointed out, even to comprehend what peace means is not easy. As her lifelong experience told her, the many military campaigns had not brought peace and security, only increased poverty and an escalating spiral of violence and discrimination (see also Uganda Human Rights Commission 2003: 24).

DEVELOPMENTS ON THE GROUND

In the most recent years, many technological innovations and new developments have reached Acholiland. One notable example is Western Union Money Transfer; another is the mobile telephone network. Yet another recent development is a new, private hospital built in Gulu town, financed by concerned, wealthy Acholi in the diaspora. The hospital is well equipped, and the most advanced services will be offered, such as cardiac, laparoscopic, and cosmetic surgery, assisted reproduction, mammography, endoscopy, computerized tomography, and magnetic resonance imaging. Sports injuries will be treated at a special clinic (Gulu Independent Hospital n.d.). Perhaps the most important development is Gulu's new university, established in 2003.

At the same time, many young people in the war-ravaged north with expectations of a better future regarding education and work, expressed an experience of being increasingly betrayed, a feeling of being severed. For them, Gulu University stands there as proud evidence of modernity and development in Uganda, but few have the means to go for higher studies. Governmental scholarships remain few. The scholarships are often delayed, and are anyway inadequate for the few selected students' everyday survival. Additional private sponsorship is often needed. Similarly, few had consulted Gulu Independent Hospital. The initial fee, equivalent to about ten U.S. dollars, was just too high.[2] So the university and the hospital also came to represent young adults' disconnection or humiliating exclusion, and even their abjection, from the promises and expectations of modernity—as Ferguson (1999) writes in an analysis of the industrial downfall and economic crisis in the Zambian Copperbelt. Rather than a lack of future possibilities promised by development and modernization, Ferguson suggests that most people experienced a loss of, a disconnection from, these very possibilities.[3]

In the words of Evelyn Grace Anywar, a performing artist and an Acholi who lives in Nairobi, "The Acholi feel rejected. The Acholi feel hated. The

Acholi feel unwanted" (quoted in Leopold 1999: 228). Despite the burden on life added by structural adjustment programs, cost sharing, and war, many young adults continue to cultivate their dreams of higher education and good careers. From my informants' point of view, to be able to benefit from health care and education is a civil right. In a more profound sense, frustrated young people claimed, it is a question of citizenship and democracy in everyday life. If a person lacks the funds to obtain health or educational services from private sponsors, this must not limit the citizen's right to exercise them in Uganda's public sector. Yet, as Whyte (1997) shows for eastern Uganda, people have lost confidence in the government's public health care, which they find insufficient and infested with increasing demands for extra money. As I will show, the LRA/M rebels raise exactly these issues in their manifestos.

The Ugandan government admits that the northern region is one of the poorest regions in the country, where 63 percent of the population live below the poverty line compared to the national average figure of 38 percent (*New Vision*, February 16, 2005). But my discussion of young adults' discontent and their experience of abjection is not based on statistics about unevenly distributed development measures in the aftermath of the various structural adjustment policies (for this see SAPRIN 2001). Instead it is based on my informants' lived experience. The war is, of course, an obstacle to many development schemes in the north, and some development agencies have relocated their projects to other areas of Uganda. For example, the United Nations has long argued that all people need access to safe drinking water and basic sanitation and declared 2003 the international year of fresh water. In 1997 a feasibility study by the Uganda National Water and Sewerage Corporation proposed Gulu town as suitable for a water supply expansion project, but the German financial institutions turned the proposal down and instead requested the Ugandan authorities to locate an alternative area for the project. The reason given was insecurity in northern Uganda. The Ugandan independent daily, the *Daily Monitor* (December 19, 1997), reported the episode. Typically, as some Ugandan friends noted as we read the paper, a German delegation visited Kampala and Jinja in central Uganda but did not bother to visit Gulu town to assess the possibilities on the ground. "There is not much to say," one of the readers, a young man, told me, "the article speaks for itself." In his view, this was a common feature of development in Uganda. "The field assessments are done in Kampala," and possible projects are all "cancelled from Kampala," he concluded.

The terror and violence committed by the rebels over the years tend to take focus away from the lived frustrations of the noncombatant population. The war is frequently described as one of those bizarre African wars that really cannot be comprehended. Well aware of this powerful version of the situation, young informants were often careful when they expressed their views on the public arena, and it took quite some time for me to gain their confidence so that they could freely share their feelings, views, and ideological standpoints. Again without being able to provide any proper or final statistics, I want to question the conclusion by Gersony (1997: 59) that of the Acholi people, "more than 90% do not respect, welcome, encourage, support or voluntarily assist the LRA." Another consultant concludes that he "could find no one in Acholi who would admit to having any sympathy for the LRA as such" (Weeks 2002: 11). But frankly speaking, who would welcome war? And who would openly admit support for the LRA/M rebels or their predecessors, as it is possible, even likely, that such public support could result in treason charges?

By the mid- to late 1990s, Uganda's political environment had turned increasingly hostile (Human Rights Watch 1999), and the political situation in northern Uganda had become very volatile. With this in mind, I suggest that there is a measure available to assess Gersony's figures. In the 1996 and 2001 presidential elections, fewer than 10 percent of the voters in the north supported President Museveni and his no-party Movement system; in 2006 some 16 percent did so.[4] The number of people who have welcomed the Movement government, then, is basically as small as the number who welcomed the LRA/M rebels.

In the official discourse, it is often claimed that Acholi people, especially the young, willingly join the government to fight the rebels. This was claimed, for example, by the late Amaza (1998: 132), a Movement insider and the author of a biography of the NRM/A of Museveni. During the course of fieldwork, and despite a politically volatile situation, I was struck by the daring with which young people publicly questioned the government's failure to end the war. Over and over again, informants refused to accept the government view that civilians should organize paramilitary local defense units (LDUs) and home guard troops to counter the rebels.

Around Christmas time in 1999, reports reached Gulu town that the rebels had entered Uganda in great numbers from their bases in Sudan. Within a few days they were in the environs of the town, and one night in late December, the bursts of a rocket attack woke most people in the town. In the morning, I learned that a rebel unit had attacked the resident district commissioner's house. Two weeks later, the district commissioner, who narrowly survived the attack on his residence, spoke to a crowd a few kilometers from the town center, at another scene of unexpected rebel presence. The previous night rebels had patrolled the area well before sunset. They did not harass the people, who took them for a Ugandan army unit. After sunset, however, the rebels looted a shop and abducted some young people to carry their plunder.

Visiting the scene the following morning, the commissioner angrily told the crowd, "We are going to kill all rebels." He further ordered civilians to get spears and knives and immediately start tracking down the rebels, eventually to kill them. "You continue to kill the rebels," he ordered the civilians present. A man in the crowd objected, "Enough is enough." The man argued that such an operation must be the mandate of the army, not of the civilian population. His objection annoyed the commissioner. Pointing his finger at the man, a rude gesture in Acholi society, the commissioner let the whole crowd (including the bystanding anthropologist) know his opinion about the objection. "You! You are a rebel!" the commissioner countered with a raised voice. The crowd went silent, and many people shook their heads, disturbed by the commissioner's words. They all remembered the violent consequences of previous orders to civilians to carry knives and chant antirebel slogans. Now as had happened before, people feared that government counterinsurgency tactics would turn civilians into military targets of the rebels (Branch 2005: 15–20).

People in Acholiland also questioned the common conclusion that the rebellion was a peripheral matter, or simply an "Acholi 'question,'" as Kabwegyere (2000b: 41) suggests. Such a conclusion proposes that the war is a local rebellion, initiated by Acholi, and consequently for the Acholi themselves to end. But whether they supported the rebels or not, my informants strongly held that the LRA/M rebellion is not some kind of "tribal uprising" (see also Leopold 1999). In expressing their frustration, people frequently referred to a particular statement, allegedly from the mouth of President Museveni. In one of his public speeches, so the story goes, he evoked the metaphor of the Acholi as grasshoppers in a bottle, where they will eat one another before they find the way out through the bottleneck. Of course, people were distressed about this wartime ethnic stigmatization.

The rhetoric of a local northern conflict in which Acholi kill fellow Acholi like cannibalistic grasshoppers, reflects a more general Ugandan conception of the Acholi as violent and war-prone. So does Museveni's claim that the rebels are "culturally backward" (quoted in Omara-Otunnu 1992: 457; see also Leopold 1999: 223–224). In this way, commentators in powerful positions legitimate and contribute to oppression in ethnic terms.

Fratricide, it must be admitted, is a lethal dimension of the war. Ladit Arweny, a clan elder, summarized a discussion held among a group of about fifteen influential clan elders. The elders shared the frustration of the younger generation, and the clan elders had come together to discuss the war and related issues:

> We [Acholi] are commonly being spoken of, throughout Uganda, as grasshoppers. Now, we Acholi feel that what is being said in other parts of Uganda, by other tribes of Uganda, is not totally right. Now, in the bush, the composition of rebels is composed of *all* the tribes of Uganda, except that the majority are the Acholi, and leadership is again an Acholi leading. . . . In the real sense, *the real sense*, the war is not between Acholi at home and Acholi rebels. No! As I said, you can find all tribes there [among the rebels]. Even Banyankole, Museveni's tribe, they are also there! (Gulu town, January 1998)

Ladit Arweny then referred to the dilemma he shared with most noncomba-tant Acholi:

> We sitting here also have our relatives in the bush, but they don't consider us relatives. They fear us, you see? And when they come they can kill anybody, they know, these are really enemies, because they belong to the government. So it is not totally right to say that Acholi are killing themselves.
>
> So definitely, when you hear of confrontation taken place, you find the dead bodies are all Acholi. But the rebels don't consider killing the Acholi, they consider killing the supporters of the government.
>
> Lastly, you could consider this an Acholi war, because the war is being fought on Acholiland. The children abducted are the Acholi people.

The war, it is true, is being fought in Acholiland, but it ought to be understood from a wider perspective. The elder's reference to an "Acholi war" is, in this context, synonymous with a war *on* the Acholi. However, external observers, helped along by government propaganda, have for many years regarded the conflict in northern Uganda as a local problem only, preferably ethnic, which I hold differs little from the grasshopper metaphor.

GOD'S GOSPEL AND THE MEDIA OF CONFLICT

In an undated manifesto that was most likely written in the beginning of the 1990s, and under their former rebel name, the United Democratic Christian Movement/Army, the rebels wrote that they wanted to "see an end to the use of witchcraft and sorcery by the promotion of the Ten Commandments" (United Democratic Christian Movement/Army n.d.; quoted also in Nyeko and Lucima 2002: 18). Rather than being the expression of bizarre fundamentalism, the claim echoes more than one century of missionary teaching in Uganda. In an interview in 2006, Vincent Otti, LRA/M's second in command, when pressed on the issue, replied, "I cannot deny that. These are the 10 commandments of God. Which one of them is bad? The first commandment? The second commandment? The third commandment? It is the truth because it is God's truth. It is God's commandments. They must be followed." Before addressing other, more deep-seated issues of contest in Ugandan political history, he even recited some of the commandments, asserting their universal value beyond Christianity: "thou shall not kill, thou shall not covet thy neighbor's possessions, thou shall not steal" (interview in *Black Star*, July 4, 2006).

Wars are partly what the media make them (Allen and Seaton 1999: 3). Not surprisingly, in the media the consensus is that the LRA/M rebels fight for the sole reason that they want to rule the country on the basis of the Ten Commandments. One typical media report claims, "The LRA, a group whose beliefs are rooted in Christian fundamentalist doctrines and traditional religions, has been fighting President Yoweri Museveni's government since 1987, with the aim of establishing its own rule based on the Biblical Ten Commandments" (UN/IRIN online news, November 20, 2002).[5]

Seldom do the media present any coherent political analysis. More often, media consumers feed on spectacular details. As Seaton (1999: 45) writes, "Stories of wars in faraway places have to attract audiences to sell to advertisers in competition with soap operas and game shows." With reference to war-torn Sierra Leone in particular and Africa in general, Richards notes that ethnic strife all too often ends up as the explanatory model, a powerful but reductionist conclusion that seems to attract the interest of the outside audience: "According to outside assumptions, 'proper' rebellions in Africa should have 'people' (an ethnic identity), contiguous territory under unambiguous control of the rebels, and an announced programme that the world at large can understand. In short, they should be Biafra-like 'mini-states' in waiting" (Richards 1996: 59–60). The idea of ethnic sentiments as primordial is affirmed. Culture is understood to be an essential and durable feature of human activities, a final product with its meaning inscribed once and for all, a bounded entity, like a painting on the wall or a dress in the wardrobe, so to speak. From this essentialist perspective, different cultures and civilizations are naturally prone to clash (e.g., Huntington 1996). Quite often, hand in hand with this interpretation goes the pseudoanthropological assumption that a kind of culture of war and violence tends to prevail in the non-Western world. Eventually this simplistic logic will fail, and the most convenient interpretation that media then mediate seems to be the opposite. Complex civil wars in Africa and other non-Western settings are reported to be the expression of a new kind of barbarism, where chaos has allegedly replaced almost every aspect of culture and sociality, and violent anarchy has replaced any political dimensions (Richards 1996; Allen 1991). As the lived complexities thicken and ethnic stereotyping fails, the world press typically loses interest.

Allen (1991) and Ehrenreich (1998) have characterized the prevailing media representation of the LRA/M as the heart-of-darkness paradigm. The conclusion made from this paradigm, Ehrenreich notes with frustration, is only too familiar to the Western public and thus highly seductive. The Western media consumer will conclude that "the conflict is bizarre, but Africa is simply Like That" (Ehrenreich 1998: 84).

A documentary called *The Mission* (1998), screened in various European countries, is perhaps the ultimate manifestation of the heart-of-darkness paradigm.[6] In the opening part of the film, which is set in 1997, some Kampala journalists are about to travel north to gather information about the LRA/M and its enigmatic leadership. Landscape scenes along the road as the group travels from the capital toward the conflict area are screened almost endlessly. A local tune and some Africans dancing in the dark night, illustrations that return as the central theme throughout the film, are the only commentary on the journey. The viewer encounters unfinished buildings along the road, not uncommon features in countries like Uganda, as well as burnt-grass landscapes that are common indeed during the dry spell. Still, the less-informed viewer gets the impression that the houses and the surrounding landscapes have been destroyed by war.[7]

Toward the end of the film, the viewer is presented with low-quality archival video material of the LRA/M from the peace talks in 1993–1994, which eventually failed. The film provides no information about these talks, and the jump backward in time from 1997 to these earlier talks is left without comment. Joseph Kony, the rebel leader, at one point addressed the elders for three hours during the talks. According to Ladit Arweny, an elder who attended, Kony wanted to make sure that the LRA/M was received well by the community. "He gave assignments to the elders to make all traditional arrangements for their return home," reports Arweny (n.d.: 22). The rebel leader also spoke about previous peace talk failures and raised the sensitive issue of some high-ranking rebels who accepted an amnesty in the 1980s, only to die in unclear circumstances. The fate of these rebels has become a dominant feature in the collective memory in Acholiland today. Especially remembered is senior rebel commander Mike Kilama, who agreed to lay down his weapons to take advantage of the amnesty, only to be shot dead when, as Ugandan military officials claim, he tried to escape to Kenya in 1990. His death occurred at a critical time, when a number of former rebel commanders were arrested on treason charges and others fled Uganda, contrary to the terms of the peace deal signed by both fighting parties in 1988 (Lamwaka 1998: 157–158; Okuku 2002: 34–35). The untimely deaths of several former rebel commanders have remained a critical issue throughout the years, but the viewer of *The Mission* is left in ignorance of all this. Most of the rebel leader's comments are left without translation. Only parts of his speech to the team of peace negotiators are translated into English, and these parts almost exclusively concern his references to the Bible, but again no context is given to his comments. There is no immediate logic comprehensible to the Western audience, only undirected fragments of apparently bizarre statements.[8]

As the central theme, the film follows the fearless and untiring struggle of a European nun, who searches for thirty girls abducted by the rebels from the missionary school in Aboke, northern Uganda. The altruistic struggle of the white nun contrasts sharply with the activities of the African rebels and the enigmatic comments of the rebel leader. Indeed the only lasting impression of the film is of darkest Africa.

A more recent film, *The Invisible Children (The Rough Cut)* from 2003, is a gripping and painful documentation of the plight of children who, because of security concerns, including the fear of being abducted by the rebels, in periods of high tension trek from their rural homes to Gulu town at night. There, these "night commuters," as they are called, sleep in hospital compounds, bus parks, on verandas, or wherever else they can manage. The film was shot many years after the government forced virtually all rural Acholi to live in squalid camps, officially for security purposes, but there is no proper mention of this fact and no explanatory images of the horrendous and insecure camps from which these children were fleeing every night. With a potent Hollywood horror aesthetic framing the film, this film too falls short when the historical background and sociopolitical context are considered. Lacking photo material of the LRA/M, the filmmakers use clippings from Kamajo (hunter) militia and child fighters in Sierra Leone. And when the rebel leader Joseph Kony is depicted, besides recycling the old and low-quality photos, the filmmakers use drawings. The voiceover introduces the rebel leader as "a man named Joseph in the Jungle of Northern Uganda." With its dramatic artistic dimension, the film fully plays with the heart-of-darkness stereotype.

Turning to the print media, the Belgian journalist De Temmerman (2001) authored a documentary novel called *Aboke Girls*. As with the film *The Mission*, the novel tells the story of the girls abducted from the missionary school in Aboke. Initially published in Dutch but soon translated into English, again as with *The Mission*, the story centers on the efforts of the European nun. In contrast to the film, however, the book is a well-researched and painful document on the sad predicament of the abducted young women. Still, the author follows the common trend as it replicates the thesis of the LRA/M high command as motivated solely by the Ten Commandments (e.g., De Temmerman 2001: 15, 23, 70, 156).

This one-sided claim has been recurrent also in the reporting of various human rights organizations, Amnesty International (1997: 6), for example, or the Women's Commission for Refugee Women and Children (2001: 82).[9] The typical conclusion is that the war in northern Uganda has its roots in ethnic mistrust in Uganda and in the "religious and spiritual beliefs of the Acholi people" (Women's Commission for Refugee Women and Children 2001: 81). In another human rights report it is noted that rebel leader Joseph Kony "drew from Acholi religious beliefs and incorporated Christian traditions and rituals into his movement" (African Rights 2000: 4). Of course, these reports are correct in noting that the war has taken on a religious dimension, but still other dimensions are left without commentary, notably the political, which reaches far beyond manifestations of local cosmological practices.

The focus on a single individual, the rebel leader, is also unfortunate. Such reductionist explanations encourage reductionist conclusions. If the alleged lunatic and murderer is removed, as is often suggested, the violent conflict will be no more. For example, a report by the parliament of Uganda legitimates its own militaristic agenda on moral grounds. In misquoting one of the interviewees, a European missionary, the report claims that this moral authority wanted to send Joseph Kony to "eternal peace or external exile" (in Parliament of Uganda 1997: 49). In 2006 I heard American and European diplomats repeating the message—now the only solution to the war was to have Kony "eliminated." International peace initiatives have followed the trend of individualizing a very complex war. One organization now working in northern Uganda initially sought an expert who could assist them in cooperating with the Ugandan government in the effort, as they wrote in their proposal, to "comprehend the LRA leadership's psychological makeup, as well as the spiritual aspect of Joseph Kony's and the LRA's rebellion and power base."

WAR ON TERROR AND THE WAR OF PROPAGANDA

In December 2001, the global war on terror reached Uganda as the U.S. government included the LRA/M as well as the Allied Democratic Forces, another Ugandan rebel group, on its list of terrorist groups with which no negotiations, so it is stated, will under any circumstances be initiated (U.S. Department of State 2001). The Ugandan government immediately welcomed the rhetoric of no dialogue. "We in Uganda know very well the grievous harm that can be caused to society by terrorists, having suffered for many years at the hands of Kony and the Allied Democratic Forces terrorists supported by Sudan," Museveni is quoted to have said (in UN/IRIN online, September 12, 2001).[10] As allies in the war on terror, the United States sells arms and provides military support to the Ugandan army against the rebels (*East African*, November 6, 2006; see also Otunnu Ogenga 2002; Nyeko and Lucima 2002; Twaddle and Hansen 1998). In early 2002, the Ugandan army launched a campaign called Operation Iron Fist, later relaunched Iron First II. Without parliamentary approval, the Ugandan government cabinet decided to cut by 23 percent the allocations approved by the parliament for all ministries, excluding only activities of poverty alleviation. The funds were redirected to the military campaign against the LRA/M rebels (*Daily Monitor*, October 31, 2002; *East African*, March 31, 2003). At that time, Uganda's international development partners funded around 50 percent of the country's central government expenditure, and some five years later, the percentage remained the same (Sida 2001: 6, 8; 2006: 10).

In Acholiland, young informants with dreams of education and future employment were indeed frustrated with the way that the Ugandan military increasingly absorbed national resources—resources that they would have preferred to see being devoted to the development of Uganda and especially its marginalized regions. The rebels had survived all previous counterinsurgency campaigns, and few believed that it would be any different this time.

It is beyond doubt that the rebels suffered heavily under the Iron Fist campaigns. But in the wake of these campaigns, during which fighting in northern Uganda reached levels not experienced since the beginning of the war (Uganda Human Rights Commission 2003), the noncombatant population suffered more. Human Rights Watch (2003a; 2003b), building on figures provided by UNICEF, suggested that the rebels abducted some five thousand minors during the second half of 2002 alone. In a parallel development, the Ugandan army increased the recruitment of minors into the so-called local defense units, including former rebel child fighters and other marginalized underaged people (Human Rights Watch 2003b: 19–24; see also Dolan 2002b: 69–70).

The Ugandan army promotes itself as the rational and modern party to the conflict. Again the words of President Yoweri Museveni, who is also commander in chief of the army, are significant. With reference to Alice Lakwena and her Holy Spirit Mobile Forces, the predecessors of the LRA/M, Museveni has described the rebels in northern Uganda as nothing but criminals and murderers, or at the best, victims of primitive and primordial sentiments and perverted local religious traditions. "The poor Lakwena girl was being manipulated by criminals who would intoxicate soldiers on marijuana," and supporters of previous regimes were "intoxicating poor peasants with mysticism and incredible lies," Museveni (1992: 115) writes. From his perspective, "the Lakwena peasants" used "mysticism instead of science" in their effort to fight his "modern army" (Museveni 1992: 116). References to primitive superstition and alleged drug abuse are powerful in the effort to deny any political dimension to the conflict. Instead "obscurantism," "witchcraft," and "backwardness" (Museveni 1992: 173) are said to block modernization and development in Uganda. Subsequently, Museveni used these latter epithets to describe the LRA/M, and his view of Alice Lakwena seemed to have changed somewhat. In declaring the LRA/M a brutal movement without popular support, he now sometimes contrasts it to Alice Lakwena's acknowledged popularity (Heike Behrend, personal communication).

Over the years, other influential individuals have tuned in to the propaganda of war. Major Kakooza Mutale, another military man, who is the president's advisor on political affairs, labeled some Acholi leaders as having a "diabolic and treacherous role" because of their efforts to establish peace talk contacts with the rebel leadership (quoted in *New Vision*, May 5, 1999). And Major General James Kazini, one of the president's closest military associates, concluded that "Kony is furthering no interest whether political or otherwise. He is just an agent of Satan meant to destabilise the economy and social set-up of the Acholi" (quoted in *New Vision*, October 21, 2002). Kazini also blames all military violence upon the Acholi. "If anything, it is local Acholi soldiers causing the problems," he claimed in an interview with Human Rights Watch. "It's the cultural background of the people here: they are very violent. It's genetic" (Human Rights Watch 1997: 59). Thus Kazini takes the argument back to the days of the colonialists. As was the case then, the assumption is that the Acholi are primordially violent.

President Museveni and his associates' language of denigration has taken a symbolic dimension understandable to most Africans. Now and then, Museveni calls the rebel insurgents "hyenas" (quoted, e.g., in *Daily Monitor*, February 16, 2000). The metaphor of hyenas presents them as wild creatures, which in many African cosmologies means that they have vitality and power, but more, that they represent the uncultured wilderness, danger, depredation, death, sorcery, and witchcraft. "Hegemonic groups are able to define such a vocabulary, an ability that enables them to identify opposition and protest as witchcraft, banditry, and terrorism," writes Winans (1992: 110) with reference to south-central Tanzania on the eve of independence. In a position document from the peace talks held in 2006, the rebels listed an end to abusive and insulting language as one of their immediate demands (Lord's Resistance Army/Movement 2006). Ignoring the rebels' protest, in December 2006 the

Ugandan president gave them a new epithet—"Satan's Resistance Army" (quoted by Reuters, December 14, 2006).

With a focus on the rebels' incomprehensible religious practices and gross abuses of basic human rights, and with the rebels themselves characterized as hyenas, terrorists, and agents of Satan, comprehensive peace talks for many years were repeatedly dismissed on moral grounds (e.g., Parliament of Uganda 1997). Ehrenreich, who chaired a Human Rights Watch report on the conflict, was less judgmental than the people quoted above but was still pessimistic. She noted that unlike, for example, the IRA of Northern Ireland, the LRA/M rebels "have no 'political wing,' which make public pronouncements and negotiations difficult." Instead the rebels "have apparently chosen to be silent—or, at any rate, extraordinarily vague—about their motivations and aims" (Ehrenreich 1998: 82). One report to the United Nations concludes that the LRA/M "lacks any clearly formulated political objective" (Weeks 2002: 13), yet another that "the LRA has no coherent political or other objectives" (Women's Commission for Refugee Women and Children 2001: 82). Instead it is concluded that the LRA/M follows a leader, Joseph Kony, who "has created an aura for himself and his organisation of deliberate irrationality and obscurantism" (Weeks 2002: 9).

OUTSIDE POLITICS?

Obviously, the religious dimension of the rebellion in northern Uganda has attracted more interest than the political dimension, which may be related to the gross violence of the rebels. This violence, sometimes motivated in religious and moralist terms, is to most Ugandans and outside observers spectacular in its brutality. An important consequence of this focus on spirituality and religion has been to make the wider national, political, and socioeconomic dimensions of the war marginal in many analyses.

Political scientists Chabal and Daloz argue that there are "essentially two types of armed conflict in contemporary Africa: the political and the criminal." They acknowledge the overlap between the two in everyday life, but maintain that "the conceptual distinction between them is clear" (Chabal and Daloz 1999: 83). Regarding Acholiland, most observers argue that the war in its initial phase did not concern formal politics, as it did not essentially revolve around the issue of which political system Uganda would choose (e.g., Kayunga 2000). Chabal and Daloz, however briefly, go even further. They admit that the LRA/M may have a political dimension to its religiously motivated violence, but in vague terms they conclude that the rebels' "millenarian agenda places them firmly outside the political and criminal organizations" they find relevant to examine (Chabal and Daloz 1999: 86). Bizarre and incomprehensible as it is alleged to be, the war in northern Uganda is thus left aside in their comparative analysis of Africa. Virtually by default, then, the war falls into the category of being a humanitarian rather than a political crisis.

Alternative interpretations are needed. During the years of evolving war, the political and socioeconomic dimensions have developed as increasingly central issues of debate and contest in Uganda, not only in the north of the country but nationally. The rebels feed on an increasing local discontent with neoliberal developments in Uganda, particularly structural adjustment and other development measures demanded by the donor community. Today the harsh and insensitive programs of structural adjustment and cost sharing have reached almost every sector of Ugandan society, particularly health and education, not least in Acholiland. Young Acholi men and women, especially, often communicated to me their experience of being effectively denied Ugandan citizenship. "Accountable democracy," or "participatory democracy," to repeat the commonly heard buzzwords of international development rhetoric, is defined by a government's ability to make certain services available to its citizens, such as clean water, food, health care, and education. Such democracy is obviously not found in Acholiland. In the prewar situation, livestock were sold now and then to pay school fees for young people, but the war has disrupted this and other foundations of income. In frustration, many young people desperately seek economic assistance. One young man wrote in a letter to me, "My father who was struggling sponsoring for my fees was killed by the rebel force. That is why I got stuck on the way." The writer concludes that he can only see one option for the education he was forced to abandon. "I will be compelled to join the rebel force to fight the Uganda Peoples' Defence Forces [and the] government." My young informants felt marginalized in their poverty, to paraphrase Englund's (2002b: 173–174) analysis of the political and economical dimensions of social life in the postwar Mozambique-Malawi borderland.

The frustration of young Acholi must be taken seriously. In their view, they are denied many of the most mundane and everyday aspects of citizenship that we in the West take for granted. To evoke Ferguson's (1999) argument again, they feel "disconnected" from Uganda's wider developments, even future developments. One issue often emphasized by young people in Acholiland was the importance of including the northern region in Uganda's national development and national future. As Ugandans but non-Bantu, young Acholi informants in Gulu found it disturbing when the Ugandan nation was equated with its Bantu-speaking population. Their frustration found grounds in a speech given by President Museveni in Kinshasa in honor of Laurent Kabila's seizure of state power in Zaire (Democratic Republic of Congo) in 1997.[11] The content of Museveni's speech was widely commented upon in Gulu. He said that it was now time to overcome the colonial constructs of Francophone and Anglophone Africa, and together with Kabila he wanted instead to create a "Bantuphone Africa." To many people in Gulu, this sentiment seemed to exclude the Luo-speaking Acholi people and other northern non-Bantu speakers from future citizenship in Uganda. Museveni later repeated the message on a state visit to Tanzania (the speeches are discussed also in Onyango-Obbo 1997: 36–44).

The political dimensions of the war in northern Uganda, including the complex but often violent interplay between local social worlds and larger-scale political processes, must be properly acknowledged. It is worth returning to Englund's analysis of political and economic liberalization, or liberalism, as he sometimes calls the increasing celebration of individuality and its freedom at the cost of social, national, transnational, and global relations. "If liberalism promotes neglect and marginalisation in the name of freedom," he writes, "it may also promote the historical conditions of political violence" (Englund 2002b: 185). War-torn northern Uganda corroborates Englund's conclusion.

MEANINGFUL REBELS?

"Fighters [rebels] in the north and in the west have their agenda and programme considering the political history of Uganda" a Catholic priest is reported to have said during a sermon in Rubaga Cathedral, Kampala. "But this doesn't mean I support them," he added (quoted in *Daily Monitor,* January 26, 2000). In a sermon born out of frustration with the many years of war postcolonial turmoil, I imagine, the priest emphasized the need to acknowledge the existence of a rebel manifesto as a first step toward dialogue. This appeal—which however is frequently ignored, denigrated, or silenced—has guided me in my efforts to widen public understanding of the war in northern Uganda. I do not suggest that the LRA/M political claims are less propagandistic than the official discourse, only that they are not compatible with the official discourse and thus more or less inaccessible for the outside world. The rebels' political claims threaten the ideological celebration of individuality and free choice, and the individual's alleged possibilities in the new world order of liberalized economics. For most of my informants, even for the majority who have not read any printed LRA/M manifestos, the issues raised are familiar indeed.

At the same time, my informants' practical knowledge of the violent activities of the rebels on the ground points toward another, more complex, situation. In short, the rebels do little to follow their own written endorsement of respect for human rights. In the words of the young woman who spoke up at the students' debate meeting, "I do not support the rebels, nor am I supporting the government. I am just in a dilemma. I would like to support the rebels, but they are killing my people."

It is not relevant to analyze such seemingly perplexing questions in terms of logical inconsistency, or as irrational and uninformed, as this would indicate an inability among my informants to grasp the complexity of the war. I do not agree with Doom and Vlassenroot, who describe the rebels as the "dogs of war." They write that "Acholi people at grassroots level can easily identify the dog that bites, but cannot see its master," while "better informed persons are fully aware" of the international complexities (Doom and Vlassenroot 1999: 30). The conclusion to be drawn from Doom and Vlassenroot's metaphorical comment can only be that people on the ground do not have a proper idea of the complexity of the war; that they only find the rebels to be religious but incomprehensible fanatics, as the official discourse also suggests. In all its complexity and uncertainty, everyday life is multifaceted but seldom either as unaware or as black-and-white as the heart-of-darkness paradigm proposes.

The young woman's statement is typical of the social realities of young people in northern Uganda, just as seemingly contradictory standpoints are common in every human setting. Only a contextual approach can disclose the complexities of meanings in use. Young people often tried to comprehend the discrepancy between the rebels' stated agenda and their violent military strategies on the ground. Sometimes they put forward very frank conclusions. In 2000, a twenty-five-year-old unmarried man, a teacher by profession, out of frustration concluded that terrorist attacks, sometimes even against their own people, can be legitimate when no other options are open, when the political climate has stifled any oppositional effort, "when you can do nothing." He had never been a rebel himself, nor did he seriously think about joining them on the battlefield, but he still held that in an increasingly hostile political environment, "the rebels are becoming more meaningful." Elaborating upon what he saw as a new phase in the war, he continued that "they are becoming more meaningful in the sense that they have been able to publish a manifesto, which they used not to have."

During my fieldwork in 2002, the language of young people had changed even more. Now and then I encountered young men, especially, who talked about the rebels as freedom fighters. "These are," as one young man said, "people called terrorists. The world knows them as terrorists." With them labeled as terrorists, the man continued, for all these years the Ugandan government with the silent approval of the outside world has manhandled any person who has tried to initiate dialogue with the rebels. "Which means," he further proposed, "as long as they are terrorists in the bush, the people of Acholiland can continue to suffer. . . . Maybe the world sees them as a terrorist organization, for real, which they do not still see [themselves]. These are freedom fighters!" Another young man added, with reference to the blanket amnesty offered to the rebels: "To me, this amnesty, even if the president accepted it coactively, does not apply to rebels. Amnesty only applies to gangsters, robbers, or those kinds of bandits. But to a rebel who has a constitutional right to liberate his country—because these [rebels] call themselves liberators, they want to liberate the country—they don't see that they have done anything wrong." The discussion went on and a third young man broke in, "I think they have been very wise to know that the amnesty thing was bogus."

Perhaps these statements seem strange to readers who have in mind the atrocities that the rebels have committed. Still, I want to argue that the young informants who aired these opinions did so from the experience of living with war and bad surroundings. They had little trust in the government's measures to end the war, which they saw as efforts to downplay the armed conflict as merely a northern issue, peripheral to the rest of the country. In contrast to such strategies of the official discourse, they wanted the political issues at stake to be addressed nationally. Again to quote one of the young men, "Because the [conflict] is not about northern Uganda. It is about the whole country. Of course, we are taking the upper hand. We are the ones suffering. But it is a national issue that deserves such an address."

Senior LRA/M commanders, on their side, consistently oppose any amnesty if it is not accompanied by political dialogue. From their perspective, when the amnesty law was introduced, to respond positively to it and ask for pardon equaled a capitulation. "We are not going to lay down our arms as long as Museveni is still in Uganda as president, because the only language he understands is the one that comes from the barrel of the gun," they wrote in one of their letters distributed in Gulu. "We are not going to be intimidated or baited into compromise through the Amnesty law because we have a clear agenda for fighting" (undated LRA/M letter, distributed in late December 1999, translated from the Acholi original).

Young people in the conflict area conveyed discrepancies in their own efforts to understand the violent reality they face in everyday life. In one context, therefore, they would strongly condemn the atrocities committed by the rebels as well as those of the Ugandan army. Of course, young people too sometimes conformed to the official discourse. However, in contexts that were more private many argued against the official discourse, for example, by describing the rebels as freedom fighters. In other words, the official approach of belittling the political manifestos of the LRA/M rebels, which for so many years blocked their access to the official political arena, has created frustration not only among the rebels themselves, but also among my noncombatant young friends in Gulu town.

THE MANIFESTOS

I believe that it is important to nuance the frequent claim that the manifestos of the LRA/M, on the Internet or elsewhere, are inauthentic diaspora creations and therefore "bear virtually no relation to anything actually happening in northern Uganda" (Ehrenreich 1998: 99–100, n. 14; see also Human Rights Watch 1997: 73, n. 85). Such conclusions adhere to the official discourse on the war in northern Uganda. Yet authenticity is not about where a piece has been written, but rather where it is disseminated and discussed, where its meaning is mediated and reformulated, and its relevance assessed. Also, the fact that the war in northern Uganda connects to global realities and the wider world, including the Ugandan diaspora of course, should neither come as a surprise nor be dismissed.

There can be no question that LRA/M manifestos circulate on the ground in northern Uganda, which is where I encountered them in the first place. I have also documented that a number of Acholi who were known critics of the government and therefore suspected of having copies, have perished in Ugandan prisons. This fact gives a most real, lived dimension to the manifestos. Again the official discourse of denial is violently at play. In this official discourse, not only is it denied that the LRA/M has manifestos but people who dare to voice the contrary run the risk of being imprisoned. As reported by the Uganda Human Rights Commission (2003) and Human Rights Watch (2003a), a growing number of people countering the official line have been arrested on charges of treason or suspected terrorism, but denied court trials. Locked in army prisons or detention centers commonly known as "safe houses," they have disappeared from public view. Some are suspected to have died in custody, under conditions that most of my informants find mysterious and "bad," or in any case not natural. This was notably the case with rebel commander Kilama and others who surrendered, only to die. The fates of these individuals have had a profound impact on Acholi people, who remember the violent rule of Idi Amin in the 1970s. Now as then, as Robben (2000: 96) writes with reference to the better-known case of Argentina, "Violent death was taken away from the eye and control of the people, confined to the secrecy of the detention centers, and spread through society." As happened in Idi Amin's Uganda, in Argentina thousands of people alleged to be in opposition to the military government of the time disappeared between 1976 and 1983.

By relating the written manifestos of the LRA/M to the viewpoints of my young informants, I suggest an alternative to the simplistic representation of the LRA/M in media and government rhetoric. At the same time, in my analysis I aim at "re-politicizing war," to use a phrase of Allen and Seaton (1999: 4). They describe the opposite, the depoliticizing of war: "Ethnic mythologizing by protagonists and by journalists is precisely a means of taking the politics and the history out of wars, and reducing them to fantastic emanations" (Allen and Seaton 1999: 4). Protagonists and journalists often reach for the easy way out. Recall the images of the Acholi as grasshoppers, or the LRA/M rebels as the biting dog, or of the Acholi as collectively unable to properly understand the war or take any national responsibility. The frequent reference in the official discourse to the rebels' religious practices and gross human rights violations feeds on such reductionist conclusions. At the same time, in the official discourse contested issues of political dignity are efficiently side-stepped, even silenced.

Kayunga writes that it was only in the process of the evolving war that insurgents in northern Uganda were forced to frame their ambitions in terms of a struggle for multiparty politics and democracy, "if only," as he holds, "to win international sympathy and support" (Kayunga 2000: 112; see also Lord's Resistance Army/Movement 1997c: 3). In response, it is important to add, however, that this support must also be won locally and nationally, not only internationally, and it is not analytically satisfactory to reduce the political manifestos of rebel groups in Uganda as being addressed only to external forces. This Kayunga actually acknowledges. "As the LRA lost popularity especially after 1991," he writes, "it began to embrace multiparty propaganda" (Kayunga 2000: 115).

Friends in Gulu have told me how they occasionally have been stopped at rural roadblocks manned by the rebels. After hasty political lectures by the roadside, they have been given written manifestos with the order to continue their travels and tell fellow Ugandans about the rebels' claimed agenda. In 1997, during fieldwork, I was given one such manifesto. The one-page document promotes, first, the immediate restoration of multiparty politics and, second, the introduction of constitutional federalism. Following these opening statements, it expresses support for human rights, stresses the need to develop nationwide socioeconomic balance, and promotes restoration of nationwide peace and security and of ending corruption. The next items express the need for free and fair forthcoming elections, the establishment of good relations with neighboring countries, improvements in the judicial system, and demands that the military organization be separated from the judiciary and executive. Finally, the manifesto argues for the reform of parliament so that it can become capable of tackling "critical political and economic issues of the country" (Lord's Resistance Army/Movement 1996a). A subsequent and much longer manifesto also promotes human rights, as well as "national unity" and the restoration of "political pluralism" (Lord's Resistance Army/Movement 1997b). Again it can be noted that at this point of time, informants felt skeptical about the rebels' claim to support any human rights, because of the many abductions and atrocities that rebels continued to commit.

In late 1999, I came across another printed political manifesto, again shown to me in Gulu town. This undated pamphlet repeats many of the issues put forward in the previous manifestos. But at eighteen pages in length, it also included much more detailed criticism of the practices of Museveni's Movement government. Among other things, Uganda's armed involvement in the Congo was questioned, and multiparty politics were promoted. The pamphlet, which is an obvious continuation of previous manifestos, furthermore acknowledged that structural adjustment programs are necessary but questioned how they were being implemented in Uganda. It argues that people at the grassroots level suffer the most, especially in peripheral areas in the north and the east. The manifesto also includes brief descriptions of LRA/M's economic programs and proposed policies on education, agriculture, health, land and natural resources, infrastructure, commerce and industry, and defense. Finally, the pamphlet questions the concentration of the executive, legislative, and military powers in Uganda in the hands of a single individual, the president (Lord's Resistance Army/Movement n.d.).

"WHAT WE ARE NOT . . ."

It is notable that representatives of the LRA/M often find it necessary to write against the official discourse. For example, the organization denies that it is motivated by any fundamentalist Christian ideologies. On one of the LRA/M Internet websites, under the title "What we are not . . . ," the LRA/M is described as not a religious movement or a Christian fundamentalist group, or a terrorist group of any sort. The now defunct site declared: "The name 'LORD's' was adopted by members of the Rural Population who decided to pray for divine intervention in order to prevent the countless pogroms and massacres of the peasant population by the National Resistance Army now known as Ugandan Peoples Liberation Army [sic, for Uganda Peoples' Defence Forces] headed by Major [now full] General Yoweri Kaguta Museveni. Thus the name is a representation of the people's Plight and Agony" (accessed September 15, 1999). In the printed manifesto circulated on the ground in northern Uganda in 1999, a note signed by the LRA/M leader Joseph Kony serves as a preamble to the political issues raised. Again the effort to deny the fundamentalist label is central. "There have been miss informations about this Movement, its name, objectives, policies and even its entire membership including leadership," Kony writes. The movement is for all Ugandans, he furthermore claims, and the term "Lord" is explained as a simple thanks to the "Heavenly Father" who has made it possible for the movement to resist Museveni's army, which nevertheless "is always armed from tooth to nail." The rebel leader continues, "While a big percentage of the Movement's members are ordinary and Practicing CHRISTIANS, I would like to strongly deny that these members are or in any way have the intention of becoming Christian Fundamentalists" (Lord's Resistance Army/Movement n.d.: 5).

As indicated, a great discrepancy exists between the alleged agenda of the LRA/M as mediated through media and Ugandan state propaganda and what is contained in the written manifestos of the LRA/M. A former LRA/M political commissary gives his version of the movement's name. "The group constantly prayed and thanked god for keeping them alive," he writes. "In appreciation for the mercy and protection God had shown on them, these survivors gave the name LORD'S RESISTANCE MOVEMENT/ARMY (LRM/A) to their liberation movement" (Lord's Resistance Army/Movement 1997c: 3). Again the movement's spokespersons try to distance themselves from the issue of the Ten Commandments. The argument is put forward in yet another rebel document. "Serious reflection on moral codes and religion may help us now and in the future," it is claimed. However, the document continues, prayers "are not compulsory" and Uganda needs "freedom of association and belief" (Lord's Resistance Army/Movement 1996b).

Most external observers agree with the Ugandan authorities in questioning the authenticity of LRA/M Internet sites and printed manifestos. When in 2000 I inquired among government officials in Gulu, the response was a solid denial of the existence of any LRA/M manifestos, past or present. Already in late 1999, however, as it became evident that the rebels had distributed a printed manifesto to religious and political leaders, as well as to some international NGOs, it soon attracted great interest from the public. One of its main authors, who eventually left the rebel movement and thereafter could tell me his version, claimed that two thousand copies were printed and distributed to several national and international NGOs as well as to foreign missions in Kampala. The same manifesto was retyped and published on the Internet.[12] Some known critics of the Ugandan government were arrested on the allegation of having copies. Frustration with this government response among the noncombatant population, I noticed during my fieldwork, grew along with their curiosity to hear what the LRA/M really had to say. At that point, influential local government officials such as the resident district commissioner of Gulu, the Local Council 5 (Gulu) chairperson, and the Gulu District Movement chairperson admitted to me that the rebels did indeed distribute a political manifesto, which they did not, however, show me. In separate interviews, they all vaguely described the rebels' manifesto as nothing but a copy or duplication of the ruling

Movement's recent Fifteen Point Program (as outlined in Movement Secretariat 1999). Their replies to my questions in May 2000 were well coordinated.

The only official representative of the government apparatus who told me that the rebels had their own manifesto was a local council youth representative. The manifesto had been shown to him at a district meeting with various government representatives. He had also been given the opportunity to listen to a tape with the rebel leader speaking, which, however, was kept from the public. The district authorities forbade the local radio station to put the tape on the air, because, as the then local council chairperson and political leader of Gulu district claimed in a public speech in February 2000, "It will only disturb [people's] minds." The youth representative was of another opinion. "The manifesto looks very good," he told me as he recalled the meeting that preceded the public speech. Then he added, "But all in all, what matters is what is seen on the ground," indicating that the rebels' violent practices pointed in another, opposite direction.

Today the Kampala region is booming and expanding rapidly. As noted by Leopold (1999) and Tangri and Mwenda (2001), Uganda is widely regarded, among both academics and influential organizations such as the International Monetary Fund, as a success story of reconstruction, structural adjustment, and economic liberalization. In 1999, I discussed these issues with a colleague, an expatriate anthropologist in Kampala. "You will find no academic in Uganda who is critical about the structural adjustment programs," he commented when I brought up the issue. As my report of local discontent in the north shows, however, peripheral regions were lagging behind; my informants said that that area had benefited only partially from the development, privatization, and alleged prosperity of the country. Indeed, donor agencies, private enterprises, and other financial institutions have been reluctant to invest in the northern region because of armed fighting and recurrent periods of insecurity. I therefore suggest that a majority of my Acholi informants shared with the LRA/M rebels the experience of mistrust, created by war and uneven development. The criticism is outlined in one of the rebel manifestos:

> LRM/A recognize the importance of the World Bank and IMF Structural Adjustment Programs. However, we also recognize that these programs have concentrated on achieving low inflation and deregulating markets to the exclusion of other considerations. The resulting deflationary pressures have undermined prospects for economic recovery, compounding in-

equalities, undermining the position of women, and failing to protect poor people's access to health and education services. They have contributed to high levels of unemployment and the erosion of social welfare provisions for the poor. Meanwhile market deregulation have brought few benefits for those excluded from markets by virtue of their poverty and lack of productive resources. (Lord's Resistance Army/Movement n.d.: 11)

The Ugandan government is said to be "selling off" the country and its public and natural resources. The claim is not unique to the LRA/M rebels or even Uganda. From the perspective of one of Diawara's (1998: 106) informants, a taxi driver in Senegal's capital Dakar, African presidents are increasingly becoming mere ambassadors, ordered around by the "real presidents" of the West. Regarding Uganda, Tangri and Mwenda (2001: 132–133) show that the extensive privatization programs initiated during the 1990s, more often than not infested with corruption, have "promoted the creation of a tiny wealthy class" rather than following the objectives to "broadening the basis of ownership" (see also SAPRIN 2001). Even more vulnerable to such developments, of course, are people who live with war and bad surroundings, when little can be done with private means to improve the prospects for the future.

With such developments in mind, it is notable that the LRA/M manifestos present a critical stance against "the New World Order" as described by the sociologist Zygmunt Bauman (1998). He does not refer to Uganda in his book; but interestingly, Bauman (1998: 66) quotes rebels in Chiapas, Mexico, when he tries to put his finger on the frustrations in the so-called peripheries in today's "process of a world-wide *restratification*" (Bauman 1998: 70), which benefit only the very few. What illustrates the new world order is not, perhaps, the weakening of states, as many have suggested, but rather, at least in the Ugandan case, the militarization of the state and its elites in particular (see also Sluka 2000). So even if most government officials as well as external observers have dismissed the rebel manifestos as diaspora creations disconnected from Ugandan realities, it must be noted that these documents pinpoint the issues relevant to most people in Acholiland in particular and in Uganda in general. This does give them a certain degree of authenticity. The leaders of the LRA/M delegation, voiced their frustration in thier opening remarks to the peace talks held in 2006:

> Your Excellency, over the years, it has been suggested and the leadership of the NRM/A [of Museveni] has shouted it from the roof tops to per-

suade the international community, that LRM/A has no political agenda. In our view, to say so is to underrate our national problems and to give a false impression that the regime in Kampala is the most sagacious in the world. Failure of the LRM/A to have access to the mass media to express its political agenda loudly in intellectual form does not mean the lack of it. (Reproduced in *New Vision*, July 15, 2006)

OSAMA BIN LADEN IN UGANDA

As mentioned, in December 2001, the U.S. government included the LRA/M on its list of global terrorist groups. The global war on terror had reached Uganda, and the Ugandan government welcomed the rhetoric of no dialogue. The LRA/M rebels, on their side, perhaps frustrated with yet another effort to silence their political agenda, occasionally reciprocated the rhetoric of the global war on terror. As the rebels were maneuvering their way to Gulu town in mid-2002, a rebel suspect arrived in the middle of the day in a neighborhood on the north side of town, allegedly to survey the area. Typically, as they are obliged to do, some people reported their suspicion about the rebel presence to the local army unit. But the military withdrew, leaving the matter to the police. The police did nothing. The rebel suspect disappeared, but his rebel unit came back in the middle of the night. They broke into houses, arrested people, and looted food and clothes. They remained for several hours and they went about their careful work undisturbed. One local government functionary who tried to escape was shot dead. Eventually the rebels decided to pull out, still without having encountered any Ugandan military response. As is common, some local people were forced to carry the plunder toward the rebel hideout. As they withdrew from town, the rebels asked their abductees if they knew who they were, and why they had come. "You are the rebels, the LRA, I guess," one young abducted man answered. "Yes, we are. We are strong. And we are Osama Bin Laden. We will come back within a few weeks. Remember that!" he was told repeatedly before he and his fellow abductees were released (they were not taken to the hideout itself, so that they would not be able to disclose its exact position). They walked back to town, where I recorded the story the following day.

In the official discourse, it is often claimed that today's rebels in Uganda have been trained in camps run by Osama Bin Laden and the al-Qaeda network (e.g., Global Witness 2003: 13). This is apparently the firm conviction of President Museveni, who regards Joseph Kony and the LRA/M rebels as "al-

Qaeda trainees" (quoted in *Daily Monitor*, March 6, 2003).[13] Regardless of whether or not this is the case, the LRA/M field unit above reciprocated the rhetoric. Simultaneously, many of my informants were convinced that the rebel leader Joseph Kony, after many years of being told that he is a terrorist—something that his actions confirm him to be—has now decided to be one. As one informant put it in 2002, when he imagined Joseph Kony's way of reasoning, "They say that I am a terrorist. Well, let it be so, and let me then give them terrorism." Perhaps such a self-conversion to terrorism can be interpreted as an effort to recover political agency, otherwise denied in the official discourse.

On August 26, 2006, the rebels and the Ugandan government signed a cessation of hostilities agreement. This was something that the rebels had long insisted as necessary for serious peace talks. Listening to some of my informants over the phone, and to those who live in the Swedish diaspora, I could hear them voice their skepticism—or rather lived realism—based on personal experiences and a history of failed talks. They were apprehensive, but I could also sense hope. I especially remember one political refugee living in Sweden, who had suffered tremendously in Museveni's prisons. From our exile in Sweden, we had both done our best to follow the talks in Juba, southern Sudan, and when the cessation of hostilities agreement was signed, he immediately called me. It was a simple fact, he argued with some excitement, that in signing this initial agreement with the LRA/M rebels, the government had finally, after so many years, recognized the LRA/M as a political force in Ugandan politics. So too did the outside world, he added later on, when Jan Egeland, the United Nations undersecretary-general for humanitarian affairs, visited Sudan and met with Joseph Kony in November 2006.

After the September 11 attacks on the United States in 2001, however, one can only conclude that the official and dominant discourse became more black and white than ever. As the leader of The Moderate Party, Sweden's biggest conservative party, stated, echoing U.S. president George W. Bush's militant stand after the attacks, "Either you are with us, or you are with the terrorists." When I pressed the conservative party on this issue, presenting the example of Uganda, a party secretary responded to my questions by reiterating the argument. It is a matter of being for or against terrorism, I was again informed. He also commented upon the issue of poverty reduction, something he did not regard as particularly important in the effort to counter terrorism. The September 11 terrorists were well educated and relatively well off economically, he argued, and thus not recruited from the marginalized poor. But the politicians' black-and-white rhetoric, indeed common in today's global politics, with its two possible alternatives, narrows young people's ability to maneuver their way in life.

If, however, we turn our eyes away from the most spectacular terrorist deeds of today, and focus instead on small-scale dirty wars like the one fought in northern Uganda, it becomes apparent that the assertion that Osama Bin Laden is a rich but evil individual is not analytically satisfactory. The liberalist and modernist celebration of "the individual self as the locus of consciousness and experience," Englund (2002b: 183–184) holds, "fails precisely because *it renders relations invisible*—from personal relationships to transnational and global relations." In other words, instead of the all-too-common obsession with single individuals like Osama Bin Laden, Saddam Hussein, or even Joseph Kony and their individualities or personal biographies, we need to pay attention to the power relations and structural circumstances that promote such persons' positions. Sometimes these relations boil down to the issue of distribution and redistribution of global wealth. Most modern services offered in Gulu town these days, for example, those of the brand-new private hospital that wealthy individuals could take advantage of, have less relevance for most people than the LRA/M manifestos do. To put it bluntly, rather than being satisfied with the fact that cosmetic surgery can be done today in Gulu town, most of my young informants would vote for LRA/M's (n.d.: 15) promise to provide "free basic primary health care for all." This is not to say that these informants actively support the LRA/M, or that the LRA/M is an organization that they think is able to realize its promises. But they experience, again as taken up by the LRA/M (n.d.: 11), that the "population at the grassroots are hardly feeling the economic achievements of the Museveni regime."

This may be a provocative parallel to draw, but it is essential if we are to better grasp the kind of lived political milieu that has kept the LRA/M rebels motivated for two decades (see also Branch 2005). It is not surprising that the logic of war alienates people in the war-torn region from the central government. To put it simply, the more violence the rebels commit against the noncombatant population, the more the government will be blamed by the same exposed people for its failure to protect and provide for its citizens. A growing number of young people feel that the war increasingly excludes them from the various modern developments in Uganda, in other words, that their right to exercise citizenship is denied them. They feel severed from the Ugandan nation and its economic, legal, and educational services. To young Ugandans living in the marginalized north, then, manifestos like those of the LRA/M are increasingly attractive, while the official heart-of-darkness discourse on the LRA/M only adds to their frustrations. In the words of the unmarried teacher also quoted above, "As citizens we shall not accept injustices to continue. If we continue to point out the wrongs and yet there is no change, then we shall look for other options. The present rebellion can be used." Either you are with us, or you are with the terrorists, as George W. Bush said.

Chapter 4

DISPLACEMENTS

BAD SURROUNDINGS

"For God and My Life." The writing on the wall on one of the many huts in Palaro camp for displaced people and uprooted families is a direct and remarkable rephrasing of Uganda's national hymn, "For God and My Country," included in the preamble to the country's constitution. By replacing one word, the writer relates the lived predicament of the camp's inhabitants to the wider, national context. Perhaps, it may be suggested, the writer wanted to emphasize a feeling of being severed from the rest of Uganda and from Ugandan nationhood, a development from being in the world to bare life (Agamben 1998).

In war-torn Uganda, worldwide flows of imagery, weaponry, and humanitarian aid entangle with local developments of war and displacement, something that is common in most dirty wars everywhere on the globe. Alliances on the regional and global levels contribute to the complexity of the local conflict scene. These are the lived realities that people inescapably are caught up in. "The surroundings are bad," as my informants say, summarizing the situation. As displaced people, I propose in this chapter, try to orient themselves in life on the existential level, they also actively try to comprehend what is going on. Yet the domination

FIGURE 4 Children in Palaro camp, Gulu district. Photo by author.

that people experience is so forceful that there will be little the displaced people can do to escape their sufferings or steer their way in life.

These most obvious features of life in encampment have inspired anthropologists to explore the structural dimensions of the enforced domination, often with inspiration from Michel Foucault's well-known writings. For example, in discussing the predicament of Hutu refugees resettled in Tanzania, Malkki (1995: 236–237) sees the refugee camp as a "technology of power" that helps "to constitute 'the refugees' as an object of knowledge and control." Uganda is illustrative. The army escorts, protects, and controls most humanitarian convoys going to the camps in the rural areas. But also, humanitarian assistance comes hand in hand with military oppression. Encampment, relief dependence, and military control obviously limit and restrict people, but, as Malkki adds, camps are never immune to productive indiscipline and creative resistance to the imposed order (see also Nordstrom 2002: 276). Such resistance is not to be romanticized, however, especially when the immediate surroundings, even the camps themselves, are battle scenes, as has been the development in northern Uganda. Most often life is more about sheer survival than anything else.

Again, these are the conditions that structure life in displacement. By highlighting the structural dimensions of violence, I aim to draw attention to the extreme level of individual and collective suffering among the displaced people. Eventually, I want to propose, cultural and social agency diminish as the logic of domination and violence enter the most private spheres of everyday life. Such a displacement regime undermines the agency and individual subjectivities of the displaced people, and ultimately even takes their lives.

This is the preliminary and only conclusion that can be drawn from my structurally informed analysis of displacements in Acholiland. People live with a harsh reality. They exercise little or no control over their surroundings or even over their lives. Agency is experienced as being in the hands of others.

However, I will also focus attention on resilience and coping strategies among the displaced people, in their microcosms. Despite chaotic developments, people try to control the situation and the surroundings. In reconfiguring their social worlds, individuals struggle to handle dirty wars that degrade and destruct their local worlds. I find here an irreducible contradiction. There are stories of survival, and stories of death. Sometimes the structures of domination and violence take people's lives; sometimes the individual defies, even defeats these structures. Refugees and displaced people, write Allen and Turton (1996: 10), "will attempt to carve out some area of personal autonomy, however trivial, in which to exercise independent choice. The more rigid and impersonal the structure within which they are forced to live, the more likely it is that they will exercise this choice in ways which challenge the structure."

In 2005 the displaced numbered some two million Ugandans. Of the Acholi, more than 90 percent were displaced. At this moment in history, about one thousand people died every week in the camps, but only some 11 percent of these died because of direct violence being inflicted upon them. The overwhelming majority died of curable diseases and malnutrition (World Health Organization et al. 2005). Another 40,000 Acholi have fled across the Nile River to Masindi district, south of Gulu district, thus leaving the immediate conflict area. Others, obviously, have left for the Kampala region, have moved west to the West Nile region, or even left Uganda altogether. Gulu town, which harbored some 40,000 people before the war, today has a population of around 140,000. In periods of intense fighting, many civilians seek night sanctuary in towns. Children especially have trekked to the towns in search of safe night havens. For example, St. Mary's Missionary Hospital in Lacor, located a few kilometers outside Gulu town, harbored more than 40,000 people each night during a peak in the fighting in July and August 2002.

In international and humanitarian jargon, most of these people are "internally displaced persons" rather than refugees. To say that they are internally displaced obviously indicates that they have moved but remain in their country of origin. The term "refugee," in contrast, is usually restricted to a people who have fled their country of origin. Their refugee status is acknowledged by international law, but also, the refugee becomes "a disquieting element" who "brings the originary fiction of sovereignty to crisis" (Agamben, quoted in Orford 2003: 210–211). Internally displaced families do not pose such an explicit threat to Uganda's sovereignty.

As a sad irony of the international and humanitarian jargon, internally displaced persons are completely dehumanized in the frequently used short form, "IDPS." I will not reproduce such short forms, or even make any analytical distinction between internally displaced persons and refugees. The internally displaced persons in Acholiland, I hold, are refugees in their own country, uprooted and scattered families. Unlike most other refugees, however, they have not fled the crisis that caused their predicament. They are thus not refugees in the sense that they have found a safe haven.

A virtual flood of humanitarian reports assessing the situation in the camps has been released over the last years.[1] Despite all these reports—or perhaps because of them—people on the ground feel more and more like animals in a zoo, subjected repeatedly to assessments. To them, the outcome is unclear, the feedback often too abstract. There are also growing frustrations among Ugandans in opposition to the politics of war and displacement. Paradoxically, as report after report discusses how humanitarian aid to the camps can better be organized, or when yet another development scheme sets out to educate uprooted people on how they may farm more efficiently on ever shrinking pieces of land, but effectively shun any proper analysis of the political crisis and its deep-seated grievances, they will be regarded as reports and schemes that are licensing the status quo (see also Dolan 2005: 165, 232). For example, in commenting on the UNICEF deputy executive director's address to the U.S. Congressional Caucus in March 2006, Samson Mande, exiled representative of Uganda's biggest opposition party, argued that it was a "poor report whose recommendations aim at keeping our people permanently in the camps rather than take them back home."[2]

THE CHRONIC EMERGENCY

International organizations operating in Uganda have become entangled in the structuring of the camps, and eventually in a catch-22 situation. As the war has evolved over the years, there has been a growing discrepancy between the claims of the relief organizations and their implementing practices. Humanitarian relief is most often stated to be neutral and nonpartisan. Yet it is always intrinsically entangled with local politics. One notable example is when military and influential members of the government campaigned in the camps, claiming that they were the actual providers of the relief aid. According to them, the government provided the relief. In their exposed situation, sometimes informants in the camps have absorbed this claim. For example, some people in Palaro told Tonny and me that the Ugandan government had sent the International Red Cross to the camps. According to their conclusions, these outside agents were in some kind of alliance. And during the campaigns for the 2000 referendum, in which Ugandans were to choose between the existing no-party Movement system and a multiparty system, politicians supporting the ruling Movement government benefited extensively from logistics provided by the Ugandan army. Again, I found out, people in the camps were told that relief and humanitarian assistance would be withdrawn if the Movement system were to be changed for a multiparty system. The political opposition, on the other hand, was stopped from campaigning by the Ugandan army and police. When the elections approached, few opposition politicians were even allowed to leave Gulu town. Some of these malpractices were repeated in the campaigns for the 2006 presidential elections. Again people in the war-torn north were told that humanitarian aid and military protection would be removed if the sitting president lost.

The presence of central state authorities, both political and military, remains strong. The Ugandan authorities continue to influence and even apply conditions on relief or humanitarian activity by the various international organizations, making the relief situation very intricate and by no means neutral. Humanitarian aid and relief programs are the response to a state of emergency, when something acute must be done. They are by definition temporary (Harrell-Bond 1986: 67). But after two decades of war, it is increasingly difficult to talk about a state of emergency in any conventional sense, as such a state has become chronic, no longer the exception but the rule. Some of the camps for uprooted and displaced persons in Acholiland have been in existence for more than a decade, and so have the international organizations' measures to lessen the human suffering in these same camps. Chris Dolan, who did extensive research in the camps around the same time that I did, argues that the situation has developed into a form of political mass persecution, or, as he elaborates upon at length, "social torture" perpetrated by the

Ugandan government against its citizens in the north, paradoxically with the international community as bystanders of a sort. Uganda's international partners in aid and development, he concludes, "while talking of good governance, are in fact complicit in this process" (Dolan 2005: 24).

Even if the people who have been forced to live in the camps feel excluded from Ugandan nationhood and citizenship, as suggested by the written words on wall of the hut in Palaro, they could not escape the war. Rather, the camps for the internally displaced soon became magnets of fighting that was previously more geographically dispersed. The rebels have attacked the Ugandan military as well as the vehicles of several humanitarian organizations. More than anything, however, they have targeted the displaced people in an effort to break up the camps. Again dirty war is made manifest. Throughout the years in Uganda, both state armies and rebel forces have used terror to control the noncombatant population. It is the displaced people, rather than military personnel, who are the tactical targets in the effort to establish control. In a telephone interview broadcast on the local FM radio in Gulu in 2003, Vincent Otti, the rebels' second in command, threatened to increase the attacks on the camps, which he maintained were inhabited by "government agents" (see *New Vision*, May 5, 2003). Such threats from the rebel leaders have been frequent throughout the war.

In mid-2002, the rebels seemed to have initiated a new strategy, at least for a time, when they outnumbered the Ugandan military in the rural areas. Typically, as I could observe, during this period they would arrive in the camps in the morning hours, when people were typically more relaxed than usual after the uncertainty of the night. Frequently the Ugandan army withdrew after only a brief encounter with the rebels. The rebels would then address the displaced people, allowing them a week or so to leave the camps before they attacked. After a week the rebels would come back to carry out the threat. Hundreds of huts could be set on fire within a few minutes. The rebels often allowed people to flee before their huts were set on fire, with the explicit order that people must go back to their villages of origin. According to Acholi beliefs, however, it is seriously bad to burn down a house. Such an act of destruction must be cleansed ritually and for this a goat sacrifice is needed. Otherwise diseases and even epidemics will eventually spread throughout the neighboring surroundings (see also Olaa 2001: 110).

Obviously, and to the frustration of the many people who once again are displaced, no proper ritual retraction can easily be performed if hundreds of huts are burned. My own field experience confirms this. One early morning in July 2002, for example, the rebels arrived in Pagak camp. They had been in a nearby camp some days before, and they had warned the people there that they would soon go to Pagak as well. They had appeared in the environs of Pagak the previous evening, something that the local Ugandan army personnel knew. Eventually, when they attacked the camp, the rebels went straight to the army barracks and burned them down. Then the commanding female rebel ordered the people of Pagak to leave the camp with their belongings, after which the rebels started setting the camp ablaze, destroying 312 huts within minutes. After some time the army arrived with helicopter gunships, and witnesses claimed that bombs were dropped indiscriminately, on both rebels and fleeing civilians.

When visiting the scene after the rebels had left, the district government representative again promised army reinforcements. He took the opportunity to promise that the international organizations would soon arrive to provide food and new shelter. Tired with their impossible situation, the people in the camp abused him. "You are only coming when we have problems," he was told.

People everywhere try to achieve a sense of control over their position in the wider surroundings of life and death. This struggle is an ongoing dialectic of orientation, disorientation, and reorientation, inherent in the human condition. In 2002, as war intensified, I recorded several cases of what people called "rebel scares." Always suspecting rebel attacks, people experienced lessened control over their surroundings. Even the most mundane happenings, which people who live in peace would not even reflect upon, could result in a rebel scare. In one such case, in the middle of the night, as a thunderstorm was approaching, lightning struck a building in a camp near Gulu town. Some people took it for a rebel attack and fled. They were soon joined by others, and some ran all the way to Gulu town. Soldiers from a nearby Ugandan army detachment, for their part, started to fire into the night, increasing the panic. It was only in the morning hours that people realized that thunder, not rebels, had struck the camp. "If you are asleep and you hear people running, you just take off with them," a young man in another camp said. If people hear noises, shooting and screaming during the night, indicating that rebels or wartime thugs are arriving, they will run into hiding in the bush.

For displaced people who live with these bad surroundings, everyday priorities by necessity shift with the changing conditions of war. To identify with the wider nation while in the camp, or to exercise the rights of citizenship, is just impossible. In the crisis of internal displacement, to follow Jackson's (2002b: 122) writing on displacement, "life is ad hoc, addressed anew each day, pieced together painfully, with few consoling illusions." He continues: "To get through the day, or through the night until morning, little or no thought is given to what is true, meaningful, or correct in any logical or ideological sense; one's focus is on what works, on what is of use, on what helps one survive. Under such circumstances, cultural and national identity, imagined or imminent, are . . . luxuries the poor cannot afford" (Jackson 2002b: 122). At the end of the millennium and during my second period of fieldwork, the armed conflict in northern Uganda had lasted for almost a decade and a half, oscillating between full-scale war and low-intensity dirty war tactics with only sporadic ambushes. After a wave of abductions in Kitgum district in January 1999, most of the rebels withdrew to their base camps in southern Sudan. Only pockets remained, especially in rural Gulu and Amuru districts, but it was difficult to differentiate rebels from groups of wartime bandits. Despite the bandits and pockets of rebels, it seemed that things slowly went back to normal. Displaced people in the camps started to move back to their villages, a few permanently, but the great majority only for the daytime hours. When Tonny and I traveled along rural roads in late 1999, we frequently encountered rural people who were walking the five to twenty kilometers from the camp to the home village to work in their gardens. They did this on a daily basis. On one occasion, as Tonny carefully wheeled our small motorbike through the many people walking along the road with their heavy loads, he asked rhetorically, "So, they call this peace? People are walking ten miles to collect food. What kind of peace is that?" His experience, more than mine, told him to regard these new developments skeptically.

Then, toward Christmas 1999 and after almost a year of lull in the fighting, rebels again entered Uganda in large numbers. A diplomatic deal between the governments in Khartoum and Kampala, facilitated by the Carter Center, had effectively excluded the LRA/M, one of the most important parties to the region's conflicts. Just back from our safari to Kitgum and Agoro, in northeastern Acholiland, Tonny and I spent the Christmas holiday in Gulu town. Rumors soon circulated about the fresh rebel intrusion. After a mechanic had checked our motorbike, always in need of new parts, we did our best to assess the situation before we refueled and headed northward, now to Baker's fort and the nearby Palaro camp. The distance meter of the motorbike, which a mechanic in Kitgum had fixed for us, indicated that we had traveled forty-nine kilometers from Gulu town when we arrived in Palaro. The camp housed more than 15,000 people. There we could only confirm the news. All over Acholiland, we learned, the Ugandan army was responding to the rebel intrusion by ordering rural civilians to return immediately to the camps. People who were found outside the camps would be treated as rebel suspects. This time the army announced a forty-eight-hour deadline, after which the areas surrounding the camps were shelled and bombed (Human Rights Watch 2003a: 62, 67).

In Palaro we met some relatives of Tonny's, his mother's stepsister's family. The old woman and her family invited us for a drink. We shared a bottle of locally distilled *gulugulu*, the little they could afford to share with us, again manifesting the Acholi hospitality that I so often encountered. They told us that the rebels had arrived at Palaro two days earlier. They interrupted the Christmas celebrations, looted foodstuffs, and abducted a man from a celebration party to be their guide. The rebels later killed him. Simultaneously, some other people who fled another group of rebels that was approaching Palaro ran into an army ambush. The army shot a woman and her child dead.

"We are worried," Tonny's old relative told us. "We worry about the rebels, if they are coming back. Where shall we go to collect our food? We fear going home to collect food now." As war escalated, most people obeyed the army's orders and decided to return to the camps. Again the lived surroundings went from bad to worse.

As Tonny and I traveled back to Gulu town, we met army lorries with soldiers, armored vehicles, and an army commander's pickup, all heading north. In town, army helicopters and some new tanks had arrived, indicating the seriousness of the situation. Soon, information reached town that the rebels had spread all over Acholiland. Tonny remarked, "When I hear this thing, I feel sick. Because I don't know how to dodge this war for another ten years. This will finish the whole of Acholi." Memories of war surfaced. The war was again a most real aspect of life in Gulu town. The authorities often prevented buses and lorries from traveling north, and the Kampala buses were delayed every day at army roadblocks. The Gulu-Kitgum road was closed from time to time, and rebel ambushes were frequently reported. The army forced travelers to slash the roadside bush, when points of rebel ambushes, real and imagined, were eliminated. An extortion business soon took root, and people sometimes paid their way through the army's roadblocks. But to what use, Tonny complained after that he and all his fellow travelers along Gulu-Kitgum road were forced off the bus to slash, as the same thing would only be repeated at the next roadblock further ahead.

THEY CALL THESE PROTECTED VILLAGES

Crowded in camps
Herded like cows
In a huge kraal
Cramped all together
In a foreign fashion
Not of their choice

The Lutum people
Have no gardens
Have no granaries
Eat from charity
Handed out
By white men
In deep silence.

The Lutum people
Are weary and tired.
(ORYEMA-LALOBO 1999: 2)

Christine Oryema-Lalobo's poem follows the style introduced by another Acholi writer, the late Okot p'Bitek. The book-length story describes a fictive people who live with war, destruction, and displacement. Oryema-Lalobo calls them the Lutum people, which I suppose is a sad play on words, as *tum* refers to those who are finished (after *tum*, to be finished).

It was after about ten years of war that the Ugandan government decided to forcefully resettle a large number of the population into camps. Most of my informants in the camps held that information about the policy of protected villages prior to the relocation was vague. Instead, threats and violence were common. Those who first refused to move were sometimes beaten until they did move. In some cases, the Ugandan army shelled villages whose inhabitants refused to leave (see also ARLPI 2001: 6–10). The Ugandan president officially announced the policy of moving the rural people to camps on September 27, 1996, but the army had evidently forced people to the camps earlier than that (see also Gersony 1997: 49; ARLPI 2001: 11; Weeks 2002: 19). Concentrating large numbers of civilians in camps has been an intrinsic part of the Ugandan army's counterinsurgency warfare. When people try to go back to their home villages they are occasionally beaten by the army, informants complained.[3] Again, it seems that Ugandans fail to escape the recent past, and it is only too seductive to suggest that history is repeating itself, which was how many informants interpreted the developments. For also in the early 1980s, as the then government army tried to counter Museveni's guerrillas, its counterinsurgency forced great numbers of noncombatants into internal mass displacement (Kasozi 1999: 183; see also Mutibwa 1992: 159).

Some time after the establishment of the camps, the government presented a five-point program for the displaced people. This included primary schools, water and sanitation, health care, food distribution, and tractors so that large-scale farming could be initiated near the camps.[4] People were also promised military protection; thus the camps were officially called "protected villages." To implement such a program, however, is of course both costly and difficult. In most camps, the five-point program was inadequately implemented. In early 1998, I attended a public meeting in which government officials urged the international community to implement the program in the camps. After visiting the region, the United Nations' chief humanitarian officer, Jan Egeland, said that "northern Uganda must be one of the worst humanitarian crises in the world." Since then—and this is of course good but still paradoxical—world media have frequently reported about "the most forgotten crisis in the world," as Egeland also labeled it (in *New Vision*, November 11, 2003; *Daily Monitor*, November 11, 2003). The crisis was held to be humanitarian rather than political.

As already indicated, calls to help have been listened to, and numerous international agencies assist the displaced people in their daily survival. The relief organizations have ended up in a difficult situation. They are actually implementing the Ugandan government's policy of forced encampment, while the rebels disallow the creation of camps. The rebels have frequently issued written threats to the international organizations, sometimes even attacking their convoys. As they write in one of the many letters they distributed in Gulu in December 1999, addressed to the local people:

> Today several UN agencies like UNICEF, other human rights organizations and NGOs like World Vision are masquerading as relief workers during trouble and times of war. But these organizations operate on a set agenda to deplete your natural resources. Those operating among you are actually the shield and spears for Museveni against you. You should know that they are in Gulu, Lira, Kitgum or Apac not as relief workers, but to fulfill the agenda of Museveni. Do not be deceived that we [the LRA/M] have no political agenda. Where were the UN, the human rights agencies and UNICEF at the time you were herded into the camps? (Translated from the Acholi original)

The forced mass movement of people to the camps must be understood, then, in terms of a military strategy. Museveni, the Ugandan president, has repeatedly promised to dismantle the camps. Yet it is no secret that high-ranking army officers want the camps to remain as a valid military strategy, as they regard all Acholi as potential rebel supporters who must be controlled and monitored (Branch 2005: 19; ARLPI 2002a).

Restricting the rural people to bounded and defined areas made it more difficult for the rebels to get intelligence information and move freely in the countryside. Arthur, the former rebel controller, testified that in the early 1990s the rebels had lost most of the intelligence information and cooperation from people in the villages, while the Ugandan army was "everywhere, moving in great numbers." He recalled that there were Ugandan army personnel at virtually every point of water supply, and the Ugandan army had started using its effective and feared helicopter gunships as well as armored personnel carriers called Mambas and Buffaloes. The Ugandan army intended to take and eventually keep control in rural areas, but it also seized the opportunity to loot foodstuffs, cattle, sheets of iron, and other valuable items from deserted villages and rural schools. New buildings could be seen in Gulu town. As people pointed out to me, some of them were obviously roofed with old, rusty iron sheets, something that informants connected to the Ugandan army's looting in the rural areas.

"Release my people from the camp. Let them go home," Tonny once said to

FIGURE 5 Tonny in front of our home in Anaka camp, Amuru district. Photo by author.

me, perhaps not unintentionally paraphrasing the late reggae star Bob Marley or Exodus and Moses and Aaron's request to Pharaoh.[5] Tonny was referring to his relatives and friends in Anaka camp, a place that we now failed to revisit. Rebel ambushes along the road to Anaka as well as attacks in and around Anaka on an almost daily basis made travel a great risk. We had to cancel our plans to travel there both when my parents visited us in the field in 2000 and when my fiancée, Helena Edin, traveled with me to Uganda in 2002. Tonny, like many others, blamed the government and the Ugandan army for forcing the people to go to the camps. "I will not support them in this," he said, "because my people are suffering. So, who is protecting whom? What is this? And yet they call these protected villages." In 2005 I again decided not revisit Anaka. Now the rebels had issued an explicit threat to kill Westerners, whom they indiscriminately labeled as associates or supporters of the International Criminal Court, a response to the court's warrants of arrest for five top rebels.

"It is the people protecting the army," people told me, with reference to the geographical structure of the "protected villages" that came to prevail for many years—an army detachment stationed in the center of the camp, from which location it was supposed to protect the thousands of people surrounding it. To live in the camps, informants argued, is to be a living shield (*kwot*) between the two fighting forces. Over the years the army showed little willingness to do anything about the situation, and persistent rebel attacks undermined not only people's trust in the army but also in Uganda's leaders, and ultimately the president (Doom and Vlassenroot 1999: 28).

A HISTORY OF AUTHORITARIAN CONTROL
AND STRUCTURAL VIOLENCE

Part and parcel of British colonialism was the wish to delimit and control the movements of the many "tribes" in Uganda in separate districts. The British confined the Acholi population to an administrative entity called the Acholi district. The creation of Acholi district, as well as other tribal districts in Uganda, indeed manifested the colonial concern for keeping the people in the places they were believed to belong. Already in 1913, the colonial authorities forced numerous Acholi into internal displacement. Postlethwaite, the first district commissioner to Acholiland, "embarked on a policy of compulsorily moving large numbers of the population of Western Acholiland and concentrating them beside the main road" running in a south-north direction (Girling 1960: 175). The reason given was that areas affected with sleeping sickness were to be evacuated, but as Girling notes, Postlethwaite obviously aimed also to make the task of administration easier.

In the more recent history, resettling the population in camps was not primarily, as officially claimed, an effort to protect the population against rebel attacks. Nor was it only an immediate military strategy of the Ugandan army. Resettlement has also been enforced domination and an effort to control the population. This aspect was often emphasized by informants living in the camps. The Ugandan government, as understood by the displaced population, is imposing its rule by regulating everyday life; by controlling food resources and food distribution; by evening and night curfews; and by abusing the displaced people (see, e.g., Human Rights Watch 2005). In some camps, the curfew starts as early as five or six p.m., but it fluctuates locally, depending on how the army defines the "security situation." In the mornings, people are not allowed to leave for their gardens until late. People obviously prefer to do heavy garden work early in the mornings, but now it has to be done under the equatorial midday sun. In many camps women are not allowed to go to the water pump to fetch water in the evening, although boreholes, sometimes only one in each camp, tend to run dry during the day because of heavy use. For example, Palaro camp had only one borehole at the time of Tonny's and my visit, but the hand pump was not functioning properly. Most women chose to go to a spring located a few kilometers away from the camp. They told us that the Ugandan army had forbidden them to go there, after an incident when rebels abducted some young girls. If they went to the spring anyway, or if they went to the borehole after the night curfew, army soldiers would sometimes beat them, the women said. Rather than feeling protected by the army, the women felt abused and prevented from doing what they saw as their responsibility as women. In one instance, army soldiers arrested a woman who had gone to the bush to defecate. At gunpoint they forced her to smear her head with her own feces, after which they made her go from camp to camp, warning others not to disobey their orders.

Since the mid-1980s, war in the north has deepened regional divides and the process of ethnic reification already fostered by the colonialists. Forced movement of millions of civilians to displacement camps has taken reification and restriction to its extreme. The argument of Galtung (1969), who coined the concept of structural violence, is illustrative. It is not only the most basic human rights of the Acholi that are violated. The displaced individuals are further violated physically:

> Under physical violence human beings are hurt somatically, to the point of killing. It is useful to distinguish further between "biological violence," which reduces somatic capability (below what is potentially possible), and "physical violence as such," which increases the constraint on human movements—as when a person is imprisoned or put in chains, but also when access to transportation is very unevenly distributed, keeping large segments of a population at the same place with mobility a monopoly of the selected few. (Galtung 1969: 169)

The so-called protected villages could not be better illustrations. People's movements have become restricted, and survival and food security are controlled by the Ugandan government and outside organizations. Humanitarian organizations take the census of the population to be able to assist them. Basically, the number of needy individuals is calculated according to rough criteria of what makes households. Direct violence that targets individuals in everyday life goes hand in hand with indirect violence without obvious actors or persons who commit the violent acts.

Forced encampment has undermined Acholi ways of organizing life. As my friend the late Caroline Lamwaka wrote to me, expressing a common opinion among Acholi people, "I don't call the camps protected villages because the flimsy grass-thatched huts do not reflect the true traditional set up of home-steads in Acholi." Young men and women complained that there is no guid-ance from more senior people, while older men and women saw few possibili-ties to guard and guide the youth. Thus traditional values, cultural knowledge, and social institutions of everyday life are threatened. For example, the com-pound fire (*wang oo*) of evening meetings, and a place of tales and teaching-stories, from where the young can grow and carry with them "all the libraries of facts and happenings" as an elder described it, cannot be lit. The camp curfews forbid this. People also fear that such gatherings would attract rebels or wartime bandits.

Even the wider balance between the living and the dead, or between the human and extrahuman worlds, is jeopardized. Kopytoff (1987) notes that many African social groups have the capacity to carry their ancestors with them as they migrate. African roots of belonging, he generalizes, are not conceived to be in an unchangeable place, as Westerners often define theirs, but rather in kin groups, in ancestors, and in a genealogical position. Indeed, this was an important aspect in the history of migrations on the African continent. Writing of the aLuund in southwestern Congo, De Boeck shows that place is reproducible and allows for the repetition of social relations in new locations. Lineage ancestors dwell in the ancestral *muyoomb* trees, or "living shrines," which are firmly woven, as elders are, into "the wider networks and pathways of socio-cultural and natural textures" (De Boeck 1998: 29, 48). These trees can be replanted in new locations, and locality can be moved through space. As the trees grow, a living memory of history and belonging also grows.

This is valid also for Acholi society (see Girling 1960: 46; Malandra 1939: 30). Yet, in situations of great social unrest and violent conflict, it is not easily achieved. Clan elders in the camps often argued that they did not have the means to do this. To move an ancestral shrine (*kac* or *abila*) is a costly busi-ness; goats and chickens ought be sacrificed to make the ancestors satisfied and thus willing to move along.[6] Ideally, it should be an occasion of joy and festivity, with a treat of food served to all participants, including the ancestors.

Also, I was told, clan elders must be in complete consensus about the move, and the clan gathered so that the ritual might be conducted.

A case can illustrate the complexity of these affairs in the midst of war. A chief (*rwot moo*) was to be anointed and ritually installed. However, most of the prominent people of the clan were displaced to Gulu town, including the chief-to-be. Because of information about fighting in the area of the clan's origin, they decided to anoint their chief in the compound of his new home, a few kilometers outside town. To complicate things, there was a need to perform the last funeral rites of the previous chief and his wife before the new chief could be installed, and their ritual huts had to be constructed at the new site. A goat sacrifice was needed for these rites. Furthermore, the ancestors were to come along to town. So the clan elders also needed to erect an ancestral clan shrine and plant an ancestral tree (called *fix* or *kitoba* tree) at the place of the coming anointment. The new clan tree should preferably consist of a cutting from the ancestral tree of the place from which the clan migrated.

On this occasion, a small faction of the clan did not show up, and I was informed that no consensus had been reached on the candidate chosen for installation and anointment. The absence of a certain old man was particularly commented upon. The man had also been missing at a funeral the previous week, I was told, something that indicated that there was rivalry in the clan. Despite the war, people of his faction still lived in the rural area where most people of the clan had lived before the war. I was left with the impression that the choice of chief was not of prime concern among these dissidents, but that they objected to having the ritual event moved to Gulu town. Certainly, some may have wanted to be present but failed to come because of the difficulty of travel in the rural areas. At the time, rebels frequently ambushed civilian vehicles along the roads, and people naturally feared this. Nonetheless, it was decided that the initiation was to be conducted.

During the early-morning preparations for the upcoming rituals, a large *mafinis* fruit dropped from a tree and hit an old man, invited as visiting observer from a different but allied clan. He was not seriously hurt, but he left the scene immediately, without a word. Murmuring spread through the crowd, particularly among the women. This was a bad omen, my friends Otim p'Ojok and Tonny told me. The preparations, however, continued. The new clan shrine was erected, and the ancestral tree was planted next to it. The necessary sacrifices were prepared. A he-goat and two chickens were to be sacrificed in front of the shrine and the tree. The throat of the goat was slit in front of the shrine and the ancestral tree (some people suggested that two sacrificial goats were called for, one for the shrine and one for the tree). Then the throat of the first chicken, a black one, was slit. When it found final rest, it fell in a position with the throat and the head facing away from the shrine. The second, white chicken ended up in a similar position. The crowd again murmured, as the performance of the dying chickens indicated some kind of ancestral dissatisfaction. Tonny whispered to me that the ancestors must be unhappy with the split in the clan. Otim p'Ojok nodded in agreement.

The anointment ritual was performed, however, and Tonny and Otim p'Ojok continued to point out "bad signs" and mistakes made. The whole affair was a total mess and the clan very disorganized, Otim p'Ojok concluded. Both Tonny and Otim p'Ojok focused their criticism upon the hurry in which the ritual was conducted. Indeed it was a pressed time schedule. Not only was the anointment to be conducted, but the ancestral shrine had to be erected as well within a single day, and everything completed well before dusk, as people wanted to leave for home early in fear of rebel attacks or reprisals.

In peaceful and good surroundings, the installment would have been halted when so many bad omens occurred, and diviners (*ajwaki*, sing.: *ajwaka*) consulted to find out the dissatisfaction of the ancestors so they could eventually be appeased (see Malandra 1939: 37–42). Now, with these bad surroundings, the situation did not allow the diviners to be consulted.

Because of the war most rural Acholi face great challenges in coping with violence and social stress, although in theory, Acholi cosmology allows people to move or migrate, bringing their ancestors along. There is a difference between the retrospective, historical perspective in which issues of contest have fallen into oblivion, and the unfinished, contested and violent reality of the contemporary. In the above case, no consensus was reached, and the whole affair ended up being quite costly. Goats and chickens were sacrificed to the ancestors, and clan members and other visitors needed to be properly fed. In the camps, of course, such costly feasts are among the first things that are set aside, as daily survival always comes first.

THE HUMANITARIAN REGIME

Life in the camps has put its inhabitants almost entirely in the hands of the Ugandan government, the army, and the international relief organizations.

Slowly people have been made dependent on these outside authorities and agencies for survival.

Besides being socially destructive, the long-term situation will not be sustainable if international emergency aid operations become essential parts of the established administration. In the humanitarian efforts to structure and thus handle a refugee or displacement situation, Daniel and Knudsen (1995: 3) observe, variations in kin relations as well as personal background and biography are ignored and individuals' needs are made equal but also identical (see also Jackson 2002b: 79). Age and gender differences are also neglected as lived heterogeneity is handled homogenously. In Malkki's (1996: 378) terms, the displaced persons are constituted "as a singular category of humanity within the international order of things." In the humanitarian effort to serve the displaced people, Malkki adds, life in camps is often dehistoricized and thus depoliticized. In Allen's (1996a: 239) words on the refugee situation in the mid-1980s among the Madi who live northwest of Acholiland, "local people often ended up being perceived as amorphous recipients of things given out." Perhaps innocent but still sad is the example when one of the international organizations distributed second-hand bras and women's underwear in some camps, leaving the male recipients angry but with little dignity.

The staffs in charge are often from the Western world. They usually work according to their personal preferences and past experiences of the best methods of relief distribution, and they work on time-limited contracts. Even if a particular officer has a great deal of knowledge regarding relief distribution, this knowledge is more often based on experiences from several different places around the globe than it is from long-term involvement in a particular area with its particular problems and social or political structures.

When I first arrived in Acholiland, in 1997, the Ugandan Red Cross, whose members were hired as volunteers by its international mother-organization, kindly encouraged me to travel with its team to rural areas that would otherwise have remained inaccessible for me. On such a journey to Kitgum, perhaps only a week after my arrival in the field, I took the opportunity to ask the international field officer in charge, a Briton, about the war. Newly arrived in Uganda, I was eager to collect information that could assist my understanding. But his answer was brief. "What do I know?" he said. "I'm not interested, I'm just a relief worker."

Eventually I was to observe how this kind of promotion of relief as essentially unembedded in the local reality—and thus allegedly neutral and nonpartisan—created misunderstandings, friction, and suspicion among the relief organizations, the particular relief officer in charge, the locally hired staff and volunteers, and the people who were supposed to benefit from the relief distribution. Time constraints do not always allow misunderstandings to be unraveled at the point of distribution. Delivered in politically volatile surroundings, the distribution of relief is, by its very nature, often carried out in haste and in a top-down style. In Acholiland, during periods when the rebel presence was high, international organizations sometimes simply dumped the relief in the center of the camps so they could take off as soon as possible. Sometimes the local volunteers and the lorries were left behind in the camps overnight, as expatriates and other staff members hurried back to town. This situation of great time constraints makes the importance of preparation and follow-up essential, in an environment where opinions can be freely ventilated. As always, however, this is easier said than done. On one occasion, after which some of the volunteers were sacked—unjustly, as they saw it—the entire crew of Ugandan Red Cross volunteers in Gulu town threatened a collective strike. They had been accused of dragging their feet in assessment work, but also, more severely, of having failed to implement the orders of the expatriate officer in charge. The field officer's closest associate, who also functioned as an interpreter, was very authoritarian in style, and he added to the social distance between officers in charge and the volunteers. The volunteers claimed that they had indeed followed the instructions, but that the methodology of assessment had been changed without notice.[7] When I naively asked my volunteer friends why they did not air the criticism with some other expatriates at the organization's town office, or ask direct questions when instructions were not clear, I was told that they did not dare to do so. Better, then, to remain silent, they concluded.

The International Committee of the Red Cross soon restricted me from recording any interviews with camp inhabitants, or even using my camera for documentation. I guess that they found my research to be too political. With these restrictions on my work, I decided to rent a motorbike and travel without their assistance, accompanied only by a close coworker. Once when I visited Co pee camp, north of Gulu town, I met again with the Red Cross in the field. The organization was there to conduct a population assessment. Later on, when this information had been properly compiled, they were to return for actual distributions. The situation in Co pee was rather chaotic. We soon gathered that rumors had circulated that some international organizations, notably the Red Cross and the World Food Programme, were to come to assess the situation.

It was obvious that the number of inhabitants in and around the camp had increased considerably since the previous Red Cross assessment in the camp. A great number of people on the outskirts of the camp had constructed temporary grass shelters (called *alup*, to hide in the bush) but not proper huts made of mud bricks, which is otherwise more common. Most displaced people, when first arriving at a camp, construct these temporary shelters until a proper hut can be built. But the expatriate Red Cross field officer in charge of the assessment was frustrated. He threatened to withdraw immediately to Gulu town. People in the rural surroundings of the camps, even from Gulu town, had constructed temporary shelters so they could profit from the forthcoming distribution, the relief officer concluded. "Well, if that is the case," I said to him, "you must admit that people are creative in their strategies to cope with the situation." He countered, "Strategies of creativity? No, it is just strategies to try to screw us!"

From his point of view, of course, he was correct. But we both knew that the international relief organizations are commissioned to distribute relief only to the places defined as "protected villages" by the Ugandan authorities. People trying to cope in villages surrounding the camps were not included in many of the relief programs, while the Ugandan army, for its part, often treated people who refuse or otherwise tried to dodge encampment as rebel suspects. Given the difficult situation, the many people who had arrived at the Co pee camp demonstrated a strategy of turning dependence into resourceful ingenuity. "And yet these very strategies," Allen and Turton (1996: 10) note, "by which they seek to maintain some degree of control over their own lives, are likely to be classified by 'the system' as inappropriate and undesirable." Instead camp policies were enforced and the status quo licensed.

The logic of domination is more complicated than simply including the described dimensions of Uganda's official policies and the international community's responses. The rebels, as mentioned, have regarded the population in "protected villages" as supporters of the government. The situation has fueled the mistrust of the Ugandan government and its local measures. In the long run the situation whereby the great majority of the Acholi population is forced into camps or other displacements is socially and physically destructive. High levels of mistrust and dissatisfaction among the displaced people, and the risk of increased violence—on both structural and individual levels—is inherent in the harsh living conditions. Galtung writes: "That structural violence often breeds structural violence, and personal violence often breeds personal violence nobody would dispute—but the point here would be the cross-breeding between the two. In other words: pure cases are only pure as long as the prehistory of the case or even the structural context are conveniently forgotten" (Galtung 1969: 178). For a long time my friends in Pagak camp—Olwor Reuben, Atek Mary, and little Tekkwor—refused to accept the increased restrictions of life. Instead Reuben started a small business. He also supervised the soccer club in Pagak. In their everyday life, he and his friends planned for the days to come. They were thinking about tomorrow (*tam pi diki*), as they said. However, these initiatives were eventually crushed with great brutality when somebody threw a hand grenade into their house. That no one can point with certainty to who threw the grenade in the first place only adds to the fact that personal violence and structural violence often feed each other in a tragic mutuality, adding to the seriously bad surroundings.

A STORY OF SURVIVAL

"In the frontier realities that mark political upheaval," Nordstrom writes, "the people, goods, and services that move along shadow lines are often closely and visibly linked to the most fundamental politics of power and survival" (2001: 216). These shadow economic and political links "move outside *formally* recognized state-based channels" (Nordstrom 2004: 106), but are at the same time deeply intertwined with the formal structures of the state. Many of the local agents of the state, notably soldiers, are also powerful actors in the shadow economy. Various international organizations are also entangled with the shadow economy, since trust and personal ties are important aspects of the nonformal exchange. The shadows and the formal state practices intersect in a myriad of ways, "*but they do not give up their own identity in this intersection*" (Nordstrom 2001: 230).

In other words, a government soldier who gets involved in the shadows of war will in most situations remain a government soldier. Indeed, this was also the conclusion drawn by my informants. And personnel of the international relief organizations who get involved in the shadows can never fully detach themselves from the organizations they represent, at least not in the perspective of my informants. Nordstrom (2004: 73) quotes Nietzsche's "the doing is everything."

War realities are always global but still violently emplaced in local war zones, as is the case in northern Uganda. Contemporary experiences meet and intermingle, locality meets and fuses with translocality, the global is manifested in the local, exiles and diaspora groups are involved for political and/or humanitarian reasons, as are Western agents and foreign interest groups, and the character of particular conflicts constantly evolve and change over time. As Nordstrom argues, the shadows are also a place of power and sociopolitical transformation.

The camps in southwestern Acholiland lie on the border of Murchison Falls National Park, along the Karuma-Pakwach highway that connects Kampala with the West Nile region. The wild game in the park is a source of luxury food for the people in the area: not only the Acholi but also people from the West Nile region enter the park to poach game. In the camps, game meat is a welcome addition to the monotonous diet of home-grown vegetables and relief food. Of course, it is illegal to hunt these animals.

When ammunition and guns are captured from rebels or found in hidden rebel armories in the bush, they are taken to the local army quarters before being shipped to Gulu town to be registered. At times, Ugandan soldiers will keep some of the captured weapons for highly dubious personal use, such as night robberies and petty harassment carried out by the notorious *boo kec* bandits, often with the tacit agreement of the local army commanders. In the camps, army soldiers will sometimes lend captured guns to young men, who sneak into the national park to hunt. In return for the loan of weapons the soldiers demand half of the meat, while the hunting party shares the remaining half. Obviously, on their poaching missions the young men have to avoid not only park rangers but also mobile army units, which may take them for armed rebels. They may also encounter rebels.

In late 1999 Olak, who lives in one of the camps, went to the park as a porter for a Ugandan army soldier we shall call Opoka, who had a machine gun. This was not the first time Olak had gone hunting in the park, and several other young men came along as porters as well. This time, however, they returned from four days in the park without any meat, and Opoka parted company with Olak and the other porters. After about a week, soldiers came to investigate rumors that Olak had a gun. They did not find Olak at home, as he was away working in his garden. Instead they arrested his younger brother and another young man. When Olak heard of this, he went into hiding, but the soldiers eventually located him. He was arrested and ordered to confess where the alleged gun was hidden. In the effort to make him talk, they set Olak's hut on fire, destroying his camp shelter. This is Olak's story:

> I was arrested and taken to the army barracks together with another boy called Olum. Some person claimed that we had a gun. We told the soldiers that the gun was not ours, but the owner of the gun was an army man called Opoka. So they refused our talk. They start beating us, and they tied my arms and my legs. We were beaten seriously, and they burned our bodies with a melting plastic cup. They continued beating us before taking us back to the army jail [in the camps, most often an empty pit latrine]. We were ordered to disclose the identity of the man who had the gun. We agreed and we were taken to his place, but the man was not around. So the soldiers thought that I was deceiving them, and then they start beating me again. They start firing their guns. They just emptied two magazines, and two bullets hit me. From there they took me to the army barracks again, where the commander again ordered the soldiers to shoot me, as he claimed that I still did not tell the truth. However, the soldiers now objected, and I was eventually brought to [a local] hospital, where I stayed for two days. After that I was taken to Lacor [Missionary] Hospital.

The army commander did not allow Olak to leave the camp, but after two days in the camp's hospital, a sympathetic police officer provided him with a letter authorizing him to travel to the missionary hospital in Lacor, outside Gulu town, where his bullet wounds could finally be tended.

Olak's hunting missions reflect his everyday existential struggle with extreme poverty. Yet the ramifications of such illegal hunting sorties extend beyond the camps and the destinies of young men such as Olak. The game meat travels farther. To augment their income, Ugandan soldiers usually sell their share of this meat in Gulu town, or in the camps themselves. The potential buyers are visitors to the camps who have the means of transport to smuggle it back to town, and who are not stopped at the army's roadblocks. In town I met a Western staff member of the International Organization for

Migration, who told me that he occasionally bought bushmeat from the soldiers in the camps, which he put in the back of his white NGO pickup and took back to Gulu town. His account was not unique. "Those who may be on the forefront of aid may as well be in the backyard of profiteering," as Nordstrom notes (2001: 226, n. 6).

The displaced people in the camps, of course, take careful note of such exchanges. My expatriate informant told me that he consumed some of the meat himself, but took some to Kampala, where he sold it to friends and colleagues at the Kampala headquarters. For him the profit must have been insignificant and the risks equally negligible, but I was left with the impression that the whole process boosted his ego, as he was able to offer friends and superiors some exotic wild meat. His meaning in use was rather different from Olak's orientations in life. For at the other end of this illegal trade route, it is the young men in the camps who take the full risk on themselves. The buyers in Kampala know little, perhaps, about the young displaced men who put themselves in jeopardy. If caught, as Olak's experience shows, they may be taken for rebels, while the providers of the guns will deny any knowledge of the affair.

RELIEF AND THE REBELS' SHARE

In rural Acholiland, people often told me that "you can't plan your life. It is impossible to plan beyond today. You don't know anything about the coming days." Any long-term planning is indeed extremely difficult. And again, to arrange social gatherings around the compound's fire (*wang oo*), children and youth listening to the stories of the elderly as they all join the "family theatre" (p'Bitek 1962: 21), nourishing the roots of cultural belonging, is unthinkable. Such gatherings, as people knew from experience, could attract rebels or wartime *boo kec* bandits, or invite army harassments.

During the time of my fieldwork, in most camps, people would hide during the days that followed relief distributions by the International Red Cross, the Norwegian Refugee Council, the World Food Programme or some other well-known international agency that works in the war-torn region. The rebels have eyes, camp inhabitants said, and they know when the relief agencies have been in the camps with their large lorries. It would be little more than three days after a distribution before rebels arrived to loot, people argued with experience in mind.

In my introductory field endeavor in 1997–1998, when I had no independent means of transport, I visited several camps together with the Red Cross. During my interviews, I asked people living there if they thought that rebels would be coming the following night, something that I had heard of. "They will not," people responded if I had arrived in a Toyota Land Cruiser. But if I came in a loaded lorry the response was different. Quite naturally, in its assessment missions the Red Cross did not use its lorries. However, people in the camps knew that the rebels registered such movements. The rebels would then wait until any of the relief organizations came back with lorries for an actual distribution of aid.

In a strategy to cope with the situation, people in the camps would leave some of the distributed goods in their huts, hide some of it in the bush, and themselves sleep in the bush during the nights following the distribution. If people did not leave something "on display," as they said, the rebels would search for camp inhabitants and most likely beat them until they found the goods. If the rebels found a cooking pot with remains of newly prepared food they forced camp inhabitants to tell where they had stored the rest of the food. "We are only coming to take our share," rebels told people. "It is essential to obey," young people in several displacement camps told me. Yet, if camp inhabitants hid the goods they had received in several places, they hoped that the rebels would loot from one place only.

That rebels are coming for their share is as simple as it is sad. If there were no rebels, there would be no relief distributions. Cynically speaking, the distributions exist because of forced resettlements in camps that have made it difficult for people to grow food themselves. The camps, in turn, are the consequence of rebel activity, and consequently some of the distributed goods and food belong to the rebels. This is what the rebels say to the people in the camps when they come to loot.

CLASHES OF INTERPRETATION

The increase in atrocities committed by the rebels since the beginning of the 1990s has alienated the local population. Abductions of minors and the killing and maiming of civilians, including cutting off lips, ears, and noses, have been widely reported (e.g., Amnesty International 1997; Gulu Archdiocese 2003b; Human Rights Watch 1997). Moreover, suspicion and lack of confidence in the Ugandan army remains as its passivity and misconduct continue.

In June 2002, war again reached Purongo camp, located next to Murchison Falls National Park on the important truck route from Kampala via Karuma to the West Nile region. Of course, it was not the first time physical fighting had affected Purongo, but as in many areas, people had experienced a lull in the fighting for more than a year. This time the rebels burned some fifty huts and killed a local government councilor and at least one Ugandan soldier. As usual, they also abducted a number of people to carry their loot. When the Ugandan army realized that the camp was under attack, the soldiers withdrew, only to shell the camp from a distance. At least one mortar hit a hut, and a married couple and their three children died on the spot. When we investigated the case, Tonny and I were told that some fifteen people died in the crossfire, soldiers excluded. But in the Ugandan media, one could read the usual dominant-view conclusion. "Kony kills 18 in game park," as a headline of the *Daily Monitor* (June 30, 2002) said.

In another encounter in Kitgum district, the army ambushed the rebels when the latter were fetching water from a river. Most rebels managed to escape the ambush, but for the abducted children escape was more difficult, as they were tightly tied together with ropes. About thirty children were shot dead by the army from a very short distance, about ten meters away. In the *New Vision* (March 18, 1998), the Ugandan public could read soon after that the Ugandan army had been successful and killed many of the rebels, but that no children were killed.[8]

Das and Kleinman (2000) point out that power relations on national and global levels will influence the subjective experience of violence as negotiated in the local social world. In other words, a particular political subjectivity takes shape. Supplementary to this conclusion, Englund (2002a) points out that global power flows, often regarded as disconnected and nonlocal, and imagined by many academics to have a kind of life of their own, actually are concrete and very real, always situated and interpreted in specific contexts, always involving people's social worlds. Actual social networks and exchanges as well as specific historical circumstances provide the inescapable "emplacement" of global forces, to use Englund's (2002a) terminology.

Again, a story from Acholiland can illustrate the emplacement and entanglement of global realities in a local context. In November 1997 a group of rebels attacked the outskirts of Pabo, a trading center located some twenty-two kilometers north of Gulu town that has been turned into a congested camp with a population at the time of nearly 50,000. During the attack, which went unnoticed by the local army personnel who were supposed to protect the population, rebels stabbed fourteen people to death. Elderly women and men as well as children and babies were among the victims. The attack in Pabo seems to be extraordinary in its brutality, without apparent logic or rationality. However, most often the rebels' violent strategies contain messages to the local people (see also Branch 2005: 6). Rebels had been in Pabo earlier, that time to loot foodstuffs. They had stolen a sack and filled it with beans. When they reached a rebel camp, the beans were cooked and eaten. In investigating the matter, I was told that eight rebels died after eating the looted food. Surviving rebel commanders then assumed that the stolen sack, in which the beans had been carried, was bewitched and therefore poisonous. The rebel commandant sent a unit of six rebels to Pabo to take revenge on the people responsible for the witchcraft. Thus the massacre.

Even if they were not bewitched in terms of Western logic, the beans had somehow been made poisonous. They were distributed to the people in Pabo as relief aid, as seeds to be planted. As seeds they were chemically treated, something that might have made the people eating them sick or even killed them. Beans are vulnerable to insect pests and so are often treated with pesticide. Beans might also contain high levels of cyanide, which makes it important to prepare them carefully, with long cooking. However, looted food is often prepared in haste, and it is indeed possible that people under pressure, such as rebels in a hurry, unintentionally poison themselves (Paul Richards, personal communication). Now and then I read in Ugandan papers about people who died because they consumed seeds handed out by humanitarian organizations.

To observe that the rebels often have their own explanations and interpretations for their actions is not to excuse their terror. But the observation highlights that international relief, most often held to be neutral and humanitarian only, immediately becomes entangled with the practices and politics of war. Humanitarian organizations have virtually operated as local administrators, coordinating and planning activities. As these organizations have taken over many of the functions of the Ugandan government, they will also be perceived, as the government is, as a parallel partner to the army, seldom neutral in the eyes of the locals.

For example, when a truck of the World Food Programme (United Nations) drove through Gulu town loaded with armed and uniformed government troops, people in the town just shrugged their shoulders. But the incident was not without implications. When I asked about the lorry, people related it to the wider international context, where the United Nations and the international community are said to be allied not only with the Ugandan government, but also with political actors such as the United States and the rebels of southern Sudan. The objective of such alliances, informants along the street argued, is to counter the government in Khartoum and the alleged expanding Islamism of the Arabs, and more recently, global terrorism. This is done with Uganda and more particularly Acholiland as the necessary stepping-stone. Standing in opposition to this political body is not only the LRA/M, but also the sufferings of the Acholi people, who have found their homeland turned into a battlefield and an arena of international politics. The LRA/M rebels, for their part, at times have not hesitated to ambush the United Nations, the World Food Programme, UNICEF, or the various international organizations working in the area. In a press release the rebels accuse the United Nations and UNICEF of providing "poison food aid to the northern population" (Lord's Resistance Army/Movement 2001).

DISPLACED SPIRITS OF THE DEAD

On the road from Kitgum toward the Sudanese border is the wreck of a lorry and an antiaircraft gun once belonging to the south Sudanese rebels who tried to regroup their forces from Uganda, ambushed by the LRA/M rebels. The battle had been fierce. Together with the bodies of the many dead, the burnt wreck was left to rust by the roadside. When Tonny and I passed a year later, in December 1999, only skeletons and rusty pieces of metal remained.

As the fieldwork proceeded, I was able to better understand Tonny's uneasiness at the site of the burnt lorry. As usual, he took me to Rufina Labol, his old mother who once practiced as a healer (*ajwaka*, plural: *ajwaki*). She said that we had exposed ourselves to *cen* at the scene of the ambush. *Cen*, she explained, are the spirits of people who died violently. p'Bitek (1971) translates *cen* as "vengeance ghost" or sometimes "ghostly vengeance," a kind of shadow existence rather than only a spirit or a soul separated from its body. Odoki (1997: 40) uses the term "troublesome spirit" to describe such deceased persons in search of rest and peace. So the scene of the ambush was a place of great unrest, with no silence, inhabited by roaming spirits of the dead (*lu-cen*).

According to Acholi beliefs, the shadow being of a killed person might return to disturb its killer. If you have "killed too many people," as Tonny put it, this will have a profound and malevolent influence on your behavior. He used the metaphor of butchery, "If you slaughter cows all day, you will end up dreaming about it." In addition, the spirit of the one who died violently will also disturb the person who found the body. People who merely witness or otherwise experience the violence of war can be disturbed, with repeated nightmares and other daily flashbacks that assail their memories. Thus there is a continuous and destructive challenge to ordinary, quotidian life. There is a quantitative dimension to this—the more cen you experience, the greater its effect. A violent shadow world unfolds before you. The result is that the exposed person will start behaving asocially, amorally, and eventually in violent and destructive ways.

Perhaps, if the term of Western psychiatry is used, one can talk about post–traumatic stress disorder (PTSD), always framed and articulated, however, in locally informed spectra of distress and bad experiences. Ghostly vengeance will also expand socially, in space and time, and to other people. "Cen will not only haunt the killer," Tonny explained, "but the whole clan, for generations. Children produced will be sick, even insane." In other words, traumatic memories, disturbance, stress, and destruction do not refer only to the intrapsychic processes of individuals with traumatic experiences, which makes it ineffectual to talk about any objective and universal set of diagnostic criteria that defines post–traumatic stress. Traumatic memories also involve cultural orientations and are part of the structuring of social life, group identity, and collective memory. Examples from around the world show that traumatic memories may be passed on, actively and passively, from one generation to another (Bracken 1998; Suárez-Orozco and Robben 2000).

With the help of healers like old Rufina Labol, individual problems can be solved and a wider societal balance achieved. The healers are able to communicate and negotiate with and eventually capture cen and release the victim from its grip. The healing session is a public event that involves the local community and relatives of the exposed victim. Apart from the healer (or healers) in charge of the divination and communication with the spirits, there will be a drummer and some women singing various songs that invoke the spirits and encourage them to make themselves known. Clan elders are also consulted, as are ancestors, mostly about the local sociohistory that led to the unfortunate situation, and curious children gather to follow the session, which is not only one of individual healing but also a process of socialization in which the victim is incorporated and reconciled with the community of both living and dead. Various old and new conflicts in the neighborhood can be aired. In other words, the traumatic memory of the individual victim is socially constructed so that it also can be socially deconstructed. Through practice, the traumatic memory is "made real" (Young 1995: 8).

As always with cultural orientations in life, meaning emerges socially. In such situations, children gradually build up their own understanding of cosmology, morality, unlawful violence, and healing. "It may be supposed, indeed, that attendance at [seances] has an important formative influence on the growth of witchcraft-beliefs in the minds of children, for children make a point of attending in them and taking part in them as spectators and chorus," as Evans-Pritchard once noted with reference to the Azande. "This is the first occasion on which they demonstrate their belief, and it is more dramatically and more publicly affirmed at these seances than in any other situations" (Evans-Pritchard 1937: 154).

However, rebel children grow up in a milieu in which senior rebels agitate militantly for a new moral order. As a result, these children may not easily be receptive to the efforts of diviners and other arbitrators of the local moral world whom they have learned to mistrust. As a former female rebel told me, "I do not like *ajwaki* [diviners], because when I was in the bush we did not listen to any ajwaki. The teachers said that they are bad." As is common, she referred to the rebel commanders as teachers (*lupwony*, sing.: *lapwony*). According to the instructions of these teachers, the diviners are bad and therefore held to be legitimate targets of military violence. "Teacher" is also the name frequently given to the Christian missionary, and much missionary teaching, as we know, again contains a strong denunciation of the work and practices of the diviners like Tonny's old mother. The former rebel girl experienced the nightmares so typical among most former rebels, which revolve around the themes of killing people again or being reabducted. Despite these dreams, she did not feel comfortable with the idea of consulting the diviners. Similarly, but with reference to the fact that she was now a born-again Christian, another former female fighter said she would decline any assistance from the diviners.

Maybe my role as researcher made me a child in this context, because my informants' stories about cen and the possible and dangerous exposure at the scene of the ambushed lorry gave me, although I was an outsider, a framework for understanding my own worries about staying and moving around in a war zone. As an anthropologist with a special interest in the lived cosmology—that is, the everyday process of social contest and human creativity—I found personal relief in collecting ethnographic data on cen. And I discovered that Tonny was most eager to assist me in this aspect of the research.

Young people who have fled or otherwise left rebel ranks are typically offered some rudimentary assistance through one or another of the organizations that work with reintegration. After medical checkups and counseling, some are offered primary schooling, others various skill training. World Vision is the largest of these organizations, but its explicit born-again Christian ideology leaves little room for the moral discourse on cen or ghostly vengeance. In a report to the organization, two local researchers, who define themselves as born-again Christians, conclude that Acholi beliefs and practices "are still being very effective in dealing with trauma problems" (p'Anywar and Rubben 1999: 33). Still, they adhere to a common Pentecostal claim when they propose that the "relationship between Christian faith and traditional Acholi approaches towards counselling the traumatised can be equated to mixing oil and water." Acholi practices are compared to witchcraft and sorcery, which "can not be in conjunction with Christianity" (p'Anywar and Rubben 1999: 32, 33).

Despite initial assistance and counseling at the reception centers, the predicament of the formerly abducted children is not very different from that of other people in the war-affected region. Most often they eventually end up in one of the many camps, or in towns like Gulu. Besides the uncertainty, idleness, and the lack of proper nutrition or even schooling and healthcare that they share with most people in the camps, some of their problems are particularly worth noting. The returnees are often told that they have been exposed to "bad things in the bush," indicating that they are morally tainted. Close relatives are usually as supportive as they can be, but more distant kin and other neighbors are often more judging, using "bitter language." Such bitter language implies that the returnees "have cen in their heads," something people fear will affect also the wider surroundings. "We don't like you people who have stayed in the bush," one young woman was told by her female age-mates. Another young female returnee claimed that especially women of the neighborhood were rude to her. Again the issue of cen, or ghostly vengeance, was prominent. Neighbors avoided her. "Cen, cen, cen! You have cen!" she now and then heard. I encountered many painful stories along these lines, like the one of the man who refused to allow a young, orphaned ex-rebel niece to bury her dead child in his compound. The child's father was still with the rebels.

Some young male returnees in Koch Goma camp felt abandoned. Neighbors and other people avoided them, again saying that cen had made these men dangerous to their surroundings. "You have come from the bush with so much cen in your heads," they were told. "The people fear to stay with us," one of the boys told me, because "they fear that their minds will be changed because of us, who are from the bush." The former rebels in Koch Goma tended to stay together, and they found solidarity in a shared past as rebels.

To live with the spirits of the dead, and to have to encounter the bitter language from the surrounding community, are not the only problems that returnees face. Also, as latecomers to the camps, the returnees have most often found shelter on the outskirts of the camps, and any field where they can dig will usually be located some distance away, as nearby areas are already taken. Thus the returnees have risked ending up as a buffer between civilians and the rebels, their former comrades in arms. What they fear most is to be reabducted, and working in faraway gardens adds to this fear. They also fear that neighbors in the camps will tip off the rebels if they arrive. "Don't kill us, but go to your former colleague who stays over there," neighbors will say in an effort to save their own lives. Explicit threats like this are frequent, returnees claimed. Sometimes the rebels have come to camps expressly to collect returnees, whom they regard as their children.

In addition to this, Ugandan army personnel, senior to these returnees but sometimes with a rebel background themselves, frequently approach young men who have escaped from rebel ranks. Patterns of rank reemerge, invisible to most outsiders. In some cases that Tonny and I investigated, the same army soldiers who rescued them from the rebels in the first place later harassed them. Various demands are made of them. The soldiers may demand money, or, if the young male returnees sell locally grown tobacco in order to raise a little money, they demand free tobacco. In one instance, some young men bought some sugarcane with the little money they had managed to raise, only to have it taken by the soldiers. Similar accounts are legion. Also, Ugandan soldiers frequently approach male returnees to recruit them into the army or the local defense forces. The returnees are held to have important information on hidden rebel bases, their routes, and strategies. Sometimes they are given a salary, but sometimes they are just forced. Even minors are taken as far as Sudan in the army's hunt for rebels (see also ARLPI 2002b).

THE PEOPLE ARE WEARY AND TIRED

Structural domination imposes itself on people's social worlds, making it difficult for them to control or even grasp their own fate. Domination is violently enforced by both the Ugandan government and the rebels. Obviously, people in the camps live with mixed feelings. They are most grateful to receive aid, food, and cooking equipment. On the other hand, they know that this creates a situation of dependence.

When rebels were active, people also know that the nights following a distribution would be most uncertain. Part of the distributed goods would probably be looted. Also, people might be abducted in the process and forced to carry the looted goods. As long as the rebel units were moving inside Uganda, "there is no major problem," some young men in Palaro told me with voices of resignation. Abducted people were most often released soon after, so that rebel hideouts were not exposed to nonrebels. However, things got worse as the rebel units headed toward Sudan. Looting increased. Many people were abducted to carry the looted goods, and children were abducted and taken to Sudan for rebel initiation and military training.

As 2006 drew to a close, after a year of almost no rebel attacks, there was still no easy solution to the difficult situation for the displaced people. Even though they want to leave the camps, until any final peace agreement is reached they also fear leaving them. A common desire in the camps has long been that the international community should intervene, and arrange and guarantee everyone's safe repatriation. Ironically, instead the United Nations and other representatives of the international community have upheld the displacement structures, adding another dimension to the enforced domination of the displaced people. International relief has long been distributed exclusively to camps that are officially recognized, on the orders of the Ugandan government. The displaced people eat from charity, handed out by white men in deep silence, as the Acholi poet Christine Oryema-Lalobo has it.

In these circumstances, the humanitarian apparatus has become intimately entangled with the Ugandan army's strategies of domination and control.

Resistance to this control, for example when people in the camps refused to offload the relief lorries, has typically been met with sanctions and increased authoritarian control. So even if there are examples of people defying the representation of themselves as being only anonymous and passive recipients, the majority of displaced people cannot negotiate anything without jeopardizing their own survival. In one confrontation, when the people in Anaka camp did not meet up with the relief lorries, the leaders of the camp had to publicly apologize to the district government leaders over FM radio, before the intentional humanitarian organizations resumed distribution. The rebels' violent practices add to the victimization of internally displaced persons and families. So far, most people in the camps have survived. But more than the threat to their physical bodies, perhaps, life in terror and encampment has threatened their humanity, which ultimately has been reduced to bare life. "The Lutum people / Are weary and tired," writes Oryema-Lalobo.

Chapter 5

WARTIME RUMORS AND MORAL TRUTHS

TOO MUCH *RADIO KABI*

War, violence, displacement, and political persecution in Acholi-land have very much set the framework within which action and coping are possible. Rumors are also part of this framework, forcing people to construct their own truths as they try to achieve some sense of governing their own fate. In this chapter, my aim is to contextualize my informants' stories in the effort to demystify them. Simply speaking, in everyday life people invoke meanings they find relevant, as they try to comprehend and live the wider, unbounded world that they are caught up in. It is, however, a paradoxical situation. In the context of dirty war people can exercise little or no control over the wider surroundings or even their individual fates.

Rumors are central to the propaganda machinery in all war settings, I believe. They link the personal with the political, and the local with the national and even global. During my second fieldwork period in 1999–2000, it was rumored that the rebel leader Joseph Kony was terminally ill with AIDS, now spending his last days in a military hospital in Khartoum. "Kony sick, in army hospital," the front page of the *Daily Monitor* read in big, black letters on December 7, 1999. The article suggested that the rebel leader had expressed the wish to meet his parents before he died. A few weeks later another rumor surfaced, this time that Joseph Kony had lost one leg in battle. Quoting a Ugandan minister, the front page of the same newspaper now suggested that the rebel leader had been injured and crippled (*Daily Monitor*, December 31, 1999). "Kony very sick, coughing blood," the *Daily Monitor*'s headlines again stated on August 2, 2006.

As most rumors cannot be confirmed, they just "added salt to the wound," as my informants said, to the uncertainty of everyday life. My friend Otim p'Ojok explained with a fictive example, "Say that five rebels enter from the Sudan, then you say, oh, five hundred rebels have passed from there!" In Acholiland, people call unconfirmed rumors *radio kabi*, after the toy radios that children some-times make and play with. For the antenna, the children use a straw of sorghum (*kabi*). So news that is not really fully reliable is often taken with the caution "It is news from the children's toy radios." Information is shared on a daily basis whenever friends meet. After a day's work, people sometimes come together to have a chat and share a pot of sorghum beer, which is consumed with straws. When such social gatherings continue for a good number of hours, and the women who have prepared the beer keep filling up the pots with more beer, many stories and pieces of news indeed will be aired, checked, and coun-terchecked. Their relevance for everyday life is assessed and reassessed. "There is too much radio kabi," Otim p'Ojok commented about a discussion we had had with some clan elders the day before. "But in the end radio kabi becomes the truth," he added, not without frustration.

Rumoring often manifests the paradoxical search for control and balance in life, perhaps more so in war and threatening contexts. Tonny told me that radio kabi could predict danger. Indeed, radio kabi assisted us greatly when we traveled along rural roads. The bicycle mechanics who had their rural stands strategically placed under big, shady trees at almost every road junction be-came our main sources of information regarding rebel movements. Their customers had often traveled far, and the mechanics' stands were obvious points where information was shared. In this variant, radio kabi lessened our uncertainty and gave us a sense of control.

In Acholiland, there are also rumors of a more profound potency that find their way into the social memory of collective suffering. These rumors too, I suggest, mediate the existential uncertainty of quotidian life. They also say something about political asymmetries in Uganda and beyond. One concerns the alleged occupation and subsequent colonization of Acholiland by non-

Acholi agents, something alleged to be going on in the shadows of war. Displacement of the great majority of the rural Acholi into camps has meant that people have had little or no possibility of maintaining their fields and gardens or watching their land. By forcing all these people into the camps, many of my informants argued, the Ugandan president took revenge on the Acholi for their alleged involvement in Uganda's violent past, especially in Luwero in central Uganda during the war in the first half of the 1980s that brought the current government to power.

Other rumors negotiate the experience of the various new health threats, which informants sometimes concluded are targeting the Acholi collective through its most vulnerable individuals. Examples of such health threats are the HIV/AIDS and Ebola epidemics, but also relief food of questionable quality, as when the recommended last date for consumption, always clearly printed on the sacks or cans, has expired. A final set of rumors concerns other forms of indirect domination and the government's alleged revenge, which my informants again held was an additional factor in the slow annihilation of the Acholi people. Recall Ladit Arweny, the elderly man who talked in terms of a war on the Acholi because of the fact that the great majority of the casualities are Acholi. In his eyes, the rebels' fratricidal terror and the Ugandan government's lack of commitment to ending the war were both aspects of this war on the Acholi. Again the ghost of Luwero seems to haunt the Acholi collective. As Pirouet (1991: 205) writes, "Many Acholi would argue that they are now suffering what the people of the Luwero Triangle suffered previously, and that insecurity has merely been shifted from one area to another."

All these rumors figure strongly in the current social memory in Acholiland, deepening the idea that the Acholi are being subjected to a slow and secret genocide, staged by the central government and other outside powers, even when the involvement of the international community as status quo is licensed (e.g., Otunnu Olara 2006). Sometimes informants suggested that the government's hidden agenda was to have the war continue by every means, a war that for so many years was good business for high-ranking army officers but ultimately was believed to be the end of the Acholi people.

A GREAT CONSPIRACY OR A SOCIAL BARRIER?

My aim is not to discuss the rumors in terms of a great conspiracy. Such a reductionist conclusion, I propose, adds to the exoticism that is only too common in reporting on the war in northern Uganda and wars elsewhere in

Africa. Theories of conspiracy often end up with metaphors borrowed from psychology and the medical sciences, and from their various diagnoses of mental and physical unhealth, such as paranoia, mass hysteria, or alcoholism. A diagnosis of unbalanced individual personalities is transferred to whole groups, to describe or diagnose collectives and societies as well, even cultures and continents. Illustratively, the film *The Invisible Children* (2003) contains a part called "The mental state." Pictures of four mentally ill persons, all well-known characters in Gulu town, frame the narrative. One of them is even interviewed, and he is evidently drunk. Motion pictures of child-soldiers from West Africa are used to illustrate the film's narrative.

In an influential article on Cameroon, translated from the French original and soon published in three English versions, the historian Achille Mbembe presents an intriguing but still illustrative conclusion on the postcolonial situation in contemporary Africa. Alienation is African postcoloniality par excellence, he holds, and the postcolony is nothing but a hollow pretence, a regime of unreality and simulacrum, a mere idol, a fetish. He continues, "The postcolonial polity can only produce 'fables' and stupefy its 'subjects,' bringing on delirium when the discourse of power penetrates its targets and drives them into the realms of fantasy and hallucination" (Mbembe 1992b: 16). The postcolony is characterized by the loss of any limits or sense of proportion, he holds.[1]

The psychoanalytical jargon is seductive but nevertheless a fiction, at least for the social worlds of my informants. In refusing to describe my informants as living in abstract worlds of paranoia, delirium, fantasy, or hallucination, I aim to highlight instances of shadowy power relations, actual social relations, and symbolic transactions that have led some of my informants to conclude that the Acholi people are disappearing, even that they are being subjected to a genocide.

The uncritical transference of individual diagnoses to the collective has long been debated in anthropology. As Adam Kuper concludes on Ruth Benedict's view of the concept of culture, "For Benedict, the integration of a culture was comparable to the crystallization of a personality. Cultures had their own collective personalities—the Dobuans, for example, were paranoid, the Kwakiutl megalomaniac—and they impressed a modal personality type on the individuals who were raised in that culture" (Kuper 1999: 66). Kuper proceeds to quote Edward Sapir, a contemporary critic of Benedict: "I suspect that individual Dobu and Kwakiutl are very like ourselves; they just are manipulating a different set of patterns. . . . You have to know the individual before you know what the baggage of his culture means to him" (from a lecture by Sapir, quoted in Kuper 1999: 67). I want to avoid labeling the discourse on genocide, common among my informants, as paranoid or perverted, something that however has been the official Ugandan government response to this discourse. Instead, I want to highlight how rumors are made manifest in context of everyday discussions and conversations. Understanding people's predicament in life is important to the explanation of the rumors and to their prevalence. Following Sapir in this case rather than Benedict, I will draw attention to individual stories and life destinies and the role that these have in the spread of rumors. The stories on radio kabi manifest my informants' efforts to redefine the order of things, to alter the imposed legacy of violence. It is their effort to voice their concerns, to regain a sense of agency when war, destruction, and displacements leave them with the feeling that they are constantly being acted upon and that fixed meanings are imposed upon their social realities.

Hardships and crises in life often force people to rethink the very foundation of their existence, and to reorient themselves in the world. Because we are in the world, to repeat Merleau-Ponty's (1962: xix) standpoint on the human condition, we are condemned to meaning. Still, in the camps in northern Uganda, human agency is little more than bare life and the matter of survival, despite or even because of the work and presence of powerful agents such as the rebels, the Ugandan army, and international humanitarian organizations.

Recall the story of Olak, who went hunting but eventually was shot twice by Ugandan army soldiers. Also recall the soldiers, perhaps not the very same individuals but colleagues of the ones who shot Olak, who sold game meat to the expatriate representative of an international humanitarian organization. In the eyes of my camp informants, I suggest, it could have been any *muno* (European or Westerner, or better, foreigner) who purchased the meat from any Ugandan soldier, because these depersonalized forces are concluded to be in alliance. The muno especially is a rather depersonalized agent, who visits the camps only briefly and seldom engages in any dialogical communication or intersubjective endeavor with the displaced people, nor takes the time to listen to their stories and frustrations. More, the visiting muno does not generally open his or her world to the Acholi. In the view of many Acholi, visiting foreigners remain a category of people rather than known individuals because they put little effort into establishing themselves as social beings in the local moral world.

Such an attitude of distance keeping was quite strange in the eyes of my informants, but the norm in much humanitarian work. Harrell-Bond (1986) has pointedly described it as the antiparticipatory ideology. I remember when Komakech, an unmarried young man who worked with me and who also worked as a volunteer with the International Red Cross, missed his breakfast one day. With his stomach empty, Komakech went to Pabo camp to work on the Red Cross's population census. He bought some lunch at a very modest Pabo hangout, engaging in a conversation with the other customers as he ate his meal. This was against the instructions of the International Red Cross, which wanted its volunteers to maintain a distance from the receivers of the organization's relief aid. On another occasion, again with the International Red Cross but now in another camp, he was invited to share a beer with some displaced people, which he did. The expatriate staff became extremely upset with Komakech's violations of the rules, which had now happened twice, and they threatened to fire him right on the spot. He did not fail his work assignment—on the contrary—but his socializing with camp inhabitants was considered irregular by his International Red Cross supervisors.

The Acholi's two terms for Europeans and foreigners—*muno* and *lawake*—are illustrative. As was explained to me, *lawake* is like a muno who refuses to eat what is offered, or someone who does not socialize with the local people. To share a meal is perhaps the greatest manifestation of humanity among the Acholi. Once you have invited a stranger to the dinner table, or even offered the foreign traveler some water to drink, that person cannot be your enemy, Acholi say. Conflicts, on the other hand, are frequently described in terms of people who do not share food, who do not "eat or drink from the same vessel" (Onyango-Odongo 1976: 60). Informants said that a "barrier of bad atmosphere" (*ojebu*) builds up. For the international humanitarian organizations, I can only conclude, to maintain such a social barrier seems to be their naive way of keeping the image of neutrality alive. For Komakech, who was visiting his fellow Acholi in the camps, this was not really an option.

People who have found avenues for survival, like Tonny, Komakech, and other people who worked with me or with the international organizations, or others who live in Kampala or in the diaspora, show great distress over the fate of their fellow Acholi, which of course includes relatives and friends. "Release my people from the camp. Let them go home," as Tonny put it. As long as his relatives suffer in the camps, Tonny is left with no peace of mind. From an existential point of view, the suffering in the camps extends to him as well.

The rumors prevalent among my informants can fruitfully be understood from Tonny's position in life. Rumors may indeed sound absurd to the outsider and again, if left unprobed and uncontextualized, would only add to the exoticism. But the stories of radio kabi ought to be understood against the background of the fact that the surroundings in Acholiland, because of war, are seriously bad. In a situation of distress, the conclusion that the alien forces of otherness are the source of destruction and fragmentation, sometimes even a source with deliberate ill intentions, manifests itself on radio kabi. The stories of radio kabi arise in a context, as the response to dilemmas of everyday life and to other, dominant stories that are imposed on the local moral world. This conception of the other is based on lived, quotidian experience, not on disembedded fantasies reduced to Freudian metaphors.

The source of a suspicion that something or someone, even fate, is conspiring against you, Jackson holds, is intersubjective. It is experienced and made manifest primarily in "the cumulative outcome of a felt lack of recognition, of material equality, of power, and of knowledge, in one's relations to others" (Jackson 2002a: 141). If this intersubjective and contextual approach is accepted, it will hardly be analytically satisfactory to dismiss my informants' dependence on radio kabi with metaphors of paranoia and delirium. Rather, more than being absolute and static, truth is a cultural construct, realized in everyday life. It follows from this that truths are inescapably situational. Kurkiala found that his Oglala Lakota informants in North America were not primarily interested in truth in the objectified sense. "Stories," he instead notes as he reiterates the informants' claim, "are worth telling and listening to because they are relevant, that is, *morally* true" (Kurkiala 2002: 455). Stories and rumors are credible because they sound likely or are worth passing on, adds White (2000: 59) with reference to Gluckman.

Morally relevant sentiments that are transmitted by radio kabi are expressions of coping and even resistance against enforced domination. For many of my informants, the stories of radio kabi are true. Ultimately, however, these stories confirm rather than confront the experienced domination and the political order of the day. Building on Foucault's well-known argument, Kurkiala (2002) holds that resistance to domination will most often be expressed in terms that reproduce the very logic and structure of domination. Radically alternative discourses most often remain muted. In the Ugandan case the official discourse on Acholiland as the heart of darkness has almost completely silenced any alternative discourses. This discourse is indeed part of a legacy of violent conflict in Uganda. My informants' efforts to reappropriate the privilege of interpretation are thus efforts to regain a sense of control in everyday life.

MORAL TRUTHS AND LAND LOST

One issue that is immediately notable in the Ugandan public debate is the right to land. The Ugandan constitution allows any Ugandan to settle and buy land anywhere in the country. This has caused heated feelings and some tension in Tesoland, eastern Uganda, but so far little outbreak of physical violence. Some influential Iteso have accused immigrant Banyankole and Banyarwanda pastoralists of stealing their land, a theme frequently debated in Ugandan media during my fieldwork in 2002 (see also Uganda Human Rights Commission 2003: chap. 6). In Acholiland, where such a large portion of the population has been uprooted and displaced, large areas of fertile land have obviously been abandoned.

People fear that the land they have been forced to evacuate will be taken over by powerful external groups—or rich, powerful Acholi—and that the displaced people never will be able to go back to their land of origin without conflict. General Salim Saleh, the half-brother of President Museveni and formerly Uganda's overall army commander is held to be involved with an enterprise called Sobertra Construction Company. The company repairs rural roads in northern Uganda, but it has also built so-called security roads in selected rural areas. The noncombatant population has been strictly forbidden to enter these heavily guarded areas.

Now and then during my fieldwork, white NGO-type four-wheel-drive pickups drove through Gulu town, each, however, with a heavy machine gun fixed to the truck bed and an expatriate muno at the wheel. On one occasion, when two of the pickups came speeding through the central roundabout of Gulu town, almost knocking down the curious anthropologist, the soldiers by the guns had to do their best not to fall off. The situation reminded me of what I have seen in television pictures from Mogadishu in Somalia, or of Hollywood doomsday productions with action hero Mel Gibson. "Who are they?" I asked Tonny. "They are building roads with Sobertra," he answered.

The presence of the Sobertra expatriates, my urban young informants told me, proved that there were "bad things going on" beyond their control. "The government wants the Acholi tribe to be silenced," one young man claimed when I discussed the land issue with a group of young men and women. Sobertra, the man added, is in the process of taking possession of "the land of the future population of the Acholi." His friends agreed, and he continued:

> I don't see very well the motives of some of the organizations that we have in northern Uganda at the moment. Among them, we have an NGO called Sobertra. Actually, it is a company. They are based in Pabo. These people, I do not understand what they are doing, and it has taken years, they claim that they are building roads, to destinations we don't know. Ah, what I understood when I tried to inquire about it, that land [around Pabo] is seen to be a very productive land, and Sobertra is a company which was initiated by Salim Saleh. These people are there, sometimes they behave like soldiers, they drive Pajeros. The normal people of Acholi, the indigenous people, are not allowed to reach that end where these people are working, for reasons best known to them. And this is the land that even people who have gone into exile have faith and hope in, the land that they hope will be for the future generation of Acholi. So, when you begin to see this war, sometimes it is meant to depopulate us. I think it is turning to a war on the population. Just to reduce the population [in northern Uganda]. (Gulu town, July 2002)

One of the issues in the Ugandan government's five-point program on the camps was to set up large-scale farming with tractors. In late 1997, President Museveni assured some Acholi parliamentarians that funds would soon be ready for these tractors (*New Vision*, December 1, 1997). This promise never really materialized, and people naturally wondered where those tractors ended up and where the large-scale farming was supposed to be implemented. At the same time high-ranking army officers, and even a group of former rebel commanders now integrated into the army, have established big farms in the abandoned countryside.

Rather than disproving people's doubts, Ugandan authorities have occasionally performed sweeping mass arrests of people alleged to be "rebel collaborators." The mass arrests are referred to as *panda garis*, or "get onboard the lorry," as it means in Swahili. They were common during the Amin (1971–

1979) and Obote II (1980–1985) governments (Branch 2005: 10; Kasozi 1999: 146–147). Now yet another Ugandan government has used them in northern Uganda.

The young man quoted above, who aired his concern about Sobertra and the land issue, was arrested in a sweep in September 2002. He is obviously not a rebel collaborator, but as he had been openly critical of the government, his friends now thought that this had got him in trouble. He was eventually released. In January 2000, Tonny also found himself taken away in a panda gari. The military arrived in his neighborhood early in the morning, and everyone in the neighborhood was arrested, including priests, children, and women, and taken to a large field just outside town. All morning army patrols kept arriving with groups of people, numbered in thousands, the great majority young men, arrested in the nearby villages.[2] Former child rebels, known as "computers," were forced to "screen" the people arrested, one by one, in an effort to identify rebel collaborators. The majority of the arrested people were required to stand in the hot sun, passively waiting until the late afternoon before the screening was completed. At the end of the whole exercise, besides some army deserters who were caught, fewer than five people were kept in custody.

People who tried to walk away were rudely forced back by the army. Tonny subverted arrest more successfully. Always putting his words well, he strongly questioned the legitimacy of the entire exercise and he correctly claimed that all his papers were in order. He was eventually allowed to leave, but the army still confiscated our motorcycle. Later on, Tonny and I went to the soldiers, asking rhetorically if the motorcycle was suspected of being a rebel collaborator. As one of us was a muno, or European, we got it back without too much arguing. Tonny designed a rubber mudguard for the back wheel of the motorbike. *Kwo odoko tek*, it said, which means, as so many informants told us as we went for our research safaris in the rural areas, that life has become difficult.

It is in this political environment that the issues of land and other natural resources are invoked in everyday talk. Again the actions of senior Ugandan army officers add to the disaffection that people expressed. In investigating the situation in war-torn Congo, the United Nations has accused Salim Saleh and James Kazini as well as other Ugandan army generals of massive looting and illegal exploitation of natural resources, especially gold (Prunier 2004). In 2005 the International Court of Justice, the principal judicial organ of the United

FIGURE 6 *Kwo odoko tek* (life has become difficult). On safari with our motorbike in Pader district. Photo by author.

Nations, ruled that Uganda is internationally responsible for acts of aggression, looting, plundering, and exploitation of natural resources in Congo. Initially the Ugandan government dismissed the accusations as rumors only, but an increasing bulk of eye-witness reports, as well as the court ruling, named high-ranking army individuals, including Saleh and Kazini, as involved in the looting. So the involvement of the president's closest military and political associates, even his half-brother, in the shadow economy of war in northern Uganda and beyond should not be dismissed out of hand.

A report on forced displacement and the camps identifies feelings of mistrust similar to those of my young informants:

> During our consultations with people in the camps many expressed the fear that the policy of putting the population of Acholi in camps was a well-calculated move in order to grab their land. A project proposal two

years ago by the Divinity Union Ltd, owned by Maj. [now full] Gen. Salim Saleh, highlighted some large chunks of land in Acholi to be used for large-scale commercial farming. Whether founded or unfounded, the people's fear of having their land grabbed is real. It cannot be underestimated as an important factor that deepens the already existing rift between the people of Acholi and the National Resistance Movement (NRM) Government. (ARLPI 2001: 7)

In an article in the state-owned *New Vision* run on April 24, 2006, De Temmerman, the Belgian journalist and the author of *Aboke girls*, and Chris Ochowun, a Ugandan, interviewed high-ranking army and government officials, as well as a number of displaced people, who anonymously dismissed these rumors as rubbish. De Temmerman and Ochowun then blame oppositional politicians and various analyses, such as the one I am proposing, of generating panic. But they miss the very essence of wartime rumors—as long as people are not able to return to their ancestral land, make a living and plan for the days to come, efforts to disprove the rumors will only confirm them.

And much works against De Temmerman and Ochowun's conclusions, despite their failure to find any evidence of irregular land-grabbing during their "week-long journey all over northern Uganda." Saleh, the president's half-brother, not only controls Sobertra, the company that constructs roads in to which the local population are denied access, but also chairs Divinity Union Ltd., a nongovernment organization alleged to be planning large-scale farming in Acholiland. In 2003, Saleh put forward a program to create large farms called security and protection units. "The programme hopes to make use of the communally owned land system in northern Uganda and land owned by government," reports *The New Vision* (August 13, 2003). After reading the glossy, full-color proposal, which was written in a complete top-down fashion, I can understand my informants' concern that the whole thing is meant to make internal displacement permanent, in township-like rural settings inhabited with landless Acholi wageworkers, where they would be controlled rather than protected by the Ugandan army. Now and then I heard people drawing the parallel with the harsh Tanzanian *ujamaa* villagization policy in 1970s.

As the difficult life conditions in the camps have continued and become more and more apparent by the year, the alleged alliance between Saleh's establishments deepened the feeling among many of my informants that their land is being, or will be, taken away. They were also frustrated with the fact

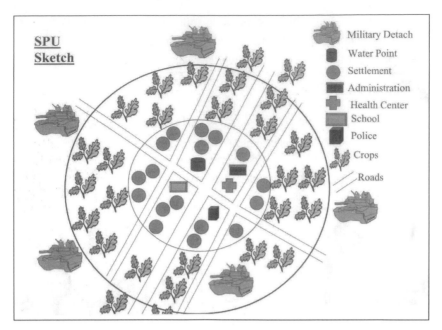

FIGURE 7 Institutionalizing displacement? The sketch of a planned security and protection unit (SPU), scanned from Salim Saleh's 2003 proposal.

that President Museveni has promoted, not punished, people accused of gross irregularities. After the 2006 elections, for example, Saleh was installed as the minister of state for micro-finance with the task to eradicate poverty. "We just call him the minister of eradication," a friend dryly concluded.

To lose their land is perhaps what Acholi people fear the most, and in the judicial vacuum that has accompanied the war, displaced people can do little to legally protect their interests. The rebels frequently address the land issue in their documents (e.g., Lord's Resistance Army/Movement 2006; n.d.). Without explicitly supporting the LRA/M rebels, informants sometimes still concluded that the LRA/M is the only power that may reverse such a development. They talked about the LRA/M as the only remaining shield (*kwot*) of protection. In some rural locations, people have even called upon the LRA/M to protect their interests, requesting them to destroy large-scale farming initiated by high-ranking members of the Ugandan army. Now and then, Kony has accepted the requests and ordered the LRA/M to destroy army-run farms and attack the vehicles of Sobertra.

For many of my young informants, stories about Sobertra and the activities of other outside organizations in areas that are no longer accessible to the displaced people were the most relevant and almost inescapable features of their social reality. Recall the panda gari mass arrests. Remember, too, that the great majority of Acholi have lost immediate access to their and their ancestors' land. In the beginning of the war, most Acholi lost their cattle. Then they experienced that they were also losing their land. The efforts of various international aid organizations to teach the agriculturalist but uprooted Acholi to farm more effectively, on ever shrinking plots of land in emerging townships, with new varieties of refined crops imported from the outside, only attest to people's fear that they will not be able to return home in the foreseeable future. In such a milieu, stories are worth telling and listening to because they are relevant and therefore true in the moral sense rather than in any objective sense. I would only add that these moral truths are based on very real experiences.

GENDERED VIOLENCE AND THE BODY METAPHOR

War obviously threatens the individual's sense of control in everyday life. It is a threat both imagined and experienced. To understand better the profound nature of such a threat in popular thought, an investigation of gendered hierarchies is illustrative. I will contextualize the argument by discussing different rumors of health threats that circulate in northern Uganda. One concerns HIV, another Ebola, and a third medical vaccinations provided to young women of childbearing age. All of these are closely associated with the forces of domination that are alleged to destroy female sexuality and women's reproductive health, and by extension, the wider social surroundings. These wider surroundings, I propose, are threatened as women's health is threatened. Again the rumors transmitted by radio kabi say something profound about the lived realities. With respect to HIV, for example, the rumors only emphasize a fact that few would deny—the epidemic threatens the future of not only the Acholi, but large parts of Africa as well.

Few if any epidemics or other collective health threats are apolitical. Rather, as people exposed to epidemics try to comprehend and cope with the human crisis that follows, the epidemics become embedded in local cosmologies and gender hierarchies of everyday life. The human body often comes to function as an evocative metaphor that communicates the interdependence between threatening epidemics and the sociopolitical order. Mary Douglas has shown that people universally evoke the human body as a model that can stand for the wider societal order and structure. In this analogy, the human body as a complex and stable system comes to represent society, which is experienced as being equally complex and stable. But this stability can also be experienced as threatened. Douglas writes of the body that its "boundaries can represent any boundaries which are threatened or precarious," adding that it can be evoked "as a diagram of a social situation" (1966: 115). More recently, Jackson has argued that the human body functions as a lived metaphor that reveals and realizes the unity of body and mind, and of self and the wider world. Body metaphors evoke meaning as they coalesce personal, social, and natural aspects of being. People think through the body, as Jackson (1989: chap. 9) has observed.

The metaphorical openness of the female body and its reproductive functions obviously makes it a powerful symbol in Africa and elsewhere. In his account on gendered violence in the Rwandan genocide, Taylor (1999a) writes that women, perhaps more than men, were targets of the violence. He explains this by reference to Douglas and feminist scholarship, from which he concludes that in patriarchal social settings, "women are often socially situated at the limen between groups" (Taylor 1999a: 43). Douglas is more specific. "In a *patrilineal* system of descent," she writes, "wives are the door of entry to the group" (Douglas 1966: 126, emphasis added). Taylor applies this argument to the Rwandan case, concluding that Tutsi women who had sexual relationships with Hutu men could be regarded as "cultural gatekeepers" and "liminal beings," because in their exposed situation they came to possess "the capacity of undermining the categories 'Hutu' and 'Tutsi' altogether" (Taylor 1999a: 43).

As the Rwandan crisis deepened, rape and forms of gendered violence became more common. Hutu and Tutsi became more reified as categories than had been the case before. Thus, if colonial powers in Rwanda, as they did also in Uganda, emphasized the reification of ethnic categories, the 1994 genocide forced Rwandans once and for all to "recognize the hegemonic character of what have become their categories" (Taylor 1999a: 50). Among Rwandans, as well as among Europeans, I understand, Tutsi women are often held to be most beautiful, stereotypically tall and slim. In an effort to break with this hegemonic stereotype, Hutu extremists ordered Hutu men to marry only Hutu women (Taylor 1999b: 170–175). And Hutu men's rape of Tutsi women, particularly during the prelude to the genocide, prepared the terrain for the coming genocide. The rape of Tutsi women undermined the Tutsi category as well as reified Hutu racism, in both practice and discourse. Rape came to shape the violence (Taylor 1999b: 184).

In war, ethnic categories more easily become increasingly reified than they were before. As part of this, the ethnic enemy is often targeted through rape and other forms of gendered violence against enemy women (and men). This has been reported, for example, from the war in former Yugoslavia, and feminist scholars have argued that rape in war manifests superior masculinity of the perpetrator, subordinated femininity of the victim, and deprived masculinity for the male enemy (e.g., Höglund 2001). Such violent acts are thus also acts of communication. In a similar but perhaps less definite conclusion on gendered modes of symbolic communication, Das notes that the female body, in situations of communal and ethnic violence, "became a sign through which men communicated with each other" (Das 1995: 56). In the perspective of perpetrators, she thus suggests, women came to be the locus of tension.

Sexual violence and rape have become common in war-torn Uganda as well. Though the rebels eventually came to rape and exploit women sexually, in the beginning of the war people attributed these activities to the government troops. This is Sabina's story:

> The [worst thing about] the NRA [government] soldiers was having forced sex with women one after the other. Men and women were collected during what they called a "screening exercise to flush out" the rebels from the community. The men and women were put in separate groups. Then in the evening the NRA soldiers started fucking the women in the compound. One woman could be fucked by up to six men; and this went on for three days. I saw these things with my own eyes, but I was lucky it never happened to me. (Sabina, thirty-six years old, former Holy Spirit member and rebel abductee, quoted in Oywa 1995: 99)

When hearing Sabina's story, the government's resident district commissioner told Sabina that women not only encouraged the rebels to continue their armed resistance but also, spread HIV. The commissioner said that the women should avoid contamination by HIV. Again Sabina: "This annoyed me and I asked him, 'How do we avoid getting infected with the AIDS virus? According to me it is the government which is intentionally spreading the AIDS virus by raping women when they go for firewood. Is raping one of the government weapons to fight the women? All these sufferings are being inflicted upon us because of our children's misbehaviour"(quoted in Oywa 1995: 99). The women's children to whom Sabina referred were of course the rebels, labeled so by the resident district commissioner. When he asked Sabina to prove that government soldiers and not rebels committed the gang rapes, Sabina responded, "I told him it was true because I saw a helicopter bring them food; the rebels never owned a helicopter!" (quoted in Oywa 1995: 99).

Of course, the victims of rape are individuals. In the eyes of the perpetrators, however, rape and other forms of organized violence target categories of people rather than individuals (Jackson 2002b: 77–78). Similarly, people in Uganda who angrily noted the many cases of rape also tended to see the rape victims as a category rather as individuals, and even so when the social distance to individual victims increases. "The Ugandan army rapes our women in the camps," I often heard men in Gulu town say (for confirmed cases, see Human Rights Watch 2003a: 5, 45–46; 2005: 32–35).

Among the patrilineal Acholi, the idea of women as cultural gatekeepers and liminal beings takes a slightly different form than the Rwandan case delineated by Taylor. Perhaps more along Mary Douglas's line of thought, women are seen as the door of entry to the group. In my informants' stories on gendered violence against the noncombatant population, it is women's role in the human and cultural reproduction that is at stake. Of course, my aim is not to replicate the Western idea of men as cultural producers and women as reproducers of human life, introduced to anthropology by Ortner (1974) and her contemporaries and severely criticized ever since. Rather I want to illustrate how such gendered divisions are reified by social unrest and wartime violence, just as ethnic divides are. To be better able to present my argument, I want to describe some local beliefs about femininity and masculinity in relation to morality, as mediated by my informants.

CONTROLLED MEN AND CRYING WOMEN

In 1997, when I first visited Acholiland, I encountered a group of Pentecostals who lived near Gulu town. Among them had settled former rebel fighters, war orphans, and a small number of others displaced by the war. The Pentecostals encouraged them to take up small-scale farming by providing land, and they eagerly assisted in the construction of huts and houses. The newcomers were also offered spiritual healing and the possibility of rebuilding social relationships. In the local Pentecostal church, former insurgents were delivered from the spiritual influence of the rebels, I was told. Local diviners, healers, and other arbitrators of Acholi cosmology were also presented with the opportunity to become purified from the many spirits that previously had assisted them in their work. Spirits and past experiences that haunted former rebels were exorcised during sermons that sometimes lasted for hours, in what was considered difficult and painstaking work. Yet, so the Pentecostals argued, in the name of Jesus Christ the evil spirits had no alternative but to leave. As a lay preacher told me, "Jesus is the only good spirit. Others exist, oh yeah, but they are evil. All of them." The evil spirits were denounced, but, obviously, the existence of these spirits was not denied. Rather, to feel protected and secure, the Pentecostals engaged the spirits, communicated with them, thus in a sense even maintained a relationship with them.

Uganda has been severely hit by HIV and AIDS, and public knowledge about the epidemic is widespread. Maybe as a consequence of this, my Pentecostal informants who expressed wishes to marry were obliged to take an HIV test. A negative result (no virus found) was used in the Pentecostal rhetoric on morality and purity. Among the Pentecostals, I met a young woman and former rebel. The Pentecostals had built her a hut, and they had given her some responsibility in carrying out certain tasks in the community. In the local church, she had been "saved" and "healed from all the bad things experienced in the bush." I asked a leading lay preacher what would happen if the saved ex-rebel girl carried HIV, but the preacher did not have an answer. When I tried to press him, he argued that a saved Christian, and thus a devoted Pentecostal, would always prove negative in an HIV test. No one who was genuinely saved would carry the virus. This was also said to be the case when it came to former rebel abductees. However, the ex-rebel girl did not express any wish to marry. On the contrary, because of her past experiences, she did not like the intimate company of men at all. So she had not yet found herself in a situation where she would be obliged to go through an HIV test. She stayed in peace with the community. When I came back two years later, however, she had left the area.

The association of the possible presence of HIV or other sexually transmitted diseases with a dubious and liminal moral status is not unique to Pentecostals. In the prewar or even precolonial context, several diseases and epidemics have been interpreted as the coming of alien forces from outside Acholiland (p'Bitek 1971: 114–120). In Acholi thought, women, to a greater extent than men, are exposed to these kinds of associations. For example, women are said to be more easily possessed by various spiritual forces than men (Allen 1991: 386, 389; Behrend 1995: 67). Most marriages are patrilocal (Girling 1960: 21).

And in the perspective of most Acholi, a woman is married into her husband's patrilineage and its wider social group (*kaka*). This makes her an outsider, a link to the outside, at least initially, until full bridewealth has been provided to her father's family and his extended patrilineage and she can thereby obtain a formal position in her new social context as a married woman. Usually, bridewealth is only provided in bits and pieces, over a long period. A newly married woman may even be dangerous, something that Acholi women of childbearing age in general are held to be. In Allen's (1994: 131) words, "She may be a sorcerer/poisoner. She is unpredictable, her loyalties are unclear, she is a threat to her husband's sisters living at home and to other wives and their children."

Today most Ugandans do not dispute the existence of the virus that leads to AIDS. However, it is still common in Acholiland to draw the conclusion that HIV and other forces of destruction, like ghostly vengeance (*cen*) and traumatic memories, target and influence women more often than men. This, it must be stressed, is nothing unique to the Acholi. Rather, the conclusion is analogous to the deep-rooted and male-biased idea in Western history of women as impulsive, prone to hysteria, and irrational, or, to put it simply, of women as the weaker of the two sexes.

To associate the spread of HIV with alleged female openness is not a conclusion made on biological grounds, although medical research does show that women run a higher risk than men of being contaminated by HIV through unprotected heterosexual intercourse. More important, and in line with the argument that I want to propose, womanhood, manhood, and the hierarchy of the genders are naturalized through social practice. "Men are more able to resist," I was told by a young man. "Women are weak," he added (see also Dolan 2002a: 61). His male friend agreed, and illustrated their standpoint by referring to funerals, where women are allowed—and men are discouraged—to cry and publicly express their agony. The funeral of Amos Sempa Alayi, a fieldwork associate of mine who died when he was hit by a speeding motorcycle, eventually came to illustrate their argument. The Christian priest opened his sermon by appealing to the people not to cry in frenzy, as several women had done when they arrived. "Let us not mourn in the traditional way," the priest said. "We must do it according to the Church. . . . If not, by sunset we will be embarrassed."

Some young men assisted the priest. Silently but firmly they took aside women whose uncontrolled anguish interrupted the sermon and the many speeches at the funeral. The young men escorted the women with a certain degree of pride. "I always keep self-control," one of the young men told me. In this context, womanhood was thus more than manhood intimately associated with Acholi cosmology and the local moral world. Manhood was associated with Christianity, even modernity.

THE *TEKGUNGO* BATTALION

With this said, I want to return to the issue of women as targets of military violence. It is commonly recognized that soldiers in Africa and elsewhere often engage sexually with local women wherever they go. When the Ugandan army withdrew from Congo after several years there, more than two thousand children fathered by Ugandan soldiers were left behind with their mothers, reports *The New Vision* (October 1, 2002). Some of the soldiers who were sent to northern Uganda to counter the rebels there brought Congolese women with them, making the situation of these exposed women even more vulnerable. In the camps in Uganda, an increasing number of young women choose the immediate but most often short-term safety entailed in having a soldier boyfriend in the Ugandan army, while other women fear being raped by the soldiers (see also Women's Commission for Refugee Women and Children 2001).

The situation conveys a special message, according to my Acholi informants, especially the young unmarried men, in which the female body functions as a sign of communication. As already indicated by Sabina's story, one powerful rumor holds that HIV-infected Ugandan army soldiers from outside Acholiland approach local girls with the purpose of spreading the virus. Twelve percent of the pregnant women tested at St. Mary's Missionary Hospital outside Gulu town are reported to be infected with HIV. This may be the highest infection rate recorded among pregnant women in Ugandan hospitals.[3]

"Terror moves silently beneath the skin, embodying the violence of the state," Kirsch (2002: 63) writes with reference to similar rumors of new health threats in politically volatile West Papua, New Guinea. In Uganda, the rumors express resistance to the central government and its army, but paradoxically enough they confirm rather than confront the political order. The rumors manifest themselves within a political discourse of domination and contest. In other words, the rumoring aims at resisting domination by means of assuming the right to interpret the lived reality. Yet the discourse of domination and resistance has a hegemonic measure to it, as the rumoring is formulated in terms understandable only within the very same discourse or political frame-work. It is in the context of the symbolic realm that people are constituted, and constitute themselves. Equally, when fixed meanings are dominantly imposed, alternative meanings will feed on a dialogue with the domination. The hege-monic moment is strong, if never final and complete. Even if such meanings will never be fully fixed or final, at least a partial fixation of meaning is necessary for communication to be possible. "Even in order to differ, to sub-vert meaning, there has to be *a* meaning," write Laclau and Mouffe (1985: 112). In other words, the domination itself will be the central point of reference, around which the construction of meanings will revolve.

With this in mind, it is likely that *rumors of resistance*—if we can call them that—"tend to exacerbate rather than ameliorate the problems of political violence," again quoting Kirsch (2002: 70). The rumor of the soldiers' deliber-ately spreading HIV to local women adds to an already harsh environment of gendered violence in Acholiland. Many other women have been raped as warfare increasingly came to target the most private spheres of civil life. Men are also infected, so the rumor goes, by a special Ugandan army battalion called *tekgungo* ("bend over," or to "bow" with "force" or great "difficulty"). Its alleged work is to rape civilians of both sexes, by this means spreading the deadly virus. The government's HIV information poster with the soldier, the gun, and the condom (figure 8) may contain messages more complex than intended, adding to the rumoring. The HIV epidemic becomes politicized through these rumors, and informants sometimes described the virus as "the silent gun." Disease, according to this understanding, is one weapon among others in "the arsenal of conquest" (Simons 1999: 80).

De Boeck notes that the aLuund people in southwestern Congo hold the female body to be more open than the male body. "As genitors and social reproducers, childbearing women are perceived as having an accessible or 'open' body (or, metaphorically, an 'open' house or 'open' field)," De Boeck (1998: 37) writes. Women of childbearing age have to close and cover up their openness, but postmenopausal women are considered as more closed, as structurally speaking more like men, and can therefore be more active and influential in the public and open arena. Allen (1994: 130) advances a similar argument for the Acholi and neighboring Madi, as did my informants when they tried to understand the consequences of and reasons behind an outbreak of Ebola hemorrhagic fever in late 2000 and early 2001. The outbreak infected

FIGURE 8 Fighting HIV and fighting a war. Poster on a government building in Gulu town. Photo by author.

at least 425 individuals and eventually took 224 lives, or 53 percent of those infected, mainly in Gulu town. According to statistics, 63 percent of the people who contracted Ebola were female (Hewlett and Amola 2003; World Health Organization 2001: 44).[4]

Ebola entered Gulu from Congo, carried by returning Ugandan soldiers, a powerful rumor among the noncombatant population held. Two years after the outbreak of Ebola, Tonny told me the following story. In mid-2000, the Ugandan army brought a dead colleague from Congo to his home north of Gulu town, with orders to the relatives to leave the sealed coffin closed. However, the relatives refused, so the story went, and they opened the coffin. Women washed the body carefully, and they shaved all its bodily hair before dressing it in nice clothes, all according to Acholi beliefs and funeral customs. Generally, I was told, when someone has died, men immediately start to dig a grave. They only assist the women in the preparation of the corpse if there is a practical reason to do so, for example, as Tonny put it, "if the deceased was so fat that the women need assistance to lift the body" (see also Odoki 1997: 37–42). When a man dies, p'Bitek (1974: 21) writes, the widow is supposed to lie down next to her dead husband, and embrace the body. When a woman dies, the husband is supposed to do the same, Tonny added. The female relatives who prepared the body that arrived from Congo, so the story went, contracted Ebola. Soon the epidemic took root in Gulu. Tonny's conclusion, which he shared with many of my informants, was that the army was responsible for the Ebola outbreak. If the scenario of the first Ebola victim, whose body was brought to Gulu and Acholiland from the outside, is interpreted in the context of the existing gender hierarchy, which I suggest is plausible, it can be concluded that women's exposed position as the link to the outside also exposes the Acholi collective. Yet, to neutralize such an exposure, I also suggest, the Acholi insist that elderly women prepare the body of a deceased person. Tonny concluded the story on Ebola, "The army brought the body to the relatives here in Gulu. But you know very well, my brother, and the army knew it too, according to Acholi culture we had to wash the body, and that was the beginning of it."

When radio kabi combines the Ebola story with the stories about HIV and the bend-over battalion, we may conclude, with Taylor's (1999b) Rwandan case, that a "cosmology of terror" finds nourishment as people try to cope with and understand extreme domination, both physical and discursive. This is not to say that Acholi culture is more likely to foster such interpretations than any other culture or ideology but the many years of enforced domination, lived uncertainty, and extreme collective suffering are. As war and terror enter the most private and central domains of people's lives, they also enter the wider surroundings and the cosmological realm. Accordingly, as Taylor (1999b: 105–106) points out in a discussion that builds on Kapferer's (1988) work on nationalism, the uncertainty of war reaches beyond only political pragmatics or psychological stress. To paraphrase Kapferer (1988: 79–80), war produces an ontology of uncertainty and stress, even terror, which eventually will be confined within the understandings and cultural orientations of the people it assaults. Such an ontology, which of course often differs from person to person, "describes the fundamental principles of a being in the world and the orientation of such a being toward the horizons of its experience" (Kapferer 1988: 79).

The rumors I discuss here are examples of individual coping with the unknown and the threatening, and invoking rumors is a mundane effort among people to cope with lived uncertainty and stress imposed by war. In these rumors and many other stories, the forces that regulate and even threaten life are located in specific situations, which means that an attempt is also being made to understand and intellectually grasp the hardships of the lived reality. Meaning is created, lived, and the alleged rationale of the order of things is exposed. For the individual, of course, the wider world is manifested in her or his particular world. To have a sense of control over the relationship and balance between these worlds is a central human preoccupation, Jackson (1998: 20–21) holds. With this in mind, I suggest that we can better understand the universal rationale for rumors that initially seem to be absurd or even paranoid. Power, in this context, is not only to be analytically located in the enforced domination that follows war and social unrest. Power is also located in the existential struggle for self-empowerment and self-mastery.

My friend Otim p'Ojok concluded of the Ebola epidemic in retrospect, "The government tried to conceal so much, so most of us believe that it came from Congo." He added, "Anyway, the Ugandan army sent soldiers from Congo to southern Sudan to counter the [LRA/M] rebels there." In his argument, regardless of the route the Ebola took, it came from outside. The LRA/M rebels, on their side, blamed the Ugandan government. "President Museveni wipes out Acholi tribes with the deadly Ebola virus while the world condemns the victims," reads the headline of one of their press releases in October 2000. Representatives of the Ugandan government and its army, on the other side, blamed the rebels for bringing the virus from Sudan, with reference to epidemiological research confirming that the Gulu type of the Ebola virus was more similar to Ebola strains found previously in Sudan than it was to those located in Congo.[5]

GENDERED BELONGING

Rebel violence has added to the exposed position of Acholi women. In addition to the rebels' moral and religious indoctrination, violently disseminated to all abductees, female abductees are often subjected to rape and sexual abuse, and to exploitation by male rebels of higher rank (see, e.g., Amnesty International 1997; Human Rights Watch 1997; Women's Commission for Refugee Women and Children 2001). Research has also substantiated that young abducted boys are sexually exploited by their senior female commanders, although it can be assumed that this is less frequent than the sexual exploitation of girls (Lucie Aculu, personal communication). To sustain an insurgency in Africa, as Turshen (2001) notes, rebels often live off the land. For this to be possible, the effort to control women's productive labor—as porters, farmers, cooks, cleaners, launderers, tailors, and sex workers—becomes an asset transfer in civil war. To handle the difficult situation, young women sometimes find security and privileges if they become "wives" of rebel commanders. Yet if the commander dies in battle, the young woman may be in trouble again. In the words of Christine, a young Ugandan with an LRA/M husband who took good care of her but eventually died in battle, "they started to treat you like a girl again and beat you. I was beaten severely and given less food." She concluded, "Unless you get another man, you suffer" (quoted in Human Rights Watch 2003b: 14).

Noncombatant informants often stressed that female rebel commanders are the cruelest of all rebels. Perhaps, I want to propose, this results from the fact that female fighters more than male fighters have sidestepped society's conventional gender hierarchy, and thus their actions are seen to be more sensational, epitomizing the worst in women. I was also told that female commanders are the brightest and bravest in battle. In July 2002, the rebels destroyed a Ugandan military convoy in an ambush just outside Gulu town. The public relations officer of the Ugandan army denied that the convoy had been ambushed, instead attributing the whole thing to a soldier's cigarette, "which heated one of the bombs," thus destroying the convoy (quoted in *New Vision*, July 22, 2002). The ambush was most daring and indeed a military success for the rebels, and most of my informants attributed the army's denial to the fact that a woman had commanded the LRA/M forces in the ambush. This, my informants suggested, was just too embarrassing for the army.

A rebel background will obviously have implications for the young women if they return home. Many of my young male informants in Gulu town claimed that former rebel girls are morally compromised, thus dangerous, and not suitable marriage partners. A group of elderly men in a displacement camp confirmed their view. "She can even kill while you are asleep, at night," one man argued. "Do not be surprised if you wake up in the morning only to find your head chopped off." However, behind the apparent absurdity of his statement, the old man was deadly serious. He concluded that any future offspring of ex-rebel women might inherit the mother's moral predicament, inflicted upon her through rape and sexual harassment. The argument is a parallel to Tonny's conclusion, that ghostly vengeance (*cen*) may haunt the clan and its new children for generations. A formal marriage with bridewealth may assist in neutralizing such threatening potentials of former rebel women. Young women and men, with as well as without education, stressed to me the importance of bridewealth. If bridewealth is provided, the woman's position in the social setting can be secured and made certain. But even when young men want to marry ex-rebel women, they seldom have the means to raise the bridewealth. In the prewar context, cattle were an important source of wealth for young men who wanted to marry. Due to the war, this and several other forms of wealth have been lost to most Acholi.

During difficult times in history, in the 1890s, for example, when rinderpest wiped out most cattle in Acholiland, bridewealth payment was made in goats (Girling 1960: 71)—although perhaps cattle were never the main form of bridewealth (Grove 1919: 158; Seligman and Seligman 1932: 119), or only became so in the later nineteenth century (Atkinson 1994: 100). Today cash is used for large parts of the bridewealth, but it is most often talked of in terms of heads of cattle. I have pointed out that Acholi generally recognize a woman as married into the husband's group from the outside. Eventually, when she bears children to her husband's lineage or clan (*kaka*), her status as an outsider will fully change to that of an unthreatening insider. She will then "become *kaka*" (Allen 1994: 131). When I asked about the social status of Rufina, Tonny's old mother, he replied, "Yes, she belongs to our kaka, because my father married her. She even uses our *mwoc*." *Mwoc* is the praise-name that members of a particular kaka use when they communicate or publicly call out their social belonging, "as a means of identification" (Crazzolara 1954: 326). However, if bridewealth is not provided to the woman's father and her brothers, many Acholi argued, the woman's loyalties will remain uncertain. She may therefore have difficulties in establishing herself as an unthreatening insider in her new social context. In addition, her partner will have neither the legal right to nor any formal responsibility for the children, adding to the uncertainty of her and the children's situation. Her liminal status may remain. As Otim p'Ojok put it, as he tried to capture what a friend had just said in Acholi, "You feel protected when you know that you belong to a particular kaka."

It seems that former rebel boys more frequently and openly face bitter talk than ex-rebel girls, while the girls, at least when it comes to explicit comments, are mostly harassed by their fellow female age-mates and by older women (see also ARLPI 2002b: 19). In a deeper sense, however, girls are also more often held to be impure sexually and thus morally more dubious, even more dangerous, than boys. Society as a whole tends to hold that female fighters in particular are morally liminal, even dangerous for their surroundings. In this respect, ex-rebel girls more than ex-rebel boys are stigmatized by society, even if mutedly. Similar stigmatization is indicated by the fact that the divorce rate among couples in which the woman has been raped by any of the fighting forces is high. One report suggests that of the raped interviewees, 83 percent were rejected by their husbands and relatives. Others had lost support from spouses, and many raped women try to keep their experiences concealed from the wider surroundings, because they "feared the stigma, and other people blaming them . . . for allowing it to happen" (People's Voice for Peace et al. 1999: 44, 63; see also Human Rights Watch 2005: 34).

In the stories of radio kabi, the reproductive capacity of men, too, is brought up for discussion. In the camps, I frequently encountered people who questioned the quality of distributed relief. In 2002, the leaders in some camps refused the maize flour that the Norwegian Refugee Council tried to distribute, because it was too old and thus spoiled (which one of the Ugandan staff members told me indeed was the case). It had to be ferried back to town. Yet it was particularly the U.S.-produced cooking oil distributed as relief, again past the last date for recommended consumption that people questioned. Sometimes, showing me the sealed cans clearly stamped with a freshness guarantee date that had passed, people would question the usability of the oil. It made men impotent, I was told. "Why do you give us this stuff, that you would not consume yourself?" was the frequent question I encountered. Again the rumor has a wider cosmological dimension to it, as the alleged spread of male impotence would make Acholi men unable to father future generations. And some of the vaccinations offered to young women as part of various health programs, I was now and then given to know, make these women infertile. Ultimately the specificity of the stories of radio kabi locates the variety of establishments, humanitarian organizations, powerful agents, diseases, and threatening events in specific historical contexts in specific places (see also White 2000: 83–84). People live with seriously bad surroundings in which all cattle are gone and where they are displaced from their ancestral land. The conclusion people advanced was that there must be a hidden agenda behind all this, namely "a war on the Acholi."

RADIO KABI IN CONTEXT

Young people especially expressed frustration over the difficulty of decolonizing the politics of regional divisions and ethnic stereotyping in postcolonial Uganda. It was a young teacher who pointed out to me that Okot p'Bitek's (1966) acclaimed poem was colored by ethnic chauvinism, as it held that the millet-eating Acholi were strong while the Bantu "who drink bananas" were weak. Young informants often wanted to alter the rhetoric of ethnic division. This, however, is not easy. For example, at an international Acholi conference in London which I attended, some senior delegates silenced a young male academic who rose to speak. To the dissatisfaction of the older people who objected, the young man had requested that his fellow delegates leave behind once and for all the issue of the atrocities in Luwero in central Uganda and instead look ahead to seek solutions to the war in northern Uganda.

The atrocities perpetrated by Museveni's National Resistance Army when it arrived in Acholiland in the mid-1980s was often locally interpreted as a form of revenge on the Acholi people. As mentioned, according to the view of many in government, as well as among many in the general populace of the south of Uganda, the Acholi are held collectively responsible for the atrocities committed in Luwero in central Uganda during the first half of the 1980s. Hence many Acholi, including some elders forcibly displaced by the Ugandan army to Labongogali camp, suggested that the present war is an act of presidential revenge. To put it simply, they suggested, President Museveni is taking revenge (*culo kwo*) on the Acholi people. The men could find no other reason why the president for so many years was so reluctant when it comes to peace talks with the rebels. It is in this context that I want to interpret the stories of radio kabi, thereby dismissing any conclusion that Acholi people are paranoid or only feeding on a simulacrum. Rather, as happens everywhere in the world, they are seeking ways to exercise control in their everyday lives. Rumors are one effort to define the wider world of the dirty war they are caught up in, even as they feel deserted by the outside world. The stories of radio kabi feed on the domination that is experienced as being imposed from the outside. Ultimately, the outside world must work against these stories if the spiral of violence and war is to be stopped. My Ugandan friend the late Caroline Lamwaka did not agree with the idea of presidential revenge, but she pinpointed an issue of relevance to most of my informants. As she wrote in a June 8, 1999 letter to me, "I personally do not believe that the trend of events in Acholi, manifest in the present day conflict situation, is a Presidential 'Culo Kwor' [revenge]. However, it is up to President Museveni to convince the Acholi people (not just through his cadres) that he does not have ill intentions towards them. This should be in both words and deeds and should be reflected at both local and national level."

When images, but not necessarily facts, of the past legitimate the present social and political order, social memory is preserved and eventually also presupposed (Connerton 1989). But meaning will never be final. As Werbner shows, the making and manifestation of officially recognized collective memories will probably also give rise to localized countermemories. In Werbner's (1998a: 7–8) own terminology, official and centralized "memorialism" will always call forth popular and local "counter-memorialism." Thus, even though the majority of Acholi would in fact question the official postcolonial claim that blames the Acholi ethnic group for the Luwero atrocities in the 1980s, many, as the men in Labongogali displacement camp do, would understand and explain Museveni's reluctance to promote peace in terms of misdirected revenge against the Acholi people. They do so, I have argued, in an effort to orient in life, to comprehend and control existentially the difficult situation in which they live. Therefore, I conclude, the stories disseminated by radio kabi, like the one of a slow and silent genocide in northern Uganda, cannot be taken lightly. On the contrary, radio kabi provides context to the official discourse and its simplistic scripts. "To keep the eyes of the world averted," writes Otunnu Olara (2006: 45), "the government has carefully scripted a narrative in which the catastrophe in northern Uganda begins with the LRA and will only end with its demise."

Chapter 6

UPROOTING THE PUMPKINS

ENGAGING THE WORLD

"Kony is my 'brother,' and Museveni is my president. I didn't vote for them, but fact is fact," Gulu politician Norbert Mao said as he addressed the "big meeting" (*kacoke madit*) in London, 1998, organized by diaspora Ugandans.

Over the years, the LRA/M movement has become increasingly isolated and alienated from society and perhaps also increasingly fragmented. The military practices of the movement have also changed considerably over time, at times very violent and terrorist in nature. Meanwhile, the Ugandan army's extensive Iron Fist operations have seriously added to the pressure on the rebels, and in periods small and extremely mobile units operate in isolation from the high command. "If the rebels face difficult battles, they will be rude to the civil population. If they don't face the battle, they are not rude," Tonny once concluded when we discussed the Iron Fist operations and the increase in rebel atrocities. But the army's tanks, helicopters, and other heavy equipment often restrict the campaign to the roads and the air. As a Ugandan newspaper editorial writer put it, "the rebels seem to be moving like sunshine, hitting every part of the north—and now far east—at the same time and with much ease" (*Daily Monitor*, June 20, 2003).

The increasing degree of isolation and marginalization may even further foster new cruelties by the rebel commanders and, most unfortunately, their new abductees.

At the same time, life goes on. In conceptualizing the wider surroundings of the living and the dead and of nature and culture as seriously bad, my informants attempted to comprehend existentially the phenomena of fratricidal violence and cultural and social breakdown, when the outside world, however, tended to blame the local culture, as the heart-of-darkness rhetoric tends to do. They furthermore aired the hope that the international community would properly address the international dimensions of the conflict. "Why do your countries in the West send us all these modern weapons?" was the rhetorical question that informants often wanted me to bring back to Sweden. The landmine, so frequently commented upon and planted almost everywhere in the surroundings, has become a symbol of these wider dimensions. In the words of Ladit Arweny, elder and a friend of mine:

> Now, what is taking place now, I think it is well known through the whole world that Sudan is being fought, and the route is through Uganda. In particular, what one can say, the Government of Uganda and other foreign forces like the Americans are fighting Sudan. And what do you think can stop Sudan from giving dangerous things to Kony, huh? The weapons that the rebels have are of international standard. That is why you can find that even ten rebels can terrorize the army. (Gulu town, January 1998)

Below I investigate how noncombatant people in the war zone understand and explain the rebels' violent practices on the ground. I want to address the more profound consequences of war, not in terms of statistics of casualties or rape and torture victims, which indeed are some of the most final costs of human destruction, but in terms of the war's impact on Acholi cosmology. To be able to comprehend what is going on, people engage their cosmology. But cosmology is not only something from the past. It is in constant flux and a process of social contest and human creativity. Cosmology encompasses the lived but infinite surroundings. As Kapferer (2002: 20) suggests, it is "a process whereby events, objects and practices are brought into a compositional unity, are conceived and patterned as existing together, and are in mutual relation."

COSMOLOGY IN CRISIS

To hell
With your Pumpkins
And your Old Homesteads,
To hell
With the husks
Of old traditions
And meaningless customs,

We will smash
The taboos
One by one,
Explode the basis
Of every superstition,
We will uproot
Every sacred tree
And demolish every ancestral shrine.
(FROM *SONG OF OCOL* IN P'BITEK 1970B)

Listen Ocol, my old friend,
The ways of your ancestors
Are good,
Their customs are solid
And not hollow
They are not thin, not easily breakable
They cannot be blown away
By the winds
Because their roots reach deep into the soil.

Listen, my husband,
You are the son of a Chief.
The pumpkin in the old homestead
Must not be uprooted!
(FROM *SONG OF LAWINO* IN P'BITEK 1966)

When the degree of war, and thus the alleged seriousness of war, is discussed in quantitative and comparative studies, war is often split into subcategories, such as "minor armed conflicts," "intermediate armed conflicts," and "war" (e.g., Wallensteen and Sollenberg 2001). Accordingly, perhaps Uganda was a scene of "intermediate armed conflict" during my first two stays in Acholiland (1997–1998 and 1999–2000). For a conflict to reach the level of an "intermediate armed conflict," the number of "battle-related deaths" is more than one thousand during the course of the conflict, but the annual death toll is less than one thousand (Wallensteen and Sollenberg 2001). During my third stay in northern Uganda, in 2002, the conflict escalated into "war," similar to the situation in the mid-1980s and 1991, with more than one thousand deaths per year.

Yet to come up with a proper figure for battle-related deaths is not easy. Typically, the many reports conclude that "scores" of people have been killed, more specifically that the rebels have "unlawfully killed hundreds, possibly thousands, of civilians" (Amnesty International 1999: 1–2), or that "tens of thousands" have died (OCHA/IRIN 2004: 7), or even that the "war has resulted in countless deaths" (Barnes and Lucima 2002: 11). Again, war statistics can only be tentative, as it is almost impossible to establish combat-related casualty rates. As it often is in dirty wars today, the majority of people will not die in direct military violence, but as a result of malnutrition and illness and in the aftermath of uprooting, displacement, and forced camp life.

Discussing northern Uganda, Doom and Vlassenroot (1999: 20) define peace as "the absence of open and widespread violence rather than a situation where all disputes are settled by procedural methods." But despite periods without violence, at least in its most direct and brutal variants, the violent pattern of dirty war continues. The fact that the rebels have withdrawn to base is also a fact of war. As long as rebel leader Joseph Kony is there with his fighters in neighboring Sudan or Congo, so experience told my informants, one could never really tell what will happen next. The only thing they know for sure is that war was not over. In 2006, for example, as is the case in any ongoing negotiations, optimistic reports seeping out from the peace talks held in Juba came hand in hand with explicit threats of war from both the Ugandan president and the rebel leadership as well as mutual violations of the cessation of hostilities agreement. Yet both rebels and government would, the next day, again assure each other and the public about their respective commitment to the talks.

Lulls over the years have given people breathing space but no peace in life, and no peace of mind. As clashes were reported from rural areas or even from the outskirts of Gulu town, experiences resurfaced as memories of previous rebel or army attacks were activated in people's minds. Memories of war may resurface in ordinary conversations, as when I was once talking with my friend Komakech. One night in late 1997, there was an unexpected thunderstorm in Gulu. Quite naturally, when the thunder woke me up, I thought of rebels and fighting. My sleepy and distorted thinking was affected by interviews conducted the day before. For a few seconds, I was terrified and completely disoriented, but I soon realized that it was nothing but thunder. However, the next day when Komakech and I were talking about the storm, he told me he had been afraid throughout the night. Komakech had soon realized that it was nothing but a thunderstorm, but his mind was assailed by the memory of his experiences of rebel violence, something that made him scared and upset.

The thunder came to function as a metaphor for Komakech's troubled state of mind. He recalled an incident some years back when he was out of town doing petty trade. Rebels arrived, and Komakech immediately left everything and escaped the scene. He also recalled the more recent memory of rebels roaming around Gulu town, even entering the central town to kill, abduct, steal, and loot. During the night of thunder, he again lived through these past experiences, which made the night of the storm seem endless.

Although there were essential differences in our respective experiences, we could communicate through the thunder as metaphor. Both of us associated it with violent experiences, except that mine were few and more easily discarded because they blended with rather nostalgic memories of bad weather back in Sweden. The conversation I had with Komakech exemplifies when metaphor functions as an evoker and mediator that effectively discloses and communicates the interdependence of body and mind, of self and world, to reference Jackson (1996: 9; 1998: 171). Moreover, as an evoker, the thunder provided the medium for interpersonal communication, and for me, an indication of how people exposed to the war experienced it.

The lack of control in quotidian life naturally frustrates people in Acholiland, but they still tried to come to grips with their fate and master it. For example, male clan elders (*ludito kaka*, sing.: *ladit kaka*) and diviners (*ajwaki*, sing.: *ajwaka*), the latter mostly women, framed the state of affairs in the context of their moral world and its wider surroundings. What is happening in Acholiland is not only bad. It is also something beyond Acholi tradition and culture, these senior members of society said. A clan elder in Amuru camp smiled at me as I asked my naive question—couldn't the spiritual world and the ancestors counter the potent but violent spiritual powers of the rebel movement and especially Joseph Kony? "Acholi spirits can only confront other Acholi spirits," he then explained. Most Acholi regard the many spiritual powers (*jogi*, sing.: *jok*) of the greater world as ambivalent manifestations, potentially with both healing and harming powers and actively evoked in the everyday interpretation and diagnosis of misfortune, illness, and the like. The man suggested however that the spirits that present themselves through Joseph Kony, the rebel leader, are alien and even evil, "not Acholi," and therefore beyond immediate comprehension.

Other informants argued that although Kony is an Acholi, the violent rebel spirits could not be of Acholi origin because there are no such violent and militant spirits or powers in the Acholi cosmological order of things. There never were. Rather the contrary, the LRA/M rebels sometimes explicitly target elders, healers, and other arbitrators of the local moral world, as was the case already with Alice Lakwena's movement in the 1980s. As her movement did, the LRA/M rebels claim that they want to establish a new moral order, with the objective of breaking with the violent postcolonial history of Uganda (see Behrend 1999a: 48–49).

Some informants argued that Joseph Kony claims to have "taken over" Alice Lakwena's Holy Spirit (Tipu Maleng) when Lakwena fled Uganda in October 1987. One could perhaps suggest that Kony might claim to have done so to legitimize his own spiritual and political authority (Heike Behrend, personal communication). According to most informants, however, Kony cannot have taken over Lakwena's Holy Spirit, because there are important differences between the Holy Spirit of Alice Lakwena in the 1980s and the spirits of Joseph Kony in the late 1990s. The elder in Amuru camp told me the following:

> The evil spirits of Kony are something new. They are beyond Acholi spirit mandate; Acholi spirits can't cope with them. During Alice's time, there were few [unlawful] killings, even though she failed [in her mission]. She failed, but then there was not as much suffering as now, with Kony. Kony is worse. Alice was fair, at least. Kony kills people who perform the spirits of Acholi. Kony's spirits are not Acholi. Kony is the root of the evils. (December 1997)

Tonny, my friend and coworker in the field, explained that Kony cannot possibly have the Holy Spirit, because "Tipu Maleng cannot kill anybody." Tonny's mother Rufina, a retired healer, agreed with her son. The old woman argued that even though it is most likely that Joseph Kony and Alice Lakwena once were presented with the Holy Spirit of God, they have both misused it to such an extent that it has now been replaced by, even transformed into, a spirit of darkness (*tipu macol*). Both Joseph Kony and Alice Lakwena are responsible for unlawful killings of innocent people and can only be regarded as evildoers and witches (*lujok*, sing.: *lajok*), she concluded. In a kind of boomerang effect, then, Joseph Kony, who at times has claimed to be fighting for a new moral order, purified from corruption, sorcery, witchcraft, and past evils, has turned into a witch himself. Behrend writes of Alice Lakwena:

> In a situation of existential crisis, the [Holy Spirit called] Lakwena or-dered Alice to heal society and to cleanse the whole of Uganda from witchcraft and sorcery. But to heal society she had to use violence, the power to kill. In doing so she, like the *ajwaka* [healer], used the means she pretended to fight. Although she was fighting witchcraft and sorcery she used the means of a witch, because she used her power to kill. And this explains why she was accused of being a witch. (Behrend 1991: 176)

Influential and powerful people may summon potent powers to harm and even kill enemies from afar, outside Acholiland, to incorporate them into the lived Acholi cosmological order of things, p'Bitek (1971: 140, 142) once noted. However, if these powers are misused, they can easily turn against their user and eventually also against the wider surroundings. Accordingly, most of my Acholi informants questioned the legitimacy of Kony's spiritual objectives and military methods. Still, many were convinced that he possessed powerful but dangerous spiritual powers that indeed can harm society. Among Pentecostal Christians, for example, rebel spirituality is equated with the devil and evil forces in the same manner that all kinds of Acholi spiritual powers are equated with evil forces that must be fought in the name of Jesus Christ. My friend Komakech confirmed this, though he is neither a Pentecostal himself nor a frequent churchgoer. "The devil exists," he said to me in 1997. "The devil is in the Bible. It is true as far as I am concerned." However, Komakech expressed his ambivalence about the rebel spirituality more clearly on another occasion: "The rebels have some kind of spirit, you know, some kind of supernatural power. Because sometimes the bullets [aimed at the rebels] will turn around and hit [the rebels'] enemy. . . . But I don't know, I haven't seen it." Alternatively, as Ladit Arweny, once involved in efforts to mediate between rebels and government, commented upon Kony's spiritual powers, "If that power is to destroy Acholi, then let that power go away." He did not deny the spiritual power of the rebel leader Joseph Kony, but he argued, in a similar vein to Tonny's old mother, that Kony is losing his spiritual power bit by bit, "because he has misused it." A young man in a rural displacement camp placed the rebel spirituality in relation to his own frustrations. Neither he nor his relatives could possibly raise the money needed for school fees, and as long as he lives in a camp, he can only drop his dreams of secondary school education. But rather than questioning the existence of Kony's spiritual powers, he questioned the spiritual legitimacy, and he countered my queries with a question, "Does this spirit develop the world and our schools?"

THE UPROOTED PUMPKINS

Military violence and terror will obviously assail the memory of their victims. Violence is not limited to the battlefield, or to the individual perpetrators and their victims, but will increasingly infest the wider surroundings of the living and the dead. However, informants commonly mentioned the Ugandan army's bad conduct and inability to protect the civilians, and the government's many years of reluctance to promote peace talks, as factors in the escalation of violence. Informants also brought up the issue of antipersonnel landmines. The Sudanese government has provided the rebels with landmines. Some of the landmines are marked with Arabic writing, as some that have been confiscated reveal. Other mines that the Ugandan army has captured from the rebels are manufactured in Belgium and Italy, the Ugandan army claims. But the Ugandan army too has planted landmines in Acholiland, especially in the Agoro Hills that border Sudan in Kitgum district. When I visited Agoro, people told me that the objective was to seal the border to make it more difficult for the rebels to enter Uganda from their bases in southern Sudan. Ugandan military authorities regard the Agoro Hills as a notorious point of entry for the rebels when they cross between Sudan and Uganda.

Ironically enough, the Ugandan army planted the mines in Agoro Hills in late 1998 and early 1999, around the same time Uganda officially ratified the international treaty banning the manufacture and use of landmines (see Landmine Monitor 2006). In early 1999, after twelve people had died in landmine blasts, and several others lost legs as they tried to collect food from their gardens and granaries, the army ordered residents of Agoro Hills to assemble in a camp set up by the U.N.'s World Food Programme. Victims had stepped on landmines on the paths to the gardens, below their granaries, and on the doorsteps to their own huts, Tonny and I were told while in Agoro. Even indoors, under the beds, mattresses, and in the cooking hearths, the Ugandan army had planted landmines. Again, war entered and defiled the most private domains of life.

In the perspective of my informants, the landmines planted in Acholiland bring death and destruction without any sense of direction, indiscriminately. Like corruption, mines are said "to be eating people." In the context of local distress, the mines are powerful symbols that capture the global character of the war. Just like the machine gun, the landmine is originally a Western invention and product. Obviously, the landmines are not manufactured in Acholiland.[1] On the contrary, informants often stressed, the landmines are of foreign origin, with a foreign character, imported to Acholiland and planted in gardens, on rural roads, and in homesteads. This was a common conclusion that I encountered—the war gets fuel from elsewhere than Acholiland, adding to the feeling of a life with bad surroundings.

"The stump of a pumpkin plant should not be uprooted" (*te okono pe kiputu*) is an Acholi proverb with multifarious interpretations. Some commonly expressed aspects of the proverb are that one should not destroy Acholi traditions, and that one ought to respect the clan, relatives, elders, ancestors, and their holy shrines. Furthermore, one should not forget about one's old friends when making new ones, for then one can always go back, if one were to meet problems in a new place. As is the case with the roots of the pumpkin, so too the roots of culture (*tekwaro pa* Acholi) and friendship ought to be nourished. Yet the rebels, and at times also the army, seem to target precisely these traditional values. Clan elders, spirit functionaries, and diviners are killed, and ancestor shrines are burned along with whole villages. As Tonny's clan brother, who lives in Anaka camp, told me, "You see, Joseph Kony is also a witchdoctor. So when he hears of another witchdoctor, he says that he or she is competing with him."

When I was visiting Anaka, Tonny's brother guided me to Ayoo Rina, a female healer (*ajwaka*) who narrated her story to us. She had worked as a healer for twenty-one years, we were told, and she had "earned a lot of money," which was invested in cattle. Her reputation as a competent healer was wide-spread. At one point, she owned eighty-eight head of cattle. When we visited, however, nothing of her wealth remained. According to her account, the Ugandan army had looted all the cattle. The rebels, on the other side, had tortured her on one occasion and killed her closest assistant. On another occasion they abducted one of her daughters, who has not yet returned. She concluded that the rebels had assaulted her and her family only because she was working as a healer. Ever since the violent encounters with the rebels, she has kept a low profile with respect to her profession.

Despite being more than thirty years old, the poems P'Bitek's wrote about Lawino and her husband Ocol, describing the encounters of development and modernization with the local moral world, seem strikingly up to date regarding the present understanding among informants about the situation in Acholiland. When I asked if Joseph Kony, the rebel leader, did not know the pumpkin proverb, informants argued the contrary. For example, a farmer in his early thirties commented upon a discussion I held with two old men in a compound a few kilometers outside Gulu town: "He knows! Because he is an Acholi, he knows. Why he doesn't follow it, we don't know. He is not following that proverb, because he now has his [own] proverbs, different from Acholi [ones]. And even the pig, the rebels don't eat it. They don't smoke; they don't drink alcohol [like we Acholi do]" (December 1997). According to the young man, the rebels were not behaving the way Acholi people ought to behave. In my informants' understanding, the seemingly alien behavior of the LRA/M rebels connects to the military support coming from the Sudanese government in Khartoum, in a deeper sense influenced by Arabic or even Islamic culture. They drew references to the rebels' policy of not eating pork, to their praying practice of kneeling on mats or plastic coverings, to their ban on narcotics, tobacco, and alcohol, especially as they prepare for battle, and to the fact that they sometimes have killed people who work in their gardens on Fridays. According to the rebels, Fridays as well as Sundays are to be respected as the day of rest and prayers. Informants also claimed a parallel to the mass killings of civilians in Algeria, which were widely reported in Ugandan newspapers at the time of my first fieldwork. The rebels are behaving just the way the Arabs in Algeria are behaving, informants often rationalized, as they tried to comprehend their own situation, in which the vast majority of people killed were unarmed civilians. The consequence seems to be the same in northern Uganda as in Algeria, people imagined.[2]

Parallel to this but earlier in Acholi history, experiences of slavery, epidemics, diseases, and social change have sometimes been interpreted as the coming of powers from outside Acholiland. Examples are Jok Ala, the spiritual power of Arab influence; Jok Omarari/Marin, the power of the King's African Rifles influence (the British colonial army); and Jok Rumba and Jok Muno, the powers of European influence (p'Bitek 1971: 114–119; Behrend 1999: 109–110). In retrospect, and in line with Jackson's (1998) phenomenological anthropology, this can be interpreted in existential terms. By engaging and incorporating the unknown, foreign or other, or by framing the alien within the existing cosmological order, one can bring it under control. Eventually, its menace can be disarmed. Yet, in the context of an ongoing crisis, this sense of control is not easily achieved. In the words of a young Gulu man in his mid-twenties, "Earlier in Acholi history foreign spirits have come and created problems and social unrest. But elders usually gathered and found ways to cope with and handle these spirits." The young man then related this to the present crisis in Acholiland, "But this time, the militant spirits [of Joseph Kony] came when our society was already disintegrated by war."

Other forces as well, though less militant, put pressure on the local moral world. Among the Pentecostals in the small community outside Gulu town—where former insurgents were offered deliverance from ghostly vengeance and the allegedly destructive spiritual influence of the rebels—local diviners, healers, and other arbitrators of the lived cosmology were given the opportunity to be released from the variety of spirits (*jogi*). In the name of Jesus Christ, so the Pentecostals argued, all these bad spirits had no alternative but to leave. This has implications for the wider surroundings of the living and the dead, of the present and the past. From the Pentecostals' point of view, it might be suggested, not only rebel spirituality but also Acholi ancestral beliefs are to be marginalized.

In the preparations for Christmas in 1993, some leading Pentecostals had gone to the sacred site of their own clan ancestors. In this particular case, the site was a tree under which sacrifices to the ancestors of the clan were made. Jackson Okech, my friend and blind Ugandan "father," was the elder supposed to care for the site, but a serious quarrel with a clan brother, which Okech said led to the illness and untimely death of his daughter, had made him lose interest in "anything to do with the clan." To his frustration, the death of his daughter had not yet been reconciled. Therefore, as the clan was already in a state of unbalance and unrest, he did not actively object when the Pentecostals cut down the tree, chopped it to pieces, and used the firewood when preparing a communal Christmas meal. The local community was invited for the meal, and people came and were said to having enjoyed it. It was only afterward that the Pentecostals informed the others that the clan tree had been used as firewood. That they all survived the Christmas meal with good health, the Pentecostals argued, proved that the power of Jesus Christ was stronger than the spiritual powers of Acholi cosmology.

Some accepted the argument of the Pentecostals, but others did not. Okech was not fully convinced, but due to his quarrel with the clan brother and the unresolved death of his daughter, he did not have the energy or will to object. It was only my queries some years later that again evoked his interest, and together we went to the site of the clan tree. Some new branches had actually developed from the stump, and evidently the tree was still alive. Okech suggested that the tree still housed ancestral spiritual powers, in his view a welcome complement to the new order of Christianity. His argument may be interpreted as a sign that the Pentecostals were not fully successful in their effort to establish a new cosmological order. An elder in Gulu town, a Catholic, argued that "even God is supporting the ancestors." Or, as an old man in a displacement camp once told me, "If Jesus does not like the ancestors, then I do not need Jesus."

WARS OF THE PAST AND WAR IN THE PRESENT

Even though healers and other arbitrators of the local moral world, as well as Christian priests and lay preachers, do their best to handle violent death and its psychosocial consequences, it would be wrong to suggest that Acholi have no problem in existentially comprehending the war. The present war, fought with helicopter gunships, tanks, armored vehicles, machine guns, and landmines, with so many unidentified killers, and with military strategies of mass abduction of minors, the burning of villages, forced mass displacement, looting of cattle, destruction of crops, and the rape of civilians in a systematic manner, is of course something new to Acholi society. Obviously, dirty war grossly abuses the nonwar moral order. Warfare in the past, as older men and women described it from the tales, was of a different kind, with clearly defined moral rules regarding the identity of enemies and allies. Women and children could never be legitimate enemy soldiers and consequently were not to be killed at all, though they could be captured and eventually absorbed into a new social setting. In the words of Ladit Arweny, the old man whose home I frequented, "If a woman displays her breasts, or if she carries a child, she cannot be killed. She can only be collected as a captive, but she is not to be hurt."

Control of the labor of women and children is a common and cruel form of asset transfer in civil wars in Africa and elsewhere (Turshen 2001). In this respect, the war in northern Uganda is not that different from the interclan feuds and interethnic fighting that occur in the tales the elders told me. In both instances, women and children have been abducted. Today, however, the number of abductions has reached unprecedented levels, and children and women are frequently killed.

These days children and women wear uniforms, carry guns, and participate in the war, which makes them legitimate targets of military violence. This is how people explained to me the phenomenon of female fighters. "These are called modern women. That is another thing," Ladit Arweny told me as he made a comparison with the nonwar moral order. As was common among my informants, he hesitated, however, to conclude that children too could be modern in this sense of the word.

The level of violence today was indeed shocking to most informants. In discussing the high levels of unlawful violence, Ladit Arweny compared the situation in northern Uganda with that of war-torn southern Sudan. During our conversation, I happened to refer to Sharon Hutchinson and Jok Madut Jok's writings on the war in southern Sudan, where, as in northern Uganda, women and children have long been regarded as mobile assets, to be kidnapped against their will. Yet they were never to be killed intentionally. Eventually, however, women and children also became direct targets of military violence (Hutchinson and Jok 2002: 99). I recounted Hutchinson and Jok's conclusions on the fratricidal violence, in which they bring up the case of Nuer rebel commander Riek Machar, who defected to the government side in 1991 (see Hutchinson 1998; 2001: 314–315; Hutchinson and Jok 2002: 98). Briefly, Machar launched a campaign to persuade his fellow Nuer soldiers that they were free to kill, as enemies, any Nuer (or other southern Sudanese) they happened to encounter. Machar argued that they were fighting a "government war" in which killings are devoid of social and spiritual risks otherwise generated by intraethnic killings. In Hutchinson's words: "What the Commander was seeking to secure with this revolutionary pronouncement was more than the unquestioning obedience of his troops to kill upon command. Certainly, he, like other southern military leaders, was intent on undermining, if not destroying, any mediating structures standing between himself and the loyalty of his troops, including, when necessary, bonds of family, kin, and community" (Hutchinson 1998: 58–59). Arweny found the comparison illustrative also for the Acholi situation. Like most of my informants, he acknowledged the difference between a government war (in Acholi: *lweny pa gamente*) and an interclan war (*lweny kaka*). The LRA/M commanders, as is clear from their written statements, use a rhetoric similar to Machar's to motivate their fighters. In its most militant form, such rhetoric obviously clashes with the local moral world.

Even if fratricide is common, the rebels seldom regard their violent practices in such terms. Child rebels have instead been encouraged, even forced, to kill adult people. Villagers will naturally beg for their lives when child rebels, who occasionally are even known to them by name and origin, arrive in the homesteads or in the camps. In an effort to evoke loyalties based on kinship, people commonly plead, "Oh, my child, do not kill me." Sometimes the children in arms persist in their deeds, angered by the plea of relatedness. "You are not my parents," they tell the villagers. Still, noncombatant informants were skeptical about Machar's claim to his fellow Nuer that some killings were devoid of any wider, ghostly menace. "It would be good for Machar to drink the bitter root instead," that is, to settle and reconcile the unnatural deaths ritually, I was told. Informants also sympathized with those who refused Machar's argument about a government war, instead emphasizing the relatedness between the peoples of south Sudan. Machar eventually rejoined the Sudan People's Liberation Movement/Army he had defected from.

In the past, I was told, a person recognized as a foreigner and enemy ran the risk of being killed in an act called *kwero dano*, the killing of a person you are not supposed to associate with, or, as one elder translated it, "a traditional enemy." In legitimate war, most people argued, "You must kill your enemy before he kills you." The killed enemy would also acknowledge this, which made ritual redress of the killing possible. To kill an enemy was a sign of bravery, and the killer was celebrated and honored in a ritual called *lameleket* that neutralized the unrest that follows the killing (see also Girling 1960: 103; Behrend 1999a: 42). But to be allowed to go through this ritual retraction, the killer needed to present the mediating elders with convincing evidence for every single killing. Obviously, today this is not easily achieved. In the heat of the battle, how can the source of the deadly bullet possibly be traced? Who laid the landmine? "What to do? You just cry and then you stop, because there is no evidence," as one old man said.

IDENTIFYING THE ENEMY WITH THE STICKS OF FIRE

In the past, I was told, the identity of an enemy could only be defined by clan elders in consensus, which led to the acknowledgment of a valid reason for warfare (see also Girling 1960: 104; Behrend 1999a: 39). After this, the leader of the war party was presented with *lapii*, the sticks for making fire, and the war party was summoned and blessed in front of the clan ancestral shrine. The fire sticks are the symbol of legitimate authority (Crazzolara 1951: 242, 272; Girling 1960: 105; Säfholm 1973: 64). The fighters were also presented with branches of the *oboke olwedo* tree, which is used as a general kind of blessing in Acholi society. And individual elders presented their sons with *laa*, a general blessing of spittle. As the war party is blessed, the enemy is cursed (p'Bitek 1971: 151–156).

Like most people—although we do not all conceptualize our well-wishing as ritual or ceremony—the Acholi perform various kinds of blessings on a daily basis. During fieldwork I met with an old man, Ladit Peter Oola, once a well-known politician in Uganda. He had worked with the district council in the late colonial days, and on the eve of independence he was among those who initiated the branch of the Uganda People's Congress party in northern Uganda. To recruit followers, he set out on a safari in Acholiland with a bicycle, claiming that he covered some eight hundred miles or almost thirteen hundred kilometers of rural roads. Everywhere he went he was quite an attraction. New-born children were named after him, and elders along the roads blessed his mission with the oboke olwedo leaves and ritual spitting (laa). In another example of blessing, collective hunting, to be successful, always had to be blessed properly. The rightful owner of the hunting grounds blessed the hunting party with oboke olwedo leaves. The blessing took place in front of his ancestral shrine (Usher-Wilson 1947: 30–31). In these cases, lapii is never an issue. People told me, however, that if, for example, a roaming lion had killed livestock or people, the expedition sent out to kill the lion was presented with lapii.

Joseph Kony, the leader of LRA/M, claims that he received the blessing to fight Museveni's government from his elders. According to Behrend (1999a: 39), Alice Lakwena too claimed to have lapii. Here I will limit the discussion to trying to track Kony's claim. According to one version, the then chief Yona Odida of the influential Payira chiefdom blessed his nephew, a certain Major Opiya of the Uganda People's Democratic Movement/Army (UPDM/A), the initial "Army of the Earth" that mounted resistance to Museveni in the north. Major Opiya was presented with the branches of the oboke olwedo tree and spittle (laa) but most likely not with the fire sticks (lapii). Chief Odida blessed Major Opiya as an uncle is supposed to bless a nephew about to leave on any kind of mission or safari (see p'Bitek 1971: 146). The blessing took place immediately after the fierce Corner Kilak battles in late 1986 and early 1987. More than a thousand people from both sides died, and the rebels eventually withdrew, defeated by the Ugandan army (see Behrend 1999a: 79–84; Lamwaka 1998: 148).

Thus, even if blessings were offered to the rebels, as is suggested by the above version, the rebels were not presented with the fire sticks, and they were thus not given the proper warfare go-ahead legitimized by any collective Acholi leadership. Today the issue of the warfare blessing of the LRA/M leader Joseph Kony is highly contested. In 1987 Kony was a spiritual advisor to the UPDM/A rebels, but it is not clear if he was present when Major Opiya met with Chief Odida. Perhaps the present chief of the Payira chiefdom, who is the grandson of the man alleged to have been the one who offered the blessing, provided me with the most likely version: "Whereas it is true that some of the [rebel] fighters had sent the late Ogoni [of the Payira chiefdom] to go and convince Rwot [chief] Yona Odida to give them that blessing, because they were at Cwero at the same area where the Rwot was, he told Ogoni to tell the fighters to hold on because it [was] a complex matter which would require him to summon clan elders; of which he never did until his death in July 1987" (letter from Rwot David Onen Acana II, July 18, 2000). It seems that the rebels also agree with this version. In the 1993–1994 peace talks, the LRA/M field commander at that time, Komakech Omona George, claimed that Acholi elders had presented them with the oboke olwedo twigs as a blessing. But when it came to the clearance for warfare, the sticks for making fire (lapii), collectively declared by Acholi clan leaders, the LRA/M commander was vague. "Our lapii is God," he claimed instead, as documented on video. The peace talks eventually failed, and in 1996, when elders tried to initiate new talks, financially facilitated by the government, the rebels killed the two emissaries who went to meet them in the bush. One of the elders who was killed, Okot Ogoni, had been involved in the 1987 effort to present the rebels with a proper warfare blessing. The second victim was Olanya Lagony, a close relative of the LRA/M's then second in command, Otti Lagony. They were killed, informants suggested, because they disputed the lapii of the rebels, and because they were "elected from Kampala" and considered government sellouts.

When discussing the matter with me, Acholi elders stated that a warfare blessing is a very serious matter that cannot easily be removed. Often my older informants compared the situation in Acholiland with the predicament of the Palestinian people, or with the Iranian fatwah on Salman Rushdie. These cases must indeed be the consequence of the Jewish and Muslim versions of lapii, elders hypothesized, because there seems to be no solution at hand at all. The enmity is too strong and too deeply rooted.

In other words, it seems as though the alleged blessing has turned against the Acholi as escalating violence and growing mistrust intensify war in Acholiland. In Acholi thought, powers to heal are also potential powers to harm, depending on shifting contexts. Indeed, as p'Bitek (1971: 146) suggests, the blessing is one side of the famous coin, of which the other is the curse. Most Acholi informants argued that the many people being killed today are not armed enemies but fellow human beings. And clan elders also argued emphatically that the many deaths in Acholiland are violations of any form of blessing, alleged or real, sanctioned by elders and the ancestors. This is especially evident, older people said, when it comes to child abductees who, in their exposed situation, lack proper guidance.

Yet Joseph Kony and other senior rebels claim that the Acholi have themselves to blame, after a prominent elder in Gulu town allegedly turned the blessing into a curse by ritually displaying his penis while condemning the rebels. His wife is alleged to have displayed her breasts. By these acts, they were asking how the rebels could turn against the parents who had once brought them into life. Imagined kinship was made most real. This older man is alleged to have voiced his frustrations over the increase in violence directed at the civilian population, saying, "If these children who are in the bush originate from my penis, I curse them."

As p'Bitek (1971: 149–150) notes, this is the gravest curse known to the Acholi. As with the warfare blessing, it cannot be retracted easily. Even if it had not been made in this particular instance—something that was contested by many informants—the mere rumors of the curse may well have encouraged the rebels to increase their violence against elders, healers, and other arbitrators of Acholi cosmology. With reference to the incident, rebel commander

Matata demanded that the elders who intended to mediate in the peace effort in 1993–1994, must "go and cleanse" before rebel leader Joseph Kony would arrive and the talks could be started. "You are, because I am," the rebel commander stressed with a touch of vagueness to the elders, as archival video material shows. Still, the message was clear. The elders should not deny the rebels as Peter did with Jesus. They were commanded to acknowledge their involvement in the war, and also to take the issue of lapii seriously. Senior rebels were also annoyed by the fact that a prominent Acholi army general and former Ugandan president, Tito Okello, had publicly "talked bitterly" about the rebels in 1993, although he had initially encouraged people to join the armed struggle against Museveni. The rebels were also bitter over the fact that some elders had joined the government in promoting local defense groups, armed with bows and arrows.

THE LION'S TAIL

More recently Joseph Kony voiced a similar argument when he called a local radio station in northern Uganda. His message over the radio is summarized in an unpublished report:

> Kony one day gave this proverb during a Radio Talk show over Radio FM Mega station about a lion and a passerby. It was raining and a young man decides to take shelter in an abandoned hut. Then suddenly, a lion enters the same hut to take shelter and lies at the door step facing outside. The young man had no choice, but to grab the lion's tail and both started to struggle almost the whole day. Fortunately another passerby came around. The young man kindly asked for help since he was already tired. He then handed over the lion's tail to the passerby while he goes to call the villagers to come and kill the lion. Unfortunately the young man went to the village and has never come back. Even the villagers are no where to be seen. (Omona 2005: 23)

Omona's report then proceeds to explain: "Kony considers himself in this conflict as a passerby who has been handed over the lion's tail. He was not the one who started the war. So any strategy in search for a negotiated settlement of the conflict should take cognition of Kony's dilemma" (Omona 2005: 23). Already in 2000, a taped speech circulated in Gulu with Kony narrating the lion story. During my fieldwork, young informants in Gulu town took a similar stand, but obviously from a different, noncombatant position. Disappointed with senior politicians and the older generation who had once encouraged young people to join the war against Museveni, a young unmarried male teacher regarded Tito Okello as a sad but typical example of "the veranda elders." In a public speech in Gulu town, the teacher, recalling that an aging Tito Okello blamed young army officers for the violence during the war in central Uganda, asked, "Now, don't you think that the elders also made the mistakes?" My friend Otim p'Ojok, at the time a secondary school student, agreed:

> I think Tito's case is one of the ugliest cases I have ever noted. It is one of the most common historical blunders that most of these African leaders make under the pretext of being elders and aged. There is that over-assumption, that an elder knows everything. An elder just knows everything, and whatever he will say, he is final. Whatever becomes a mistake, be it coincidental or a planned mistake, the elders are the very first to blame the young generation about the result which was negative. And that has been some part of politics of Uganda. If you look at the politics from Obote coming to Tito, the youths were mainly used as objects to destabilize political space. For example, there was the formation of youth wingers, like the UPC [Uganda People's Congress of Milton Obote] youth wing. So, the youths at that time also took things for granted. Still, that was the result of what the elders educated them about. You see? So they would misbehave. But the misbehavior of these youths during Tito and Obote's time is a result of the leaders themselves, the elders themselves. It was a failure, and the elders are the very first to say, "Ah, it is your failure." They never see who cultivated this failure. This has been the major mistake in Ugandan politics. The youths are used, highly used, and because they are poor, they are inadequate, they don't have the resources, so they are easily manipulated. . . . Elders capture power all the time, and they make use of youth in many ways, but all the time not for positive aspects; all the time for something that causes friction in society, social friction in society. (Gulu town, May 2000)

"And this one even caused ethnic conflicts," Otim p'Ojok concluded, again with reference to Tito Okello's military takeover in 1985. "But it was his failure. What can you do with youth who are hungry and poor?"

Most older informants refuted the idea that any general blessing of war (lapii) had been given in the form of the necessary ritual address in front of the ancestral shrines. The elder accused of cursing the rebels equally denied that he ever did so. Still, these events cannot be erased from the collective memory, and some informants' concern about the matter was profound indeed. Accordingly, the seriousness that older people, especially, attributed to the binding force of the alleged warfare blessing, manifests their existential uncertainty and a deeper crisis that may not be immediately comprehensible to an outsider.

Even though I could not establish whether the blessing or the curse had actually been performed, I will discuss the issue as a "critical event" (Das 1995) that benefits from further deliberation. A critical event forces people to rethink and reconceptualize life, relations, politics, and cultural belonging on a daily basis. An event always involves some kind of crisis, as it interrupts routine processes and procedures (Arendt 1970: 7–8). The issue of the blessing and the curse is a painful ethnographic illustration of war entering not only people's lives but also the wider surroundings and the cosmology.

The classic anthropological discussion of religion and magic may illuminate the complexity of the matter. In his discussion on the power of the "magic word," Tambiah (1990) draws on the philosopher John Austin's well-known claim that saying is doing. Tambiah takes the example of marriage vows. By quoting Malinowski, he links Austin's claim to ethnography: "Pointing to marriage vows Malinowski said that whether they were treated as sacrament or as mere legal contract, they portray 'the power of words in establishing a permanent human relation'; the average man he argued must have 'a deep belief in the sanctity of legal and sacral words and their creative power' if social order is to exist. There is thus 'a very real basis to human belief in the mystic and binding power of words' " (Tambiah 1990: 80). From this perspective, it follows that the warfare blessing, and the curse that is said to have followed some years later, cannot be seen as the mere utterance of words. Rather they were performed within the framework of the local moral world. This suggestion would explain the otherwise inexplicable escalation of violence directed at noncombatant people—something many older informants saw no other context for understanding. As mentioned, some of the actors who were suspected of having been active in the warfare blessings, or the curse that eventually followed, denied that these events ever took place. In the eyes of other informants, however, the escalation of violence proved that some kind of fundamental imbalance has been haunting the Acholi surroundings of the living and the dead.

In other words, the two-sided phenomenon of the warfare blessing and curse is profoundly embedded in the lived realities in Acholiland. A critical event of this kind essentially combines the political with the sacred in a most unfortunate way. The order of things is greatly disordered. In older people's understanding of the state of affairs, then, the escalation of rebel violence aimed at noncombatants suggests an existential crisis on both private and public levels in society. This is similar to what Hutchinson (2001: 307) reports for the war in southern Sudan, which at times was so intense, divisive, and fratricidal "that many Nuer civilians have come to define it as 'a curse from God.'"

"THEY LIT THE CANDLE, BUT THEN LEFT FOR LONDON"

My aim is not to establish whether or not a warfare blessing, which has possibly turned into a general curse, was performed. The issue is highly contested in Acholiland. Rather I want to highlight that people in the war zone tried to understand the situation of extreme social unrest and gross violence by invoking these phenomena. As an issue of contest and debate, it remains a critical event. In my informants' view—and thus their great concern with the issue, I suggest—such a blessing and curse cannot easily be undone. Yet their frustration was also a statement of hope. With time, the cosmological imbalance can be deciphered, reconciled, and thus eventually overcome. The surroundings can transform for the better.

Still, as many informants claimed, any effort to undo the blessings in the midst of strife and ongoing war may easily be counterproductive. According to one version that Tonny and I collected, elders of the Payira chiefdom, of which the late Yona Odiya was chief, tried to retract the blessing given to a group of rebels after the fierce Corner Kilak battles. Non-Payira elders demanded this. However, the retraction was done secretly, without any impartial witnesses. "It is a claim, a mere claim," a non-Payira elder said in his dismissal of the retraction. Even if such retraction had been conducted, skeptical observers questioned the manner in which it might have been done. "There are still a lot of deaths. If a blessing is incorrectly retracted, it will turn against you. And this is what is now happening! People still die. It was not done well," the non-Payira elder went on to state. He also argued that if a warfare blessing was given to Joseph Kony in person, it must be retracted in his presence as well, with his acceptance and whole-hearted participation.

Despite our hard work, Tonny and I could find no account which suggested that a retraction had been done in the presence of the rebel high command. Yet any attempt to retract any warfare blessing in secret and in the absence of the rebel leader, it was frequently suggested to us, must have angered the rebel high command. This, I propose, may partially explain the rebels' increased mistrust of elders as impartial mediators and peace bringers. Even if the rumors of lapii given by the Payira chiefdom to the LRA/M can be questioned on good grounds, it is still likely that the then Payira chief offered his general blessings of well-being to a small group of insurgents after the Corner Kilak defeat. A Payira elder himself confessed his confusion on these matters to me. He admitted that some rebels were presented with oboke olwedo and laa, but he was less certain about lapii, "It is maybe true, I don't know for sure." Still, the critical issue of the warfare blessings is hardly something that is exclusive to the influential Payira chiefdom. In the initial phase of the insurgency in northern Uganda, as I have noted, most older people encouraged young men to join rebel ranks. Again the Payira elder: "This war will take long, because most clans of Acholi gave the laa to Kony." His reference to Kony, in this case, was a general reference to various groups of rebels, including the Army of the Earth; it is only that Kony's LRA/M has come to function as the umbrella for both the Army of Heaven and the Army of the Earth.

Young men who were frustrated with the elders' inability to end the war often stressed this point to me: "Once, they encouraged us to join, but now they have turned their backs on those who did join." For young informants, however, the issue of the fire sticks (lapii) was less important than the older generation's tendency to put the blame on young people. In particular, young men and women, frustrated with the present state of affairs in Uganda, felt that the "veranda" elders' withdrawal from giving any moral support to the rebels was also a withdrawal from the political struggle for, as they put it, "genuine democracy." These young people blamed the elders, who are expected to be guides in cultural and political matters, not the young. Throughout Uganda's political independence, my friend Otim p'Ojok concluded, the older generations and frustrated politicians have manipulated disadvantaged youth and the younger generations to misbehave. Otim p'Ojok did not accept the claim common among elders that today's young people suffer from lack of guidance. According to him, the guidance is there all right, but it is destructive in emphasizing the contested and violent past rather than being constructive and directed toward the future. And my friend Tonny aired his frustrations with those who had once initiated the rebellion but later fled the country and ended up in the European diaspora. "They lit the candle, but then left for London. Now we are left here, and the bush is on fire." Some exiles are rebel supporters, some are not, and some are even government agents, but from the perspective of my informants in war-torn Uganda, when it comes to genuine peace building, they all seem to share the lack of unity and national commitment. "They are fueling the war, because they just don't know what is happening here," Otim p'Ojok told me in 2000. "They just want to maintain the rebellion, so that they can just stay there in London. They are not interested in coming home. It is like a policy that, let there be some form of rebellion which is continuous but which can maintain their positions wherever they are as exiles. You see? So if the war is going on, it is okay, because they are not affected anyway." More recently Norbert Mao, a Gulu politician, gave his commentary, "It is good those who have been backing the LRA have come out to the open but their biggest problem is that they are still stuck with the politics of 1986" (in *Daily Monitor*, October 31, 2006).

However, if exiles and rebel leaders sometimes exploit the past and the authority of elders and local knowledge in justifying their armed resistance, the image of tradition is put to political use by other actors as well. With only a vague and distorted understanding of lapii, government officials have implicitly and explicitly accused the Acholi of being rebellious. Again a homogenous picture is painted. Acholi elders are portrayed as promoters of war, and Acholi culture as primitive and violent. In this way the government has promoted ethnicity as a central explanation for the conflict and its violence, and more specifically, Acholi ethnic identity. These accusations, one elder in Gulu concluded, are nothing but political gimmicks—on the one side the rebel leader claims to have lapii, and on the other side Ugandan government officials claim that Acholi elders came together to bless the uprising against the government.

WAR AND REVENGE

Gingyera-Pinycwa has suggested that the Acholi tradition of *culo kwo* is "retribution or the wreaking of vengeance" and a "serious source for continued insecurity." Culo kwo, he continues, partly explains "much of the killing, maiming, and burning of villages" (1992: 47, n. 52). The violence is held to be specific to the Acholi.

Culo is to pay or to give, while *kwo* is an unreconciled killing, which creates enmity. It may thus be interpreted as paying a killing or, more accurately, giving compensation for a person who has been killed. This is part of the Acholi institution of settling patrilineal lineage or clan feuds, in which the clan of a killed person ought to be compensated by the offending clan (Girling 1960: 66–67). In discussing culo kwo, informants highlighted several points. When I inquired, the concept was initially translated as "revenge." However, it was soon added that culo kwo is part of a larger context. Requests for apology, reunion, and reconciliation are central elements.

Culo kwo, repaying a life, elders told me, can only be understood in the context of *mato oput*, interclan reconciliation. In other words, compensation and reconciliation rather than revenge or blood vengeance is the institutionalized Acholi way of handling disputes, homicides, and unnatural deaths. As Dwyer (1972: 53) puts it in his analysis of Acholi politics, compensation maintains order but revenge perpetuates chaos. Ladit Arweny told me the following:

> A major and essential function of traditional chiefs was to act as arbitrators and reconcilers when disputes occur in order to restore peace and maintain harmonious relations between families, clans, and even tribes. That is the major role of a chief. Should he fail to do that he is removed. The role of a chief is to maintain peace, nothing else. And killing will not make the compensation. [If] you kill a person, you compensate, you reconcile—by paying heavily, of course, but not death for death. (Gulu town, January 1998)

Presently in northern Uganda, however, children are abducted by the rebels and forced into the bush by the thousands. Others are recruited by force or voluntarily, into the government's local defense units. People, especially those who were older, frequently commented upon this situation. The problem, they said, is that there is "no good leadership" in the bush. The abductees are facing a life "without elders' control," or, "without control from the clan head." Or rather, the control is of a different order. Children abducted by the rebels are forced to kill other children, even sisters and brothers.

This is a situation of profound social and moral stress, and many child rebels have been forced to kill family members. Others have had relatives, parents, or neighbors killed by fellow rebels in ambushes and attacks. It happens that distressed rebels take revenge on the offender's own relatives, rather than confronting this rebel colleague with his or her deeds. Furthermore, a common LRA/M response when abductees manage to escape has been to retaliate by raiding their home villages. As a consequence, the abductees know that they are under constant surveillance. This makes any attempt to escape difficult to plan, both strategically and morally. Many children do not know how they will be received if they do manage to escape. They fear the community against which they have committed violent deeds, just as they fear the rebel high commanders.

Arthur, the former rebel controller, told me his account. He was eighteen years old when abducted in 1989, twenty-five when interviewed. He stayed with the rebels for more than one year, the first time very willingly and with great excitement. Right from the initial abduction from his rural home in the middle of the night, the rebels made a great impression on Arthur, with their weapons and military clothes, rugged but well-trained bodies, and dreadlock hair. In addition, the rites of initiation and the religious observances impressed Arthur. Like many young men around the world, Arthur found it exciting to learn how to crawl in the bush, fight, and handle different types of high-technology weapons. At the time, some rebel training camps were located inside Murchison Falls National Park, in the southwest of Acholiland. Thus, this was also the first time for him to see big game such as hippos, elephants, and giraffes. He liked it, and he accepted further training to be a "controller," a ritual functionary. Controllers do not usually carry guns. There may be one to three of them in each rebel unit, and their work is to protect their fellow rebels with holy water, which is kept in small jerry cans and sprinkled from calabashes. In sprinkling the water, the controllers ritually open and close the route the rebels take. The procedure will make it difficult for the Ugandan army to follow the rebels, and sometimes the controllers "close" the escape route with landmines. Controllers also secure ritually the areas in which the rebels remain.

In the beginning, most battles were easily fought and victorious. It was only later on, when things became tougher and many noncombatants were killed in the fighting, that Arthur decided to defect.

Arthur's escape was not easy. He planned his escape for "a long time." The only alternative he saw was to defect in his home area, where he could expect to find people sympathetic with his predicament. So he had to wait until he was sent for a mission there. After his escape, Arthur not only had to avoid his former rebel fellows, who he knew were present in the area, but he also had to avoid the Ugandan army, because the army commander in the area, angered by rebel activities, had promised to execute every returnee he came across. After he had spent a couple of weeks in hiding with some local home guard troops, relatives managed to take him to safety in Gulu town, where he was treated well. The days with the home guards, however, were difficult. He was given a gun and made to promise to fight his former comrades in arms, if they happened to encounter them. To his relief, they never appeared.

When discussing the present conflict situation with me, people admitted that the custom of culo kwo might have escalated the violence committed against noncombatants. At the same time, however, they argued that this is not the consequence of Acholi culture, only of societal disintegration. There are no possibilities for properly guiding the removal of ghostly vengeance (cen) and neutralizing the traumatic experiences of the fighters. For the abducted children, there is no alternative but to obey the rebel commanders. This has nothing to do with the spiritual powers of Joseph Kony, the rebel leader, or of the greater spiritual world, I was told. Informants stressed rather that the children are forced and hence innocent. Komakech, for example, argued that "young rebels have not developed their minds so they just do what they are told to do. They are just acting on command, nothing else. They are not possessed. Kony is the only one [who is] possessed." As suggested by Komakech, the abducted children have not yet fully developed their capacity as moral and social persons. They are thus not held fully responsible for their acts. In the discourse of reconciliation, then, the children's role as victims is more likely to be emphasized than their role as perpetrators.

The absence of adult guidance is regarded as a fundamental problem. Hardly an expression of Acholi traditions and norms, according to Ladit Arweny, the absence of guidance is rather a threat to Acholi traditions, the Acholi people, and the future. In his words, "I think these children in the bush are out of culture now. In fact, they don't know what they are doing. They just don't know." My Ugandan friend Caroline Lamwaka turned to poetry to express her agony. In "The Old Homestead," an unpublished poem that she sent me, she wrote:

> That young boys of yesterdays
> Should be forcefully enrolled into fighting,
> Killing, maiming, abducting
> Forced to witness the unimaginable
> The deaths of own kith and kin.

The very foundation of our culture
Has been shaken to the very depth

In other words, revenge taken by the child combatants is a consequence of the conflict, not primarily a cause. The understanding of the noncombatant population, here exemplified with the words of an Acholi clan elder and a woman poet, is thus an alternative to Gingyera-Pinycwa's (1992: 36–37), who searches for a cultural cause when it comes to the military violence in northern Uganda. Unlike Lamwaka, Gingyera-Pinycwa proposes that ultimately culo kwo is a *cause* of the extreme violence that has taken place in Acholiland. This discrepancy in explanatory models highlights the point of studies that concentrate on consequences of the conflict rather than only looking for reasons for it. "Many who write about so-called violence-prone areas or a culture of violence, often assume that powerful social scripts of vengeance or even hatred get mechanically translated into social action," write Das and Kleinman (2000: 11), as if the agency of the perpetrator is inherently determined by his or her culture. Obviously, the violent acts committed by the Acholi child abductees are not specific to the situation in northern Uganda. Similar examples can be found anywhere on the globe when children are forced from their homes into combat.

Still, violent actions, as shown in Caroline Lamwaka's poem, are often infused with cultural meanings (Whitehead 2004). Compensating for a life (culo kwo) can take several forms, people pointed out. For example, it can be the nation's responsibility to pay pensions or to compensate economically the family of a person who dies on duty. Ultimately this is the responsibility of the president, people said. Furthermore, regional divisions along historical and political lines in Uganda may also be forms of culo kwo. The looting and killing perpetrated by Museveni's troops when they first arrived in Acholiland were often locally interpreted as a form of revenge on the Acholi people. According to Uganda's official historiography, as I have discussed, the Acholi are invariably held responsible for the atrocities in the war in central Uganda during the first half of the 1980s.

TO DRINK THE BITTER ROOT

Drinking the bitter root (*mato oput*) is not simply a tradition of some glorious past. Reconciliatory rituals are conducted all the time; even in the midst of war they are conducted in Acholiland and clan feuds are settled there. In 1988, a young man tried to rape a pregnant girl. The two belonged to different clans. The incident ended most unfortunately when the girl fell badly and her head hit a rock. She miscarried and eventually died. The young man was sent to trial, legal justice was done, and he was imprisoned. He did his time and was then released, but later died for other reasons. His clan, however, still suffered as a result of his deed. "A homicide does not concern only the man who has committed it, but his close agnatic kinsmen also," as Evans-Pritchard noted for the Nuer (1940: 154; see also Hutchinson 1996: 122–127). Bad omens like death and misfortune affect the offender's clan, and their effects can continue for generations. The father of the offender was excluded from the elders' council. The barrier of bad atmosphere (*ojebu*) steadily developed between the two clans. Intermarriage, trade, and joint parties between the conflicting clans were made impossible, and the clans involved could not socialize, or share food or drink.

During the peace talks in 1993–1994, some rebels refused to drink even the bottled sodas that the Ugandan army offered. Food provided for the rebels was accepted only if it was brought as living cattle, not meat, and the rebels then prepared the meals themselves. When an agreement was finally reached—if only to fail later—the two parties did celebrate together, but the rebels went to town to buy their own crates of sodas, while the army brought theirs. Sharing food and drink, rebels insisted, had to wait for later.[3]

Yet such social barriers can be dissolved. In the case of the young man who tried to rape the girl, eventually the offender's father went to an independent group of elders in order to seek reconciliation. Bad developments, misfortune in the clan, and social pressure made him conclude that the matter needed to be reconciled. He acknowledged his son's wrongdoing and compensation was decided upon. The reconciliation ritual, which I attended, was successfully conducted outside Gulu town in early 1998. After ten years, then, the clans were reconciled and the spirits and ancestors were satisfied and thus calmed. The social barrier was finally removed, as the merry atmosphere during the ritual indeed attested to. In December 1999, I had the opportunity to participate in this kind of ritual once again. This time the compensation was low, because the killing, caused by a car accident, had not been intentional.

In February 2000, I participated once again in the same kind of ritual. This time the play of two small boys, both only three years old, had ended unfortunately, when one boy hurt the other while they were playing with a grinding stick and a wooden mortar (*pany*). One boy injured his finger, and eventually developed blood poisoning, only to die later. This was not regarded as a naturally caused death, but rather, to quote Parkin (1985: 7), a "bad death" that ought to be reconciled. The surviving boy was present during the ritual, but did not drink the mixture of the bitter root because of his young age. The fathers of the boys drank the mixture instead. During the ritual, the elders in charge of the whole thing suggested that a boy is "responsible enough to drink *oput*" when he has started picking up an interest in girls. In Acholi terminology, despite "*being* [full] human beings" (sing.: *bedo dano*), children have not yet fully "*become* [moral and social] persons" (sing.: *odoko dano*). They are thus not held fully responsible for their acts (see also Pido 2000). The Acholi say that a boy or a girl becomes a person (*odoko dano*) when he or she is able to take advice from elders and also contributes to household maintenance, perhaps bringing water or food to visitors, which is done from the age of around ten (see also p'Bitek 1986: 27). Yet in a deeper sense it refers to when young people become mature enough to have children of their own. It also refers to when they are old enough, as the discourse on child rebels as victims rather than perpetrators also suggests, to be held morally responsible for their acts, when their cultural agency is complete. Or perhaps, to paraphrase Ladit Arweny quoted above, when they are in rather than out of culture.

Reconciliation rituals can be performed between larger as well as smaller groups, even between ethnic groups, but then without economic compensation. The ritual is then called the bending of the spears (*gomo tong*). Spears from each party involved are bent in the form of a U, and then passed on to the former enemy as a proof that fighting can never again be allowed between the two groups, as was done between the Payira and the Koch chiefdoms in their mutual effort to cope with increased colonial domination. This has also happened more recently. During the Amin years, 1971–1979, Acholi people were especially targeted by Amin's state violence. After Amin's fall, soldiers in the new army took their revenge on people living in the West Nile region.

Finally, however, elders of both sides decided that enough was enough. Tito Okello, who ousted Milton Obote in 1985, was instrumental in the retraction of violence, although critics dismissed this as an unholy alliance with pro-Amin groups (e.g., Mutibwa 1992: 171–175). Revenge was turned into reconciliation when the bending of the spears (*gomo tong*) ritual was performed. Ladit Arweny, one of the participants, recorded the case: "Acholi traditional

Chiefs and Elders initiated reconciliation with the people of West Nile and peaceful reconciliation was performed on the 11th February 1986 in Palero some 26 miles north of Gulu in Acholiland. From that time there would be no war or fighting between Acholi and Madi, Kakwa, Lugbara or Alur of West Nile" (see also Gersony 1997: 75; Leopold 2005: 153–154). Since then many West Nilers who left Gulu town after Amin's fall from power have returned peacefully, and elders do their best to guard the reconciliation accord. Joseph Kony, the rebel leader who is responsible for so much suffering, can also go through reconciliation and thereafter return to a peaceful life, but only if he wants it in his heart, most people in Acholiland argued.

The fact that reconciliation rituals, especially at the community level, are performed regularly in Acholiland should not come as a surprise, I believe. These practices, far from being dislocated in a past that no longer exists, have always continued to be situated socially. They are called upon and performed to address present concerns. Of course, like any cultural practice, with time they shift in meaning and appearance.

RECONCILIATION GROWN BITTER?

Anyone who wants it in his or her heart can drink the bitter root and reconcile, I was frequently told. The rebels can thus be forgiven for any violent deed they are responsible for in Acholiland. To facilitate this, the Ugandan parliament in 1999 passed a blanket amnesty bill. It was however soon followed by an antiterrorist law and intensified counterinsurgency warfare, the Iron First operations. In late 2003 the Ugandan government requested the International Criminal Court in The Hague to collect evidence of crimes committed by the LRA/M leadership. Indeed, the rebels' human rights abuse record is horrific. The court accepted the Ugandan request as one of its first cases. Ever since, international retributive justice has become a hotly debated issue in northern Uganda (e.g., Allen 2006b). The Ugandan government's call for international justice left out possible war crimes committed by its own army. "Our position is if they [the International Criminal Court investigators] come across any allegations against government officials, they should let them be tried by the government," as the army spokesperson is quoted as saying (*Daily Monitor*, August 16, 2004). An increasing number of Ugandan commentators and academics, however, have asked why the Court decided not to proceed with its investigations of the Ugandan army's arbitrary killings and rape of civilians, torture, forced labor at gunpoint, or the forced displacement of millions of people to squalid camps, all potential crimes against humanity (e.g., Apuuli 2006; Otunnu Olara 2006). Throughout the war, also in recent years, the "undisciplined" Ugandan army "has committed crimes against civilians with near total impunity" (Human Rights Watch 2005: 2). The Court has responded to these requests and reports by claiming that "the alleged crimes perpetrated by the Ugandan government were not grave enough to reach the threshold" (representative of the Court quoted in Allen 2006b: 193).

To be accepted for trial, then, the suspected crimes must meet the court's "gravity threshold." By international diplomatic consensus, when the International Criminal Court was created its mandate excluded crimes committed before 2002. These factors give the court procedures a high degree of arbitrariness when imposed upon Ugandan realities. In addition, when Museveni launched a national truth commission in 1986 to account for the human rights violations in Uganda since independence in 1962, he explicitly barred this commission from subsequently investigating any crimes committed after his military takeover (Quinn 2004: 413). Under these two already established institutions, therefore, the years from 1986 to 2002 are left outside the parameters of accountability, a great disappointment to people in northern Uganda who have been living with war since 1986.

Just as humanitarian aid has become a dimension among other dimensions of war in Uganda, the International Criminal Court too is now part of the realpolitik of war. When the semiautonomous government of Southern Sudan, with Riek Machar as chief facilitator, invited the rebels and the Ugandan government to new peace talks in July 2006, this was the best opportunity in many years, not least because of the fact that the South Sudanese government and Machar navigated carefully the diplomacy of the region's realities, at least initially. At this point, the International Criminal Court chief prosecutor, Luis Moreno-Ocampo, dismissed this peace initiative by asserting that the rebels were only buying time to regroup. "Well," a London-based Sudanese blogger and political analyst noted with frustration as Moreno-Ocampo's words rather than those of the government of Southern Sudan hit the world news, "these are words of a politician, not of an impartial international judge. And when so important a figure gets that close to local politics, justice flies out of the window."[4] The government of Southern Sudan, on their side, had worked for a long time behind the scenes to gain rebel confidence. When Machar met the rebel leader for the first time, he intentionally addressed him as his brother, thus assuming the most basic rule in any successful peace talk—facilitating a feeling of equality between the parties. Talks commenced, and despite the Ugandan government's initial skepticism, the parties signed a historical cessation of hostilities agreement in August 2006.

Many of my informants who saw the rebel leaders' violent conduct as a primary obstacle to peace were willing to forgive them, for rather pragmatic reasons. "People just want peace, full stop," as my friend Otim p'Ojok justified his critical position on the International Criminal Court's involvement. His stand exemplifies the Primo Levian "gray zone" that he and his fellow Ugandans live with, where there are no easy divisions of black and white, and no final divisions between good and bad. Rather, it is a kind of acceptance of the situation so that life can go on (Jackson 2005).

However, and this is the main problem with the one-sided involvement of the International Criminal Court according to most Acholi informants, the representatives of the Ugandan government and most importantly the president also ought to admit killings, atrocities, looting, havoc, and destruction committed by the Ugandan army in northern Uganda ever since 1986, if any path toward a peaceful settlement of the conflict is to be opened. Having suffered in the shadows of war for so many years, victimized by both rebels and government forces, the Court's mandate and principle of gravity make little sense to my Ugandan friends.

In the effort to end the war, local politicians as well as cultural and religious leaders have frequently asked the rebels to surrender, "to come out from the bush," claiming that the war is "useless." They have also asked the local population to follow their example to forgive the rebels for "all the bad things they have done." In this rhetoric, they have frequently labeled the LRA/M rebels as "our children in the bush." The children are encouraged to flee from the rebels, and on radio broadcasts, they have been informed that they will be well received. Rebel commanders too are encouraged to surrender. Even if it has good intentions, such rhetoric suggests an imposed fixity of meaning. The opponent is regarded as a minor who needs proper guidance. For many years, Museveni frequently called upon a similar argument when he claimed that Ugandans were not mature enough for multiparty politics, a rhetoric that annoyed my friends in Gulu. "Museveni's mentality makes him a typical colonizer. An African colonizer," a young man told me. With this in mind, the almost daily request put forward by the leaders in Acholiland to the local population to forgive "the children in the bush," is somehow biased in limiting any future reconciliation to an Acholi affair only, between Acholi parents at home and their children in the bush.

In the wake of the Ugandan army's Iron Fist operations, the many arrests without warrants or a basis in the civil law, as well as an increased number of treason charges, created fear and mistrust in the blanket amnesty declared by the parliament but only unwillingly accepted by President Museveni (see Human Rights Watch 2003a: 5, 50–55). Previous peace efforts—in the local parlance called "peace jokes"—have all ended in failure as Museveni's tactic each time has been to pursue military campaigns in parallel with any talks or agreements.

It is against this background that the mistrust in the government's amnesty measures must be understood. Consequently, when the amnesty law was finally endorsed by the Ugandan president in early 2000, senior LRA/M rebels were frustrated by the one-sided request for their surrender. They argued on their part that they are fighting not for the Acholi but for all Ugandans. In arguing for this, I propose, the rebels opposed the Ugandan government's reinforcement of a hierarchical structure in the process of war and peace. In such a hierarchical structure, the political and religious leaders indirectly promote themselves as the *superior* party to the conflict, the ones to forgive the *inferior* party. The latter are the rebels, or "the children in the bush," or even, the "terrorists," "hyenas," and "bandits."

Koch and colleagues (1977) have described reconciliation in the Fijian context, where one party must surrender, remain silent during the reconciliation ritual and also accept a lower status. Such a ritual of reconciliation "serves to reinforce hierarchical structures," adds Hagborg (2001: 15), "because the superior forgives the inferior." The LRA/M commanders will not easily accept the lower status in such a hierarchy. As they stated in a letter, distributed in Gulu soon after the rebels' intrusion from their bases in Sudan in late 1999:

> You who advocate *mato oput* [interclan reconciliation] or *gomo tong* [interchiefdom or even interethnic reconciliation] with Museveni know quite well that Museveni, who came to his leadership position through the barrel [of a gun], has never admitted that he has committed crimes against Ugandans. He has never apologized. . . . It was Museveni who first attacked us. His army NRA/UPDF was the first to kill us, to destroy our homesteads including foodstuffs, rustling cattle, goats, sheep and

even children. . . . Why should the religious leaders and cultural chiefs mislead the people, but not be honest and speak the truth to the people they administer. *Mato oput* and *gomo tong* ceremonies should not be taken as joking matters. . . . People . . . are ignorant when they say that Acholi should pardon us [LRA/M]. We are not fighting Acholi but Museveni's government and all his supporters. If there is any apology at all, it should be for the Acholi and all Ugandans to demand from Museveni and his cronies. This can only be possible when they confess their mistakes publicly. (Undated LRA/M letter distributed to the public in Gulu, late December 1999, translated from the Acholi original)

Museveni must apologize, claimed the LRA/M. Many informants would agree to the arguments put forward in the LRA/M letter, and they feel that the bad things done by the Ugandan army, perhaps especially forced displacement and the mass looting of cattle, are downplayed when Western observers and Ugandan leaders with one voice condemn the atrocities and abductions committed by the rebels.

SO THAT LIFE CAN GO ON

Of course, the rebels are responsible for their gross abuses of the most basic human rights. And during the 2006 peace talks, the rebel leadership publicly asked for forgiveness. Elders and cultural and religious leaders from Acholiland and elsewhere in Uganda were invited to the rebel leaders' base camp to acknowledge this. At the same time, the rebels demanded the international indictments to be lifted before they would agree to sign any comprehensive peace agreement, adding that they would only agree to go home and subject themselves to restorative justice after a comprehensive peace agreement had been signed.

The coin has, as always, two sides. Accordingly, reconciliation also has two sides, most informants in Acholiland argued. In the interclan mato oput rituals that I have attended, there seemed to be no structural inequality between the parties. Rather the contrary—the ritual performance manifests equality. Members of both the offending and offended parties consumed the bitter root, always on neutral ground in the uncultivated bush, symbolically selected on the path between two homesteads. They were always occasions of great feasting and happy feelings, everyone sharing food and drink. Therefore, I suggest, in northern Uganda reconciliation cannot be hierarchical in the sense that one party forgives the other only. As Hagborg (2001: 15) notes for the Iraqw people in Tanzania, those who consider themselves guilty must initiate reconciliation. In the Ugandan case, this would imply that all parties involved must step out and genuinely admit their respective wrongdoings if they are to be able to promote reconciliation. Indeed, my informants held, this is necessary if peace is ever to come. In the opinion of a Gulu male senior sixth-form student, whom I met just after the amnesty law had been enacted: "The rebels cannot accept anything as long as they are denied equality. The more ignored they are; the more determined [to fight] they will be. Mato oput comes in only at a later stage when equality is established. There can be no mato oput as long as there is inequality between the fighting parties" (Gulu, February 2000). A young unmarried female teacher advanced a similar opinion: "Oput cannot work much at this time. Right now, what we need is negotiations, trying to talk to the rebels and see if they can come out. Things like oput come only much later. . . . But this time, what we need is negotiations" (Gulu, April 2000).

Reconciliation, my informants constantly remarked, can only be the final step in any conflict settlement. And to reconcile individual cases in the local community may take time. In early 2000 a young man called Otti asked some elders to facilitate the settlement of a homicide committed by his late father. A fight between the father and another man in the 1950s had ended with Otti's father spearing his rival to death. Charged with manslaughter, Otti's father was imprisoned by the colonial authorities. Legal justice was done. Some forty years later, Otti was planning to marry, but his fiancée came from the clan of his late father's victim. The fight that led to a bad death in the 1950s—that is, long before the father was married and Otti was born—now had to be settled before any marital union could be blessed. In April 2000 I joined the clans as they came together and performed the reconciliation ritual.

As Otti's story illustrates, any future reconciliation, on any societal level, must include inquiries into the complexity of the local social realities and their particular histories. Local reconciliation cannot therefore be equaled to Uganda's blanket amnesty law. According to the law, the rebels must report to the nearest government, police, or army authorities, renounce and abandon involvement in the war, and finally surrender all their weapons before amnesty can be granted (Republic of Uganda 2000). This the rebels will not easily do. As they have claimed, "We are not going to lay down our arms as long as Museveni is still in Uganda as president because the only language he understands is that of the barrel of the gun. We are not going to be intimidated or baited into compromise through Amnesty Law because we have a clear agenda for fighting Museveni" (undated LRA/M letter, distributed in late December 1999, translated from the Acholi original).

Ever since independence in 1962, the political environment in Uganda has become increasingly polarized. The prolonged war in the north has added a new dimension to this. Unless the political issues at stake are seriously addressed on the national level, amnesty laws and cultural practices of reconciliation on the local level may function, intentionally or unintentionally, as weapons of war and mistrust rather than as tools of genuine peacemaking. Neither culturally informed practices of reconciliation nor international retributive justice can replace political efforts at peacemaking, as has been the trend in Uganda. Overall and national reconciliation can come in only at a final stage in any future peace process. It would be "an act of wilful romantic naïveté," as Wilson (2001: 11) shows in the case of South Africa, to conclude that African discourses on reconciliation alone are capable of bringing peace to social settings suffering from long-term armed conflicts or extreme political oppression, even more so if they are imposed from the above.

But I am equally unsure if retributive justice of the International Criminal Court, also imposed from the above, can end impunity in Uganda, because it will not necessarily facilitate a political understanding of the structural, historical, and global conditions that caused and sustained the war. It is also a question of social injustices on a wider and much more everyday scale in Ugandan society, of access to ancestral land, and of redistribution of national wealth. As Norbert Mao, a Gulu politician, put it, "You cannot have justice if you don't have peace. You cannot talk about reconciliation when the structures which encourage violence have not been changed" (quoted in *Daily Monitor*, December 5, 2006).

There is another Acholi ritual that can perhaps be more useful to start with, the *keto ajaa* ceremony ("to cut off the grass straw"), in which the opposing parties basically agree to disagree, not reconciling but cutting off the bitter debate in order to be able to proceed. As a young man in Gulu described the amnesty law while he offered me some tea to drink, "Say that I invite you for tea, and you happen to destroy my favorite cup. Then I say *jalo*—anyway, it is okay, nothing to do. But I didn't forgive you." It is to accept the situation so that life can go on.

UNFINISHED REALITIES

SORROW AND LAUGHTER

In mid-2003, rebels were present in ten districts, all over northern Uganda. The Ugandan army's Iron Fist operations in southern Sudan and the rebels' counterattacks in northern Uganda made the situation tense. The rebels had increased their violence and abductions to reach unprecedented levels. In early September, for example, they ambushed a bus in Soroti district. Before setting the bus ablaze, the rebels killed twenty-two passengers. The Ugandan army, obviously edgy about the development, added to the violence. To give some examples: One night in late July, a pregnant woman in Gulu town became seriously ill. Her adult son and another man decided to help her get to the hospital immediately. Without warning, as they approached the hospital, all three were shot dead by patrolling army soldiers on the outskirts of Gulu town. In Katakwi district, army helicopters mistakenly bombed a funeral party, leaving nine people dead. Around the same time, in Pader district thirteen civilians died when helicopters bombed them as they were working in their gardens.

Yet another night, when Tonny was visiting Rufina Labol, his mother, who lives in Alokolum some miles outside Gulu town, nearby gunshots suddenly rocked the night. Tonny immediately decided to run to the bush to hide. He ordered his old mother to join him, but she refused. Being old and tired, she did not see the use of spending the night in the bush. "What can you do now?" she concluded, resigned. Tonny accepted her stand and ran to hide. After a night in the bush, he decided to look for a piece of land in Masindi district, south of the Nile River. He wanted to move his old mother and the family away from the immediate war zone. But many people had done so before Tonny, and good land was expensive. Obviously, he wanted Rufina to have access to water nearby, and he wanted his children who were staying with her to have only a short distance to their school. Tonny had purchased a plot of land in Alokolum for his mother and his first wife, Doreen, when life became too difficult in the rural area where they originated. For some years, Rufina had stayed in the new settlement with Doreen and the family. More recently, Gladys, the oldest daughter, had escorted the small children, Adoch Kerstin, Atuk, and Rackara, every evening to the premises of the nearby St. Mary's Missionary Hospital outside Gulu town, where they spent the nights. Solomon and Vicky, who were old enough, walked there by themselves. There, every night, they were joined by thousands of young commuters who all feared night attacks. Rufina, however, is too old to walk to the hospital on a daily basis, and Doreen has remained with her in Alokolum.

Hearing Tonny talking about these new developments over the phone, I recalled when I visited Rufina, Doreen, and the family with my fiancée, Helena Edin, in mid-2002. Like all my Ugandan friends, Rufina was very happy to welcome Helena to Uganda. During my previous stays in Uganda, I was single, something that evoked concern among many people. Ayoo Rina, the diviner in Anaka camp, had given me some roots to bring with me back to Sweden. She instructed me on how they could make any woman fall in love with me. Now I was back in Uganda with Helena. Helena was a very beautiful woman, Rufina proudly concluded. Finally her "son," as she said, had decided to leave the life of a *labot* behind. Rather than translating the word *labot* as "bachelor," my informants translated it as "a man without a woman." Writes p'Bitek:

> You might be a giant
> Of a man,
> You may begin
> To grow grey hair
> You may be bold
> And toothless with age,

But if you are unmarried
You are nothing.
(FROM *Song of Lawino* in p'Bitek 1966)

In the eyes of most Acholi, a man without a woman is not complete, and he will never be taken fully seriously. All of a sudden, and with a big smile, Tonny's old mother turned to Helena and squeezed her belly. "Now only one thing remains," she laughed. We all laughed. As elsewhere in Africa, Acholi women will gain considerable social status after they have given birth (Girling 1960: 21, 24; p'Bitek 1973: 52). Celebrating Helena's visit to Uganda, Tonny gave her the name Alyaka, "Brand New," and he bought some Ugandan-made fabric and designed a dress that a Gulu tailor made for her. Old Rufina provided some clay cooking pots. My friend Ladit Arweny, whom I visited so many times, always with more questions and queries, instructed his daughter Betty to prepare a *kikoye*, the married women's dress, for Helena. Susan, Otim p'Ojok's wife, had knotted a set of napkins and tablecloths for Helena, and Aber, the wife of Okech, my old blind "father," provided some locally made kitchen tools, things that make a proper household.

When Helena traveled back to Sweden, I spent an extra month in Gulu. Tonny, Otim, p'Ojok and I worked hard to be able to follow up some loose ends. Fighting was again escalating, and the rebels narrowed in on Gulu town. Now and then, gunfire woke me in the middle of the night. For old Rufina, the sound of gunfire was more frequent in Alokolum than it was in Gulu town itself. One night a unit of rebels arrived at a nearby displacement settlement. They set fire to forty-one huts, but another rebel unit soon arrived, and its commander told her comrades to stop immediately. They were not there to burn houses but to fight the army, the commander stated. They looted food-stuffs and clothes. Eventually the Ugandan army engaged the rebels, who withdrew into the darkness of the night. The army also withdrew. Silence and uncertainty followed. Early the next morning, Tonny came to me with the worrying news of the rebels' attack on Alokolum. We immediately set off to check for ourselves. On arriving at the displacement settlement, we listened to the stories of some of the people who had encountered the rebels, and then proceeded to check on Rufina, Doreen, and the family, who lived further ahead. They were all okay, but the nearby shooting had of course disturbed and upset them. They had not been able to go back to sleep that night, fearing what could happen.

Relieved to hear that everybody was safe, we sat down and talked. The conversation eventually came to Acholi concepts of fear and sorrow, themes that Tonny and I had been working with during the course of our research. When a relative or a close friend dies, people feel deep sorrow, called *cola* in Acholi. Like most people, in such situations Acholi people support and encourage each other to assuage the deep sorrow. But the deep sorrow also needs to be neutralized ritually, which is done by drinking oput, the bitter root, mixed with locally brewed beer, during the funeral. In contrast to the reconciliation rituals, during these occasions children too consume the bitter root. You drink the bitter mixture to swallow the sorrow, to be able to "feel free, not to think too much" as an old man explained. If the relatives of the deceased do not take at least a small sip of the bitter mixture, cola can spread to the wider surroundings—women will be barren, children will fall sick, and the harvests will fail. "If you walk to the garden with cola," Rufina told me, "the crops will burn." The surroundings will change for the worse. Odoki (1997: 55) writes that "*cola* is the result of a death throe, which sometimes is a great hindrance to the normal life and activities of the bereaved families." Deep sorrow may develop into *ojii too*, which is serious and paralyzing fear, when your heart starts pounding out of fear (literally, the fear of dying). Also the wider surroundings will die (*piny too*).

Around the time of my visit to Rufina, a gasoline truck and a bus collided in southern Uganda. The crash scene had turned into a burning inferno and more than seventy people died on the spot. A photographer took a photo of some eyewitnesses, and it was published in *The New Vision* (July 19, 2003). "Exactly," Tonny said about the eyewitnesses' facial expressions as we read the paper. "That is *ojii too*, really." They were in total agony, we could see from the photo, unable to cry or even talk. On another occasion, he had described how the body reacts to ojii too. "You feel like you are sick, drunk, very weak. Your legs cannot carry your body." I was also told that you will live with the uncanny feeling that you or some close relative will soon die. I asked Rufina if this was the feeling that kept them awake the previous night when gunfire rocked the surroundings. "Oh, no," she answered, "because no one was killed. We only feared." In describing her fear, Rufina used the word *lworo*, which Tonny translated as "ordinary fear." This, I was told, is different from ojii too.

Rufina's story is one of bad surroundings, *piny marac* in Acholi. It is a story that pinpoints not only the immediate issues of everyday survival but, more, the philosophical, religious and existential queries that my Ugandan friends struggle with as they try to comprehend and live the world. Such a struggle is of course always part of life, even when the surroundings are good. p'Bitek captures the argument. Good surroundings is "when things are normal, the society thriving, *facing and overcoming crises*" (p'Bitek 1986: 27, emphasis added).

The knowledge of Acholi cosmology that my Ugandan friends offered me, coupled with my anthropological passion to bring order in my interpretations, was also of a certain therapeutic value. Through the conversations with Rufina, other knowledgeable people, and my young friends in Uganda, some of my own worries were given a new and comprehensible context. The late philosopher Feyerabend (1993: 272) wrote that "potentially every culture is all cultures." Listening to and learning from my Ugandan friends convinced me of the validity of Feyerabend's conclusion. I felt extremely privileged to be a student of Acholi moments in history and war. For me, these were also moments of coevalness. I left Uganda with this feeling of confidence, but the bad news over the phone in mid-2003 again evoked my thoughts about old Rufina's situation in Alokolum. She had coped with the war for so many years, but now she was tired. I was relieved to eventually hear that Tonny found a plot of land for his mother in Masindi district. Again, however, she and the family were displaced. When I returned to Uganda in 2005, the family was back in Alokolum, but the army had forced them to abandon their beautiful homestead and instead move to a nearby camp, crowded and squeezed.

FOR GOD AND MY COUNTRY?

"No change" is a political slogan well known all over Uganda. It is the slogan of General Museveni, Uganda's president and commander in chief of the country's armed forces. In the eyes of most Acholi, Museveni's military takeover in 1986 brought war to northern Uganda. A woman put it that "the Lord's Resistance Army children are born under Museveni's rule." In other words, for the people in northern Uganda, the Movement government has not brought peace to Uganda. And a peaceful environment, as we all know, is the precondition for any democratic development. In the shadows of war, the Movement government has been increasingly associated with harassment and arbitrary arrests. The rebels' deadly violence adds to people's lived frustrations. As Tonny once put it, dryly paraphrasing Museveni's Movement slogan, "People are tired. We are voting and voting, but nothing happens. There will never be any change." Or as a young man said, again with an ironic reference to the slogan of the incumbent, "People have no change from their problems." As the 2006 national elections approached, some Acholi friends expressed their despair: "We cannot vote this time, it will only invite more problems. This time, it is all up to God."

Culturally, socially and bodily orientations and *meanings in use* are the main means through which war and its effects are acted upon. As Rufina's story of fear and sorrow exemplifies, this sustains the experience and memory of war, making war and its multiple forms of violence routines among other routines in everyday life. At the same time, as I have shown, my informants expressed distress about the fixation of meaning to a limited set of cultural and ethnic stereotypes that propaganda of war and chauvinistic politics impose upon the lived surroundings and the national order of things. The continuous reification of ethnic categories has been going on ever since the British first arrived in Uganda. Even today, ethnic stereotypes are uncritically promoted, imposed on the local social realities. Okuku's conclusion on the political situation in contemporary Uganda is harsh. "In fact," he writes in an analysis of the developments since 1986, "the politics of Uganda has been re-militarised and ethnicised" (Okuku 2002: 36). Young students especially were tired of hearing about the Acholi as a "primitive warrior tribe."

Uganda does not suffer from primordial and essential ethnic differences, once and forever set. Rather, by delineating some of the specific historical and political developments that have preceded the war, I have pursued the aim of repoliticizing war (cf. Allen and Seaton 1999: 4). The opposite approach, however, is more common today on the global scene. Politicians, journalists, and sometimes also academics reach for the ethnic card. In my effort to write against such conclusions, perhaps some readers will conclude that I have presented the rebels as a movement that is more coherent, both politically and organizationally, than is the case, thereby romanticizing them. I do not think I have. This is a frequent criticism that followed Richards's (1996) path-breaking study of the war in Sierra Leone. I tend to favor Richards in this discussion. In Uganda, for example, senior rebel commanders are in frequent contact with each other. Joseph Kony, the rebel leader, and Vincent Otti, the second in command, seem to be informed promptly about most developments on the ground, even when they are dislocated to neighboring Sudan or Congo. The mobile telephone network in northern Uganda has complemented the use of radio calls and satellite communication, but also paper notes nailed to trees at secret rendezvous points are used. Perhaps, the increasing degree of isolation and alienation that the rebel movement has faced has made it more coherent than it ever was previously.

In the postscript to a reprinting of his book, Richards (1998: 178) writes that the Sierra Leonean rebels (the RUF/SL) "became more sectarian through circumstances (including its bungled birth and rejection by the wider community)." In Uganda, I think, there is a parallel development. War evolves, and disintegration into internecine violence might have been foreseen by the Ugandan government and external observers, had they not so categorically denied the rebels' reasons to exist. As a paradox of life, many of the things that the LRA/M says make sense to people in northern Uganda, but their violent practices do not. In action, the rebels by necessity move in small and extremely mobile units, independent from one another. Their behavior seems to be dependent on the particular commander in charge. In Alokolum, as mentioned above, the rebel commanders disagreed over the issue of destroying people's homes. Nordstrom (1997: 51) notes that the Renamo rebels in Mozambique eventually split over ideological disagreements. Splinter groups multiplied. Similar rumors have always been frequent in Uganda, but the rebel leader seems to keep control of the great majority of influential commanders.

As I noted above, my effort to repoliticize the war in Uganda is not meant to romanticize the LRA/M; nor is it my ambition to propagate the cause of the LRA/M—something a Ugandan army representative is alleged to have said, however, about a Human Rights Watch (2003a) report. An army spokesperson "dismissed the report as the work of those bent on mobilising for the LRA," reports *The New Vision* (July 15, 2003). Instead, I make a serious effort to listen to the stories of my informants and Ugandan friends. With Allen and Seaton's idea of repoliticizing war in mind, my effort can be slightly reformulated.

As a consequence of the war, millions of Ugandans have been uprooted. During my years of fieldwork engagement, I saw the humanitarian crisis in the camps becoming a chronic emergency. Malkki (1996: 378) is worried about "the contemporary dehistoricizing" trend in much humanitarian work. Humanitarian organizations on the ground rarely consider the broader issues of war and insecurity, and neutrality is sometimes confused with an explicit antiparticipatory ideology, even ignorance. Refugees are regarded as "pure victims in general: universal man, universal woman, universal child, and, taken together, universal family" (Malkki 1996: 378). Internally displaced persons, uprooted and scattered families, herded into camps like cattle to the kraals, have become an anonymous acronym in the statistics, the "IDPs." I guess this was the reality Otim p'Ojok had in mind one day, as he wittingly suggested a new acronym for the aid organizations to take up, the "IDCs"—the internally displaced *cows* in Gulu town, the result of a few ill-planned restocking schemes; cows lingering around, eating from the garbage pits.

"The failure to explore the relationship between economic globalisation and insecurity means that the international community appears purely in the role of saviour and humanitarian," writes Orford (2003: 188). In the long run, she continues, such a course of development results in a neocolonial mode of governance, indeed an unjust new world order. A Muganda informant living in Gulu town came to a similar conclusion, claiming that the international organizations now "take a lean on the government" to the extent that they are "welcomed as its lovers." This love relationship, he told me in late 2005, is "directed" by the government "but not according to the needs . . . of the community. And that is going to cause a big-big-big problem, because people are politicizing everything now." So we need to acknowledge that Uganda's crisis is not only humanitarian. It is more profoundly, I argue throughout the pages of this book, a political crisis.

I have presented my understanding of the political and historical legacies of violence in Uganda, and my Acholi informants' stories provide the material to do so. The stories mediated my informants' efforts to engage the world so they might better comprehend existentially the phenomena of fratricidal violence and cultural and social breakdown, when the outside world, for so many years was tending to blame the local culture. Eventually, when the bad surroundings begin to change for the better, people will leave the desperate congestion in the camps to be better able to face the problems of quotidian life. Old Rufina, Doreen, and their family could then move back to their home of origin. By then, the displaced family's version of the Ugandan national hymn that I encountered in Palaro camp, "For God and My Life," may again be expressed as the more all-embracing original, "For God and My Country."

PEOPLE NEED SALT

"These hands cannot be finished" (*cing pe tum*), reads the poetic inscription I found on the same hut in Palaro. In essence, the phrase claims that the displaced people refuse to give in, despite great social unrest and lived uncertainties. As long as people have their hands, they will be able, one day, to go back to their villages of origin. With their bare hands and their bare life, they will rebuild the world. The writings from Palaro catch something that I find present in all of the stories and narratives portrayed in this book, perhaps best described as "unfinished realities," to borrow a phrase from Werbner (1998b: 99). This openness is also a statement of hope. My friend Caroline Lamwaka wrote in her unpublished poem "The Old Homestead":

> Yes, indeed it is better
> To return to the ruins of the old homestead
> Than never to return at all
> Soon all the people will return,
> And the neighbourhood will be filled with laughter and joy
> The laughter of children, running and playing
> The giggles and laughter of the girls and women
> As they joke and cut grass
> Huts will be rebuilt, and compounds cleared
> And the mango trees will blossom with fruits.

Caroline's many years of earthly struggles ended in early 2006, leaving me completely bewildered. The news reached Helena and me just as we arrived back to winter in Sweden, only some few weeks after we had spent some time with her, as we all prepared for Christmas in Gulu. So many things, in life and academia, will now be left unfinished. Caroline was among the first Ugandans who welcomed me to Uganda in 1997, who introduced me to Acholi realities, and she had been a close friend ever since. I visited her in Uganda, and she visited me in Sweden.

But I like to think that as long as the mango trees in Acholiland grow and blossom, although the Ugandan army sometimes cuts them down in the effort to deny the rebels food, Caroline's hope lives on. It must. In facilitating this, I suggest by presenting this book in memoriam of her, we need to investigate how people in war-torn settings like Uganda act upon their immediate and wider surroundings, as they try to understand not only the violent practices of the warring parties but also the international involvement. I have claimed that violence and war are socially and politically patterned rather than being mere expressions of cultural essences or something biologically innate. The war in

Uganda evokes historical antagonisms in Uganda, but more important to acknowledge, I hold, is the fact of today's global interconnectedness. Traders in war machinery, light weaponry, and the technology of violence seem to be the most mobile capitalists of today, and uncountable conflicts taking place in the world have been considerably aided by this amoral business (Sluka 2000; Tambiah 1989; Turton 1997). My informants made the same analysis of the situation. "Why do your countries in the West send us all these modern weapons?" was the rhetorical question I was requested to bring back to Sweden. I also note my informants' conclusion regarding the landmines. They are of foreign origin, imported to Acholiland. The mines have fueled the war, adding to the feeling of a life with bad surroundings. The description of bad surroundings, I therefore suggest, ought to be related to a common hope in Acholiland that the international dimensions of the conflict should be recognized by the international community.

In his project of rewriting world history, Wallerstein (e.g., 1974) summarized ideas from a growing number of studies. He advanced the proposal of a single world system with a few cores that accumulate wealth at the expense of the many peripheries that are drained. In some liberalist circles, his world systems theory is deemed faulty and outdated. Fukuyama (1992), for example, famously declared the end of history. Yet, as Turton (1997: 24) writes, "a convincing case can be made that the economic and political problems being experienced by Third World states are a direct result of their interrelations with the states of the advanced, capitalist 'core' and its international political and financial institutions." These are issues that the rebels also have tried to address. I do not conclude that people actively support the rebels, only that the rebels' claim to be fighting for "free basic primary health care for all" (Lord's Resistance Army/Movement n.d.: 15) makes sense in the view of many people. Again I want to stress that this is not to say that people back the LRA/M, or that the LRA/M is an organization they think is capable of realizing its promises. But the LRA/M (n.d.: 11) puts words to their experience: "The population at the grassroots are hardly feeling the economic achievements of the Museveni regime."

My Ugandan friends claimed that politics and accountability are about the redistribution of wealth. It is thus not necessarily the ruling Movement government per se that is bad. "Politics are based on wealth and capital, all over the world," Tonny once declared. He continued, "If people had their cattle, they would vote for the Movement. Me, I cannot vote for this Movement. They have taken my cows. But if they can give the cows back to me today, ah, tomorrow I shall vote for them." Otim p'Ojok, stating his conclusion, said, "People just want a certain degree of freedom. They are desperate, they don't even have salt. So they will go with those who give salt." Acholi mythology and tales often stress that the power of a chief can never be absolute. He must earn his position and demonstrate his ability to lead his subjects. He must show hospitality, and make sure that the people do not starve and that they can live in peace (Girling 1960: 46; p'Bitek 1971: 61). It seems like no Ugandan leader has provided the Acholi with this.

ALTERNATIVE BEARINGS

This book has described a pattern of dirty war and a legacy of violent conflict in Uganda, as it unfolds from colonial annals, historical accounts, and my informants' contemporary stories. I have invited the reader to be skeptical of the thesis that some cultures in essence are more prone to war than others. In closing this book, I again want to repeat that I do not believe the idea of war-prone cultures to be a fruitful way of analyzing cultural orientations in life. Rather, cultural orientation is a means by which people engage and try to comprehend the lived surroundings of unrest and war, and by which they continuously struggle to build hope for the future. Therefore young people, whose stories I have tried to give voice to, often listen and take advice from the older people (whose stories I also narrate). Young people's stories are comments on contemporary Uganda that place the propaganda of war in relief. Their stories are of political dignity and constitute insightful commentaries upon contemporary African societies in emerging global realities. So if we make the effort to spend some time with these young people, listening carefully to what they have to say when they confide in us, without editing their stories to better fit into the official discourse of fixed meanings, we will find that these stories uncover a more complex version of the sociopolitical reality, and eventually, it will be increasingly difficult to sustain the rhetoric of the global war on terror and its black-and-white, heart-of-darkness worldview.

In Uganda, the issue of what really happened in Luwero in central Uganda during the first half of the 1980s continuously fuels antagonistic positions. A common conclusion is that the suffering inflicted by the Ugandan army on the noncombatant people in northern Uganda was "never comparable with the atrocities committed in Luwero" (Brett 1995: 148). I really do not know how one can come to any conclusion regarding which collective suffers or has suffered the most, but still I find it interesting that most young people who suffer today want to leave the issue of Luwero behind in the name of peace building. In other words, the stories of my Ugandan friends show that ethnic sentiments and cultural orientations can be means to define a moral order against violence and atrocity that promotes reconciliation instead. A balance must be struck between the existential and the political, the local and the national, and the past and the future. As young people try to find directionality in life, they do not do so without a critical mind. They know that ethnic sentiments can promote chauvinism, which breeds further conflict and deepens regional divides. In this regard, then, as the young teacher told me, the millet eaters in p'Bitek's (1966) poem are not necessarily tougher than people "who drink bananas." Rather, they are all fellow Ugandans. As they shape their future, perhaps the young generation that grows up with war, conflict, and bad surroundings will be able to achieve this balance, exactly because of their experiences in life. "Perhaps we are at one of those moments when history moves on," Merleau-Ponty once noted. He elaborated:

> What we call disorder and ruin, others who are younger live as the natural order of things; and perhaps with ingenuity they are going to master it precisely because they no longer seek their bearings where we took ours. In the din of demolitions, many sullen passions, many hypocrisies or follies, and many false dilemmas also disappear. . . . But underneath the clamor a silence is growing, an expectation. Why could it not be a hope? (Merleau-Ponty 1964b: 23)

INTRODUCTION: ORIENTATIONS

1. The Uganda Peoples' Defence Forces (UPDF) was formerly called the National Resistance Army (NRA), but was renamed in the 1995 constitution.

2. In their press releases, manifestos and documents, the rebels refer to themselves interchangeably as the LRA, the LRA/M, the LRM/A, the LRA/LRM and the LRM/LRA. In this book, to keep it simple, I will refer to them as the LRA/M (Lord's Resistance Army/Movement in references and bibliography), as this is the most common locution in their documents and statements in recent years. I will however keep the original *titles* of their documents, and in my quotations I reproduce the original text exactly as it is.

3. Dolan (2002b) has questioned the high numbers of child abductees that various human rights organizations present to the international community. The focus on the LRA/M as a child movement, Dolan points out, enables a kind of downplaying, even neglect, of the Ugandan army's own use of child soldiers (see also Furley 1995; Human Rights Watch 2003a; 2003b).

4. The United Nations has decided upon the following categories of young people. Adolescents are between the age of ten and nineteen, youth between fifteen and twenty-four; young people are those between ten and twenty-four, and children, those below eighteen (see Women's Commission for Refugee Women and Children 2001: 86, n. 5). Official Ugandan policy defines youth as "all young persons, female and male, aged 12 to 30 years" (quoted in Women's Commission for Refugee Women and Children 2001: 9). The predicament of the many children abducted by the rebels has been widely covered by various organizations, notably Amnesty International (1997; 1999) and Human Rights Watch (1997; 2003a; 2003b), and will not be a central concern of this book.

1. ACHOLI WORLDS AND THE COLONIAL ENCOUNTER

1. To illustrate the Eurocentric bias that I want to delineate, Gray's (1951; 1952a; 1952b) series of articles called "Acholi history," published in the *Uganda Journal*, to a large extent deals with European rather than African individuals. Another account has *Early travellers in Acholi* as its title (Wild 1954).

2. Thus, even though *malo* means up or above in Acholi, *lumalo* "refers to the Acholi who descended from the hills/mountains ranges of Agoro," my friend Otim p'Ojok noted (see also Girling 1960: 6).

3. Some texts by prominent Acholi writers were published in a journal called the *Acholi Magazine*. Books were also produced. Two notable titles are Okech's (1953) *Tekwaro ki ker lobo Acholi* (The cultural history of Acholiland) and Anywar's (1954) *Acoli ki ker megi* (Acholi customs).

4. In the 1991 national census, 70 percent of the population in Acholiland listed themselves as Catholic, 25 percent as Protestant, and only 0.5 percent as Muslim (Ward 2001: 194). It can be noted that virtually all Muslims in Acholiland are non-Acholi immigrants, notably from the West Nile region. According to Ward (2001), in 1959 the figures were rather different: 39 percent Catholic and 32 percent Protestant. The figures presented by Gertzel (1974: 71) for the same period are slightly different: 30 percent Catholic and 22 percent Protestant. Lately, Pentecostalism has added to the division, and several informants who did not wish to express any explicit Christian belonging, talked about Christianity as a divider (*apoka-poka*).

5. Atkinson (1978: 523–524) suggests that the specific circumstances that led Payira and Koc to bend spears at this juncture was a conflict that erupted between the two, over control of a regional trade route for firearms.

6. Around the time of independence, the Uganda National Congress (UNC) was re-named the Uganda People's Congress (UPC).

7. The myth figures on various levels in oral history of migrations in the region (Crazzolara 1950: 61; Onyango-Odongo 1976: 31). In yet another version that I collected, the split resulted in the Luo on the one side, and the Nuer and the Shilluk on the other.

8. In narrating the myth, Bere (1947) and p'Bitek (1971: 20) refer to the missionary Crazzolara, who interpreted the parting of the waters of the Nile as the "dramatic act" that "perpetuated" the separation (Crazzolara 1950: 65–66).

9. For Acholi mythology in this vein, see Ocheng (1955: 58–59).

10. Building on existential phenomenology and psychology, Giddens elaborates on the concept of ontological security in everyday, practical life. He defines ontological security as the sense of continuity and order in events, both those directly and not directly within the perceptual environment of the individual. "Practical consciousness is the cognitive and emotive anchor of the feelings of *ontological security* characteristic of large segments of human activity in all cultures," which will "carry

the individual through transitions, crises and circumstances of high risk" (Giddens 1991: 36, 38).

11. In the 1899 colonial archives, the spelling was finally standardized as "Acholi" (see Allen 1994: 125, 138). Baker, who visited the region for the first time in the early 1860s, writes about his travels in "the extensive country of Sooli" (1866: 237, vol. 1) and his encounters with "the great Shooli tribe" (1874: 513, vol. 2). In Baker's accounts, as the "Acholi" were not yet under full colonial control, the spelling was not yet fully settled.

12. If Allen's argument is that social life in the region was entirely interrupted by the intruding ivory traders, I believe he is exaggerating. But that is just another speculation.

13. Speke's (1863; 1865) account was published in Swedish within two years of the original English publication, Mounteney-Jephson's (1890; 1891) within one year. Stanley's two accounts, *Through the dark continent* and *Darkest Africa*, were published in Swedish the same year the original English edition came out (Stanley 1878a; 1878b; 1890a; 1890b).

14. Regarding this inscription of colonial history in the Acholi landscape: the reerected fort figures in a photo, captioned "Ruins of Baker's fort at Fatiko," in a book called *Early travellers in Acholi* (Wild 1954: 20).

15. I find it difficult to comprehend fully the level of human resources put into this effort. For example, to get only one of the three steamers running on Lake Albert, western Uganda, 4,800 porters were "recruited" to carry its sections through the hilly terrain, of whom 600 were required to haul the boiler alone (see Gray 1952b: 142–143).

2. NEOCOLONIAL LEGACIES AND EVOLVING WAR

1. See, for example, Whyte and Whyte's comment accompanying Karlström's (2004) article.

2. See Gingyera-Pinycwa 1992: 4; Hansen 1977: 104–105; Karugire 1996: 77; Kasozi 1999: 110–111, 121; Kyemba 1977: 44; Mazrui 1975: 48; Mutibwa 1992: 87–88; Vincent 1999: 115.

3. Milton Obote held state power twice in Uganda. The second period is commonly referred to as the Obote II government (from 1980 to 1985). The Obote II government replaced the short-term and unstable governments that followed in the aftermath of Idi Amin's government (1971–1979): those of Yusufu K. Lule (1979), frey L. Binaisa (1979–1980), and Paulo Muwanga (1980). In this book, if nothing is indicated, I avoid implicit judgments, such as labeling some Ugandan state ministrations as "governments" and others as "regimes" or "juntas." Rather govern involves, to quote the Oxford English Dictionary, "the action of ruli continuous exercise of authority over the action of subjects or inferiors; authorit tive direction or regulation; control, rule." More specifically, it involves "the actic

of ruling and directing the affairs of a state; political rule and administration." In this sense of the word, military councils are also governments.

4. I have borrowed the concept "arbitrator" from Allen (2000), who writes about elders, healers, and other functionaries of Acholi cosmology as "the moral arbitrators of the past." By engaging Acholi cosmology and morality, one could add, they negotiate the past in formulating a future.

5. Official letter from the Ugandan army, dated January 20, 1990.

6. Amaza (1998: 62), an NRM/A insider, agrees that animosity among locals as well as within the NRM/A toward the Acholi was common. Amaza claims, however, as Mutibwa (1992: 4) also does, that the NRM/A launched a political campaign to counter the widespread animosity toward the Acholi. Indeed, in the political program of the NRM, the third paragraph makes explicit reference to the "elimination of all forms of sectarianism" (reproduced in, e.g., Museveni 1992: 279–280).

7. *Lakwena* means "messenger" or "link" (from *kwena*, "message"). Alice Auma claimed to be the messenger of the holy spirits who possessed her. In popular discourse, therefore, the medium Alice Auma is most often referred to as Alice [the] Lakwena. Some of my informants found this confusing, even incorrect, since a lakwena only brings messages between living persons, for example, in marriage preparations or other interclan affairs. According to their understanding, the lakwena is not the medium between the human and extrahuman worlds, which instead is the work of the healer and spirit medium called *ajwaka* (*ajwaki* in plural). A change in meaning of the word *lakwena* can be traced to missionaries who translated the biblical word "apostle" with *lakwena*. Not only Alice Auma but also Pentecostal Christians claim to be *lukwena* (plural of *lakwena*), in bringing the gospel of God. To make things even more complicated, Behrend (1999a: 134) suggests that the supreme Holy Spirit and over-all commander among the many spirits who possessed Alice Auma had Lakwena as his personal name.

8. In the course of time, armed resistance in northern Uganda came together under the leadership of Joseph Kony. His movement was initially called the Holy Spirit Movement. In 1988, it changed name to the Lord's Army, then to United Holy Salvation Army, and later, as some leading UPDM/A insurgents joined, to the United Democratic Christian Movement/Army. Today it is known as the Lord's Resistance Army/Movement or more commonly just as the Lord's Resistance Army (see Behrend 1999a: chap. 10; Lamwaka 1998; Nyeko and Lucima 2002).

9. The two ministers, Erinayo Oryema and Charles Oboth-Ofumbi, were assassinated together with Anglican archbishop Janan Luwum. Oryema and Luwum were both of Acholi origin, while Oboth-Ofumbi was Jopadhola.

3. REBEL MANIFESTOS IN CONTEXT

1. In 2003, the *kabake* meetings were censured by the Ugandan authorities, which instead initiated a new sort of meeting under their control, called *te yat* (under the

tree). This means, as a young man told me, that "participants do not speak their minds freely."

2. During additional fieldwork in 2005, I found out that by then the fee had been heavily subsidized, but still, to give an example, a child consultation remains three times more expensive than it is at the nearby missionary hospital. In Gulu's state-run hospital, such a consultation would be free, but again, the services are insufficient and infested with demands for extra money.

3. By introducing the terms "disconnection" and "abjection" to the anthropology of modernity and development, Ferguson (1999) aims to recapture the experience of his Copperbelt informants. Their stories of unemployment and economic decline articulate the sense that the promises of modernization had been betrayed, that people were now expelled, or discarded, from the developments of the rest of the world, notably the West.

4. According to statistics given to me in Gulu, in Gulu district (then including also Amuru) only 9 percent of the voting population voted for Museveni in the 1996 presidential elections; in Kitgum district (then including also Pader) 8 percent voted for him (see also Amnesty International 1999: 7, n. 7). In 2001, 11.94 percent voted for Museveni in Gulu (including Amuru), and 4.16 percent in Kitgum (including Pader). In 2006, 13.21 percent of votes cast in Gulu (including Amuru) were for Museveni, 18.85 percent in Kitgum, and 17.64 percent in Pader, but it is widely held in northern Uganda that these elections were rigged in favor of the incumbent. Kizza Besigye, the main challenger to Museveni in the 2001 and 2006 elections, in 2001 received 81.42 percent in Gulu (including Amuru) and 85.99 percent in Kitgum (including Pader). In 2006 Besigye received 82.37 percent in Gulu (including Amuru), 75.47 percent in Kitgum and 77.32 percent in Pader. See http://www.ec.or.ug.

5. See also, to mention only a few other sources, BBC online (October 22, 2004; March 4, 5, 2002; July 3, 2002; August 11, 2002; October 22, 30, 31, 2002; November 25, 2002); CNN online (September 14, 15, 2002); *East African*, June 23, 2003; *New York Times*, January 25, 2003. For more references to media reports in this vein, see Ehrenreich 1998: 100, n. 17.

6. Clive Gordon directed and Graham Shrimpton edited the film, which was produced by October Films for Channel Four (United Kingdom) and DR TV (Denmark).

7. As indicated by Johansen (1997), one of the volunteer researchers behind the film, the team worked closely with the Ugandan army. I doubt that the introductory clippings are from the Kampala-Gulu highway. In the film, the road that the viewer sees is mostly unpaved, not the paved tarmac that is the case with the Kampala-Gulu highway, suggesting instead that the clippings are from the team's travels within northern Uganda and southern Sudan.

8. Also translated is rebel leader Joseph Kony's praise of "Mama Betty," the only person he claims that he trusts. Betty Bigombe was the Ugandan minister who led

the talks on behalf of the Ugandan government, and to call her "Mama" was of course a gesture of politeness. Nevertheless the praise of "Mama Betty" is left without commentary, and although some brief archival clippings of Bigombe were presented at the beginning of the film, again the less informed viewer is encouraged to draw wrong conclusions, for example, that "Mama Betty" is one of the many spirits that possess Joseph Kony.

9. A notable exception is Human Rights Watch (1997: 31), which acknowledges that this idea is common in media but a misleading oversimplification.

10. See also *Daily Monitor*, October 15, 19, 23, 2001; *New Vision*, October 10, 2001.

11. This happened before the Ugandan government decided to support the military opposition of Kabila's government, which gave a new dimension to the pragmatics of the region's proxy wars.

12. The website, located on a server in the United States, disappeared from the Internet in late 2001, or around the time when the LRA/M was included on the terrorist exclusion list of the USA Patriot Act (U.S. Department of State 2001).

13. See also *Daily Monitor*, October 23, 2001; April 18, 2003.

4. DISPLACEMENTS

1. I will not embark on an assessment of the enormous bulk of material, but instead focus on my own research in the camps, conducted mainly in 1997–1998, 1999–2000, and 2002. I agree with the World Health Organization report that argues that "it seems clear that a negotiated, peaceful settlement of the conflict would be the best single intervention to reduce suffering in the Acholi Region" and that "the ethics of repeated surveys are questionable, especially when clear evidence of insufficient humanitarian assistance already exists, and precious funds could be spent on direct relief" (World Health Organization et al. 2005: 35, 37). Still, the perhaps best resource regarding humanitarians report is the Kampala-based Refugee Law Project; see http://www.refugeelawproject.org.

2. Email group discussion, received March 23, 2006. Samson Mande, an army colonel and formerly a close associate to President Museveni, fled Uganda in 2001, accused by the government as one of the masterminds behind a rebel group called People's Redemption Army. To be labeled a rebel or a rebel collaborator is a faith he shares with many in opposition to the government. He is now based in Sweden and acts for the Forum for Democratic Change (FDC) in the Scandinavian diaspora.

3. For several years, the situation for Kitgum and Pader districts was somehow different. There the moves to the camps have been carried out on a more voluntary basis, and the relation between the Ugandan army and the local population is reported to be more cordial than in Gulu and Amuru (Olaa 2001; ARLPI 2001: 10).

4. According to one report, the government waited about one month after the camps had been established before it started to develop any strategy to handle the health, sanitation, safety, and food issues among the displaced people (ARLPI 2001: 11).

5. The religious leaders in northern Uganda explicitly refer to these words of the Bible. "Let my people go" is the title of their well-researched report on the difficult plight of the people in the camps (ARLPI 2001).

6. The words *kac* and *abila* are synonyms, I was frequently told (see also p'Bitek 1971: 104, n. 8). More precisely, however, Malandra (1939: 34) suggests that *kac* refers to the sacred tree of the patrilineage or the clan, while *abila* refers to the small hut or construction to which sacrifices are presented (house of the spirit, *ot jok*), often located under or next to the ancestral tree. In support of this argument, I was told by some informants that *kac* is for the lineage or the clan, while *abila* is for the family and the homestead. More generally, informants used the word *kac* when talking about rites of solidarity between the living and the dead in context of the clan, which they contrasted with the individual salvation promoted by, among others, Pentecostal Christians. "Born-agains will not go to their clan mates' funerals," I was typically told.

7. According to the initial instructions, the volunteers were to take a sample of 10 percent of the population; later instructions, which the volunteers claimed were not made explicit to them, required a higher percentage to be selected for the sample.

8. The case was first reported by Kitgum Deanery Catholic Commission for Justice and Peace (1998).

5. WARTIME RUMORS AND MORAL TRUTHS

1. A similar version of Mbembe's article in *Africa* (Mbembe 1992b) was published in *Public Culture* (Mbembe 1992a) as well. I refer mainly to the *Africa* version, which seems to be the most elaborated one. The main difference is that the paragraph called "The domain of drunkards," from which at least one of my quotations is taken, is included only in the *Africa* version. The *Africa* version has also appeared as chapter 3 in a book (Mbembe 2001).

2. About five thousand people were netted, according to the *Daily Monitor* (January 17, 2000), Uganda's daily independent. The figure of the state-owned *New Vision* (January 17, 2000) is considerably lower. Leaving out the issue of *panda gari*, the paper wrote that "about 300 people were netted in security operations in Gulu town."

3. See *Daily Monitor* (July 6, 2003); *New Vision* (July 6, 2004). The official statistics can be compared with the statistics of the World Health Organization, which for 2001 sets the figure of HIV-infected adult people (15–49 years) in Uganda at 5 percent of the country's adult population. In neighboring Kenya, the figure is 15 percent, in Tanzania almost 8 percent. In Botswana, one of Africa's most severely affected countries, almost 39 percent are infected (World Health Organization 2002). Allen (2006a) questions the reportedly high infection rate in northern Uganda.

4. All infected cases originated from Gulu. Of the 425 confirmed cases, 93 percent (393 cases) were reported in Gulu district. Of the 27 cases in neighboring Masindi

district and the 5 cases in Mbarara district, southern Uganda, all "were initiated by movement of infected contacts of EHF [Ebola hemorrhagic fever] cases from Gulu" (World Health Organization 2001: 46). The World Health Organization sets the total case-fatality rate at 53 percent. Among infected children below fifteen years of age, the case-fatality rate was higher, 85 percent. It can be noted that far from every reported case was confirmed with laboratory tests.

5. See *Daily Monitor* (October 18, 23, 27, 2000; November 9, 2000); *Pan African News* (October 21, 2000); *Washington Post* (October 17, 21, 2000). In epidemiological terminology, "The virus associated with this [Gulu] outbreak is Ebola-Sudan and differed at the nucleotide sequence level from earlier Ebola-Sudan isolates by 3.3% and 4.2% in the polymerase (362 nucleotides) and nucleocapsid (146 nucleotides) protein encoding genes, respectively" (World Health Organization 2001: 41). Strictly speaking, however, this does not prove any particular geographical origin for the Gulu outbreak.

6. UPROOTING THE PUMPKINS

1. Informants claimed that landmines that the Ugandan army uses were manufactured in government-run but now decommissioned facilities in Nakasongola in Luwero in central Uganda, something that is suggested also by Landmine Monitor (2006).

2. Already in the 1980s, Alice Lakwena and the Holy Spirit Movement introduced some of these regulations, such as the ban on pork, alcohol, and cigarettes, for which they found inspiration from the Bible (see Behrend 1991: 168–169).

3. Most likely, the rebels were also afraid of being poisoned. During the talks, rebel leader Joseph Kony explicitly referred to failures of previous peace talks and raised the issue of some high-ranking rebels who had accepted an amnesty in the 1980s, only to die in ambiguous circumstances, some while imprisoned on treason charges despite the amnesty, and perhaps, it is alleged, poisoned.

4. John Akec, "Northern Uganda has lived on a knife's edge for too long" (July 2, 2006). See http://johnakecsouthsudan.blogspot.com.

ADF	Allied Democratic Forces
ARLPI	Acholi Religious Leaders' Peace Initiative
CAMP	Citizens' Army for Multiparty Politics
DP	Democratic Party
FDC	Forum for Democratic Change
FOBA	Force Obote Back Again
HSMs	Holy Spirit movements
HSMF	Holy Spirit Mobile Forces
KAR	King's African Rifles
KY	Kabaka Yekka (The King Alone)
LA	Lord's Army (renamed UHSA)
LCs	local councils (previously RCs)
LDU	local defense units
LRA/M	Lord's Resistance Army/Movement
NALU	National Army for the Liberation of Uganda
NOM	Ninth October Movement
NRM/A	National Resistance Movement/Army (NRA changed name to UPDF)
PRA	People's Redemption Army
RCs	resistance councils (renamed LCs)
RDC	resident district commissioner

RUF/SL	Revolutionary United Front/Sierra Leone
SPLM/A	Sudan People's Liberation Movement/Army
UDCM/A	United Democratic Christian Movement/Army (changed name to LRA/M)
UFM/A	Uganda Freedom Movement/Army
UHSA	United Holy Salvation Army (changed name to UDCM/A)
UNC	Uganda National Congress (renamed UPC)
UNLA	Uganda National Liberation Army
UNRF	Uganda National Rescue Front
UNRF II	Uganda National Rescue Front Part II
UPA	Uganda People's Army
UPC	Uganda People's Congress
UPDF	Uganda People's Defence Forces
UPDM/A	Uganda People's Democratic Movement/Army
WNBF	West Nile Bank Front

REFERENCES

Aasland, Tertit. 1974. *On the move to the left in Uganda, 1969–1971: The Common Man's Charter, dissemination and attitude.* Uppsala: Nordic Africa Institute.

Abu-Lughod, Lila. 1986. *Veiled sentiments: Honor and poetry in a Bedouin society.* Berkeley: University of California Press.

———. 1989. Zone of theory in the anthropology of the Arab world. *Annual Review of Anthropology* 18: 267–306.

———. 1993. *Writing women's worlds: Bedouin stories.* Berkeley: University of California Press.

Adimola, Andrew B. 1954. The Lamogi rebellion, 1911–12. *Uganda Journal: The Journal of the Uganda Society* 18 (2): 166–177.

African Rights. 2000. *Northern Uganda: Justice in conflict.* London: African Rights.

Agamben, Giorgio. 1998. *Homo sacer: Sovereign power and bare life.* Stanford, Calif.: Stanford University Press.

Allen, Tim. 1988–1989. Violence and moral knowledge: Observing social trauma in Sudan and Uganda. *Cambridge Anthropology* 13 (2): 45–66.

———. 1991. Understanding Alice: Uganda's Holy Spirit Movement in context. *Africa.* 61 (3): 370–399.

———. 1994. Ethnicity and tribalism on the Sudan-Uganda border. In *Ethnicity and conflict in the Horn of Africa*, edited by Katsuyoshi Fukui and John Markakis. London: James Currey; Athens: Ohio University Press.

———. 1996a. A flight from refugee: The return of refugees from southern Sudan to northeast Uganda in the late 1980s. In *In search for cool grounds: War, flight and homecoming in northeast Africa*, edited by Tim Allen. London: UNRISD/James Currey; Trenton, N.J.: Africa World Press.

———. 1996b. Review of Ronald R. Atkinson's The roots of ethnicity: The origins of the Acholi of Uganda before 1800. *Africa.* 66 (3): 472–475.

——. 1999. Perceiving contemporary wars. In *The media of conflict: War reporting and representations of ethnic violence*, edited by Tim Allen and Jean Seaton. London: Zed Books.

——. 2000. Understanding health: Biomedicine and local knowledge in northern Uganda. In *Health Promotion: New discipline or multi-discipline?*, edited by Ricca Edmondson and Cecily Kelleher. Dublin: Irish Academic Press.

——. 2006a. Aids and evidence: Interogating some Ugandan myths. *Journal of Biosocial Science.* 38(1): 7–28.

——. 2006b. *Trial justice: The International Criminal Court and the Lord's Resistance Army.* London: Zed Books.

Allen, Tim, and Jean Seaton. 1999. Introduction. In *The media of conflict: War reporting and representations of ethnic violence*, edited by Tim Allen and Jean Seaton. London and New York: Zed Books.

Allen, Tim, and David Turton. 1996. Introduction: In search for cool grounds. In *In search for cool ground: War, flight and homecoming in northeast Africa*, edited by Tim Allen. London: UNRISD/James Currey.

Amaza, Ondoga. 1998. *Museveni's long march from guerrilla to statesman.* Kampala: Fountain Publishers.

Amnesty International. 1992. *Uganda: The failure to safeguard human rights.* London: Amnesty International.

——. 1997. *"Breaking God's Commands": The destruction of childhood by the Lord's Resistance Army.* Amnesty International Country Report, AFR 59/01/97. PDF version downloaded September 10, 2002, from http://www.amnesty.org.

——. 1999. *Uganda breaking the circle: Protecting human rights in the northern war zone.* Amnesty International Report, AFR 59/01/99. PDF version downloaded September 10, 2002, from http://www.amnesty.org.

Anywar, Reuben S. 1948. The life of rwot Iburaim Awich. *Uganda Journal.* 12 (1): 72–81.

——. 1954. *Acoli ki ker megi (Acholi customs).* Kampala: Eagle Press.

Apuuli, Kasaija Phillip. 2006. The ICC arrest warrants for the Lord's Resistance Army leaders and peace prospects for northern Uganda. *Journal of International Criminal Justice* 4 (1): 179–187.

Arendt, Hannah. 1970. *On violence.* New York: Harcourt Brace.

Aretxaga, Begoña. 1997. *Shattering silence: Women, nationalism, and political subjectivity in Northern Ireland.* Princeton, N.J.: Princeton University Press.

Århem, Kaj. 1994. Antropologins mening: En introduktion. In *Den antropologiska erfarenheten*, edited by Kaj Århem. Stockholm: Carlsson Bokförlag.

ARLPI. 2001. *Let my people go: The forgotten plight of the people in displaced camps in Acholi: An assessment carried out by the Acholi Religious Leaders Peace Initiative and the Justice and Peace Commission of Gulu Archdiocese.* Gulu, Uganda: Acholi Religious Leaders Peace Initiative (ARLPI) and the Justice and Peace Commission of Gulu Archdiocese. HTML version downloaded September 5, 2002, from http://www.acholipeace.org.

———. 2002a. Acholibreaks news update January 20, 2002. Gulu, Uganda: Acholi Religious Leaders Peace Initiative (ARLPI). Downloaded February 2, 2002, from http://www.acholipeace.org.

———. 2002b. *Seven times seven: The impact of the amnesty law in Acholi.* Gulu, Uganda: Acholi Religious Leaders Peace Initiative (ARLPI).

Arweny, Levy A. N.d. Acholi traditional approaches to human conflicts. Unpublished document.

Atkinson, Ronald R. 1978. A history of the western Acholi of Uganda, c. 1675–1900: A study in the utilization and analysis of oral data. Ph.D. dissertation. Northwestern University, Evanston, Ill.

———. 1984. "State" formation & language in westernmost Acholi in the eighteenth century. In *State formation in East Africa*, edited by Ahmed Idha Salim. Nairobi: Heinemann Educational Books.

———. 1989. The evolution of ethnicity among the Acholi of Uganda: The precolonial phase. *Ethnohistory* 36 (1): 19–43.

———. 1994. *The roots of ethnicity: The origins of the Acholi of Uganda before 1800.* Philadelphia: University of Pennsylvania Press.

———. 1999. The (re)constitution of ethnicity in Africa: Extending the chronology, conceptualisation and discourse. In *Ethnicity and nationalism in Africa: Constructivist reflections and contemporary politics*, edited by Paris Yeros. London: Macmillan; New York: St. Martin's Press.

Baker, Samuel White. 1866. *The Albert N'yanza: Great Basin of the Nile and explorations of the Nile sources.* London: Macmillan.

———. 1874. *Ismailïa: A narrative of the expedition to Central Africa for the suppression of the slave trade, organized by Ismail, khedive of Egypt.* London: Macmillan.

———. 1875. *Ismailia: Berättelse om den af Ismail, khediv af Egypten, för undertryckande af slafhandeln i Centralafrika utsände expedition.* Stockholm: Albert Bonniers förlag.

Barnes, Catherine, and Okello Lucima. 2002. Introduction. In *Protracted conflict, elusive peace: Initiatives to end the violence in northern Uganda*, edited by Okello Lucima. London: Conciliation Resources and Kacoke Madit.

Barth, Fredrik. 1969. Introduction to *Ethnic groups and boundaries: The social organization of cultural difference*, edited by Fredrik Barth. Oslo: Scandinavian University Press.

Bauman, Zygmunt. 1998. *Globalization: The human consequences.* Cambridge: Polity Press.

Bayart, Jean-Francois, Stephen Ellis, and Béatrice Hibou. 1999. *The criminalization of the state in Africa.* Oxford: International African Institute/James Currey; Bloomington: Indiana University Press.

Behrend, Heike. 1991. Is Alice Lakwena a witch? The Holy Spirit Movement and its fight against evil in the north of Uganda. In *Changing Uganda: The dilemmas of structural adjustment and revolutionary change*, edited by Holger Bernt Hansen and Michael Twaddle. London: James Currey; Kampala: Fountain Press; Athens: Ohio University Press; Nairobi: Heinemann Kenya.

——. 1995. The Holy Spirit Movement and the forces of nature in the north of Uganda 1985–1987. In *Religion and politics in East Africa: The period since independence*, edited by Holger Bernt Hansen and Michael Twaddle. London: James Currey; Nairobi: EAEP; Kampala: Fountain Publishers; Athens: Ohio University Press.

——. 1998a. The Holy Spirit Movement's new world: Discourse and development in the north of Uganda. In *Developing Uganda*, edited by Holger Bernt Hansen and Michael Twaddle. Oxford: James Currey; Kampala: EAEP; Athens: Ohio University Press.

——. 1998b. War in northern Uganda: The Holy Spirit Movements of Alice Lakwena, Severino Lukoya and Joseph Kony (1986–1997). In *African guerrillas*, edited by Christopher Clapham. Oxford: James Currey; Kampala: Fountain Press; Bloomington: Indiana University Press.

——. 1999a. *Alice Lakwena & the Holy Spirits: War in northern Uganda, 1985–97.* Oxford: James Currey; Kampala: Fountain Publishers; Nairobi: EAEP; Athens: Ohio University Press.

——. 1999b. Power to heal power to kill: Spirit possession and war in northern Uganda (1986–1994). In *Spirit possession, modernity and power in Africa*, edited by Heike Behrend and Ute Luig. Oxford: James Currey; Kampala: Fountain Publishers; Cape Town: David Philip; Madison: University of Wisconsin Press.

Bere, Rennie M. 1946. Awich: A biographical note and a chapter of Acholi history. *Uganda Journal* 10 (2): 76–78.

——. 1947. An outline of Acholi history. *Uganda Journal.* 11 (1): 1–8.

——. 1955. Land and chieftainship among the Acholi. *Uganda Journal* 19 (1): 49–56.

Bond, George Clement, and Joan Vincent. 2002. The moving frontier of AIDS in Uganda: Contexts, texts, and concepts. In *Contested terrains and constructed categories: Contemporary Africa in focus*, edited by George Clement Bond and Nigel C. Gibson. Boulder, Colo.: Westview Press.

Bracken, Patrick J. 1998. Hidden agendas: Deconstructing PTSD. In *Rethinking the trauma of war*, edited by Patrick J. Bracken and Celia Petty. London: Free Association Books/Save the Children.

Branch, Adam. 2005. Neither peace nor justice: Political violence and the peasantry in northern Uganda, 1986–1998. *African Studies Quarterly: The Online Journal for African Studies* 8 (2): 1–31.

Brett, E. A. 1994. The military and democratic transition in Uganda. In *From chaos to order: The politics of constitution-making in Uganda*, edited by Holger Bernt Hansen and Michael Twaddle. Kampala: Fountain Publishers; London: James Currey.

——. 1995. Neutralising the use of force in Uganda: The role of the military in politics. *Journal of Modern African Studies* 33 (1): 129–152.

Bucholtz, Mary. 2002. Youth and cultural practice. *Annual Review of Anthropology* 31: 525–552.

Butt, Audrey. 1952. *The Nilotes of the Anglo-Egyptian Sudan and Uganda*. London: International African Institute.

Carrithers, Michael. 1992. *Why humans have cultures: Explaining anthropology and social diversity*. Oxford: Oxford University Press.

Chabal, Patrick, and Jean-Pascal Daloz. 1999. *Africa works: Disorder as political instrument*. Oxford: International African Institute and James Currey; Bloomington: Indiana University Press.

Cohen, David William, and E. S. Atieno Odhiambo. 1989. *Siaya: The historical anthropology of an African landscape*. London: James Currey; Nairobi: Heineman; Athens: Ohio University Press.

Connerton, Paul. 1989. *How societies remember*. Cambridge: Cambridge University Press.

Crazzolara, J. Pasquale. 1950. *The Lwoo, part I, Lwoo migrations*. Verona: Museum Combonianum/Istituto missioni africane.

Crazzolara, J. Pasquale. 1951. *The Lwoo part II: Lwoo traditions*. Verona: Museum Combonianum/Instituto missioni africane.

———. 1954. *The Lwoo part III: Lwoo clans*. Verona: Museum Combonianum/Instituto missioni africane.

Crisp, Jeff. 1986. Uganda refugees in Sudan and Zaire: The problem of repatriation. *African Affairs*. 85(339): 163–180.

Daniel, Valentine E., and John Chr. Knudsen. 1995. Introduction to *Mistrusting refugees*, edited by Valentine E. Daniel and John C. Knudsen. Berkeley: University of California Press.

Das, Veena. 1995. *Critical events: An anthropological perspective on contemporary India*. Delhi: Oxford University Press.

Das, Veena, and Arthur Kleinman. 2000. Introduction to *Violence and subjectivity*, edited by Veena Das, Arthur Kleinman, Mamphela Ramphele, and Pamela Reynolds. Berkeley: University of California Press.

———. 2001. Introduction to *Remaking a world: Violence, social suffering and recovery*, edited by Veena Das, Arthur Kleinman, Margret Lock, Mamphela Ramphele, and Pamela Reynolds. Berkeley: University of California Press.

de Berry, Joanna. 2000. Life after loss: An anthropological study of post-war recovery, Teso, east Uganda, with special reference to young people. Ph.D. dissertation, London School of Economic and Political Science.

De Boeck, Filip. 1998. The rootedness of trees: Place as cultural and natural texture in rural southwest Congo. In *Locality and belonging*, edited by Nadia Lovell. London: Routledge.

de Certeau, Michel. 1984. *The practice of everyday life*. Berkeley: University of California Press.

De Temmerman, Els. 2001. *Aboke girls: Children abducted in northern Uganda.* Kampala: Fountain Publishers.

Diawara, Manthia. 1998. Toward a regional imaginary in Africa. In *The cultures of globalization*, edited by Fredric Jameson and Masao Miyoshi. Durham: Duke University Press.

Dolan, Chris. 2000. What do you remember? A rough guide to the war in northern Uganda, 1986–2000. *Cope working paper no. 33.* London: ACORD. PDF version downloaded July 14, 2003, from http://www.acord.org.uk.

——. 2002a. Collapsing masculinities and weak states: A case study of northern Uganda. In *Masculinities matter! Men, gender and development*, edited by Frances Cleaver. London: Zed Books; Cape Town: David Philip.

——. 2002b. Which children count? The politics of children's rights in northern Uganda. In *Protracted conflict, elusive peace: Initiatives to end the violence in northern Uganda*, edited by Okello Lucima. London: Conciliation Resources and Kacoke Madit.

——. 2005. Understanding war and its continuation: The case of northern Uganda. Ph.D. dissertation. University of London.

Donga, J. J., and Levy A. Arweny. N.d. Brief history of Acholi from about the year 2247 BC—1997 AD. Unpublished document.

Doom, Ruddy, and Koen Vlassenroot. 1999. Kony's message: A new Koine? The Lord's Resistance Army in northern Uganda. *African Affairs* 98 (390): 5–36.

Douglas, Mary. 1966. *Purity and danger: An analysis of the concepts of pollution and taboo.* London: Routledge.

Dwyer, John Orr. 1972. The Acholi of Uganda: Adjustment to imperialism. Ph.D. dissertation. Columbia University, New York.

Dyson-Hudson, Neville. 1966. *Karimojong politics.* Oxford: Clarendon Press.

Ehrenreich, Rosa. 1998. The stories we must tell: Ugandan children and the atrocities of the Lord's Resistance Army. *Africa Today* 45 (1): 79–102.

Englund, Harri. 2002a. Ethnography after globalism: Migration and emplacement in Malawi. *American Ethnologist* 29 (2): 261–286.

——. 2002b. *From war to peace on the Mozambique-Malawi borderland.* Edinburgh: Edinburgh University Press, for the International African Institute, London.

Evans-Pritchard, E. E. 1937. *Witchcraft, oracles and magic among the Azande.* Oxford: Clarendon Press.

——. 1940. *The Nuer: A description of the modes of livelihood and political institutions of a Nilotic people.* Oxford: Clarendon Press.

——. 1949. *The Sanusi of Cyrenaica.* Oxford: Clarendon Press.

——. 1950. Nilotic studies. *Journal of the Royal Anthropological Institute of Great Britain and Ireland* 80 (1–2): 1–6.

——. 1951. *Kinship and marriage among the Nuer.* Oxford: Clarendon Press.

——. 1956. *Nuer religion.* Oxford: Oxford University Press.

——. 1965. *The position of women in primitive societies and other essays in social anthropology*. London: Faber and Faber.

Ferguson, James. 1999. *Expectations of modernity: Myths and meanings of urban life on the Zambian Copperbelt*. Berkeley: University of California Press.

Fernandez, James W. 1985. Exploded worlds: Text as a metaphor for ethnography (and vice versa). *Dialectical Anthropology* 10 (1–2): 15–26.

——. 1986. *Persuasions and performances: The play of tropes in culture*. Bloomington: Indiana University Press.

Feyerabend, Paul K. 1993. *Against method: Outline of an anarchistic theory of knowledge*. 3rd ed. London: Verso.

——. 1995. *Killing time: The autobiography of Paul Feyerabend*. Chicago: University of Chicago Press.

Finnström, Sverker. 2001. In and out of culture: Fieldwork in war-torn Uganda. *Critique of Anthropology* 21(3): 247–258.

——. 2003. Living with bad surroundings: War and existential uncertainty in Acholiland, northern Uganda. Ph.D. dissertation. Uppsala.

——. 2005. "For God and my life": War and cosmology in northern Uganda. In *No peace, no war: An anthropology of contemporary armed conflicts*, edited by Paul Richards. Oxford: James Currey.

——. 2006a. Wars of the past and war in the present: The Lord's Resistance Movement/Army in Uganda. *Africa* 76 (2): 200–220.

——. 2006b. Survival in war-torn Uganda. *Anthropology Today* 22 (2): 12–15.

——. 2006c. Meaningful rebels? Young adult perceptions on the Lord's Resistance Movement/Army in Uganda. In *Navigating youth, generating adulthood: Social becoming in an African context*, edited by Catrine, Christiansen, Mats Utas and Henrik Vigh. Uppsala: Nordic Africa Institute.

Fortes, Meyer, and E. E. Evans-Pritchard. 1940. Introduction to *African political systems*, edited by Meyer Fortes and E. E. Evans-Pritchard. Oxford: Oxford University Press/International African Institute.

Fox, Richard G. 1985. *Lions of the Punjab: Culture in the making*. Berkeley: University of California Press.

Fukui, Katsuyoshi, and John Markakis. 1994. Introduction to *Ethnicity and conflict in the Horn of Africa*, edited by Katsuyoshi Fukui and John Markakis. London: James Currey; Athens: Ohio University Press.

Fukuyama, Francis. 1992. *The end of history and the last man*. New York: Free Press/ Maxwell Macmillan International.

Furley, Oliver. 1989. Britain and Uganda from Amin to Museveni: Blind eye diplomacy. In *Conflict resolution in Uganda*, edited by Kumar Rupesinghe. Oslo: International Peace Research Institute; London: James Currey; Athens: Ohio University Press.

Furley, Oliver. 1995. Child soldiers in Africa. In *Conflict in Africa*, edited by Oliver Furley. London: I. B. Tauris Publishers.

Galtung, Johan. 1969. Violence, peace and peace research. *Journal of Peace Research* 6 (3): 167–191.

Gersony, Robert. 1997. The anguish of northern Uganda: Results of a field-based assessment of the civil conflict in northern Uganda. Report submitted to United States Embassy, Kampala and USAID Mission, Kampala.

Gertzel, Cherry. 1974. *Party and locality in northern Uganda, 1945–1962.* London: University of London/Athlone Press.

Giddens, Anthony. 1991. *Modernity and self-identity: Self and society in the late modern age.* Cambridge: Polity Press.

Gingyera-Pinycwa, A. G. G. 1978. *Apolo Milton Obote and his times.* New York: NOK Publishers.

——. 1989. Is there a northern question? In *Conflict resolution in Uganda*, edited by Kumar Rupesinghe. Oslo: International Peace Research Institute; London: James Currey; Athens: Ohio University Press.

——. 1992. *Northern Uganda in national politics.* Kampala: Fountain Publishers.

Girling, Frank Knowles. 1960. *The Acholi of Uganda.* London: Her Majesty's Stationery Office.

Glenthworth, Garth, and Ian Hancock. 1973. Obote and Amin: Change and continuity in modern Uganda politics. *African Affairs* 72 (288): 237–255.

Global Witness. 2003. *For a few dollars more: How al Qaeda moved into the diamond trade.* London: Global Watch. PDF version downloaded May 16, 2003, from http://www.globalwitness.org.

Gray, John Milner. 1951. Acholi history, 1860–1901 (part I). *Uganda Journal.* 15(2): 121–143.

——. 1952a. Acholi history, 1860–1901 (part II). *Uganda Journal.* 16(1): 32–50.

——. 1952b. Acholi history, 1860–1901 (part III). *Uganda Journal.* 16(2): 132–144.

Greenberg, J. H. 1955. *Studies in African linguistic classification.* New Haven: Compass.

Grove, E. T. N. 1919. Customs of the Acholi. *Sudan Notes and Records* 2 (3): 157–182.

Guha, Ranajit. 1997. *Dominance without hegemony: History and power in colonial India.* Cambridge: Cambridge University Press.

Gulu Archdiocese. 2001. *Justice and Peace News: A monthly newsletter of the Justice and Peace Commission of Gulu Archdiocese.* 1 (2).

——. 2002. *Justice and Peace News: A monthly newsletter of the Justice and Peace Commission of Gulu Archdiocese.* 2 (5).

——. 2003a. *Justice and Peace News: A monthly newsletter of the Justice and Peace Commission of Gulu Archdiocese.* 2 (8).

——. 2003b. *Justice and Peace News: A monthly newsletter of the Justice and Peace Commission of Gulu Archdiocese.* 2 (10).

——. 2003c. *Justice and Peace News: A monthly newsletter of the Justice and Peace Commission of Gulu Archdiocese.* 3 (2).

Gulu Independent Hospital. N.d. Gulu Independent Hospital, information brochure. Gulu: Gulu Independent Hospital. Information available also online: http://www.guluindependenthospital.com.

Hagborg, Lars. 2001. Silence: Disputes on the ground and in the mind among the Iraqw in Karatu district, Tanzania. Ph.D. dissertation. Uppsala University.

Hansen, Holger Bernt. 1977. Ethnicity and military rule in Uganda: A study of ethnicity as a political factor in Uganda, based on a discussion of political anthropology and the application of its results. *Research Report no. 43.* Uppsala: Nordic Africa Institute.

Hansen, Holger Bernt, and Michael Twaddle. 1994. The issues. In *From chaos to order: The politics of constitution-making in Uganda,* edited by Holger Bernt Hansen and Michael Twaddle. Kampala: Fountain Publishers; London: James Currey.

Harrell-Bond, Barbara E. 1986. *Imposing aid: Emergency assistance to refugees.* Oxford: Oxford University Press.

Henriques, Peter. 2002. Peace without reconciliation: War, peace, and experience among the Iteso of east Uganda. Ph.D. dissertation. University of Copenhagen.

Heron, G. A. 1976. *The poetry of Okot p'Bitek.* London: Heinemann.

Hewlett, Barry W., and Richard P. Amola. 2003. The cultural contexts of Ebola in northern Uganda. *Emerging Infectious Diseases* 9 (10): 1242–1248.

Hobsbawm, Eric J., and Terence O. Ranger. 1983. *The invention of tradition.* Cambridge: Cambridge University Press.

Hochschild, Adam. 1998. *King Leopold's ghost: A story of greed, terror, and heroism in colonial Africa.* Boston: Houghton Mifflin.

Höglund, Anna. 2001. Kvinnor, krig och mänskliga rättigheter. In *Mänskliga rättigheter: Aktuella forskningsfrågor,* edited by Göran Gunner and Sia Spiliopoulou Åkermark. Uppsala: Iustus Förlag.

Hornborg, Alf. 2001. *The power of the machine: Global inequalities of economy, technology, and environment.* Walnut Creek, Calif.: AltaMira Press.

Human Rights Watch. 1997. *The scars of death: Children abducted by the Lord's Resistance Army in Uganda.* New York: Human Rights Watch.

——. 1999. *Hostile to democracy: The Movement system and political repression in Uganda.* New York: Human Rights Watch.

——. 2003a. *Abducted and abused: Renewed conflict in northern Uganda.* New York: Human Rights Watch. PDF version downloaded July 11, 2003, from http://www.hrw.org.

——. 2003b. *Stolen children: Abduction and recruitment in northern Uganda.* New York: Human Rights Watch. PDF version downloaded March 21, 2003, from http://www.hrw.org.

——. 2005. *Uprooted and forgotten: Impunity and human rights abuses in northern Uganda.* New York: Human Rights Watch. PDF version downloaded November 1, 2006, from http://www.hrw.org.

Huntington, Samuel P. 1996. *The clash of civilizations and the remaking of world order.* New York: Simon and Schuster.

Hutchinson, Sharon Elaine. 1996. *Nuer dilemmas: Coping with money, war, and the state.* Berkeley: University of California Press.

——. 1998. Death, memory and the politics of legitimation: Nuer experiences of the continuing second Sudanese civil war. In *Memory and the postcolony: African anthropology and the critique of power*, edited by Richard Werbner. London: Zed Books.

——. 2001. A curse from God? Religious and political dimensions of the post-1991 rise of ethnic violence in south Sudan. *Journal of Modern African Studies* 39 (2): 307–331.

Hutchinson, Sharon Elaine, and Jok Madut Jok. 2002. Gendered violence and the militarisation of ethnicity. In *Postcolonial subjectivities in Africa*, edited by Richard Werbner. London: Zed Books.

Isegawa, Moses. 2000. *Abyssinian chronicles*. London: Picador.

Isis-WICCE. 1998. *Women's experiences of armed conflict in Uganda: Luwero district 1980–1986*. Kampala: Isis-WICCE (Women's International Cross-Cultural Exchange).

Jackson, Michael. 1989. *Paths toward a clearing: Radical empiricism and ethnographic inquiry*. Bloomington: Indiana University Press.

——. 1996. Introduction: Phenomenology, radical empiricism, and anthropological critique. In *Things as they are: New directions in phenomenological anthropology*, edited by Michael Jackson. Bloomington: Indiana University Press.

——. 1998. *Minima ethnographica: Intersubjectivity and the anthropological project*. Chicago: University of Chicago Press.

——. 2002a. The exterminating angel: Reflections on violence and intersubjective reason. *Focaal: European Journal of Anthropology* (39) : 137–148.

——. 2002b. *The politics of storytelling: Violence, transgression, and intersubjectivity*. Copenhagen: Museum Tusculanum Press, University of Copenhagen.

——. 2005. Storytelling events, violence, and the appearance of the past. *Anthropological Quarterly* 78 (2): 355–375.

James, Wendy. 1990. Introduction to the paperback edition of Evans-Pritchard's *Kinship and marriage among the Nuer*. Oxford: Clarendon Press.

——. 1996. Uduk resettlement: Dreams and realities. In *Search for cool grounds: War, flight and homecoming in northeast Africa*, edited by Tim Allen. Geneva: UNRISD/James Currey; Trenton: Africa World Press.

Johansen, Kim. 1997. Fra en researchers dagbog. *MS-revy Online*. Downloaded January 23, 2003, from http://www.ms.dk.

Jørgensen, Jan Jelmert. 1981. *Uganda: A modern history*. London: Croom Helm.

Kabera, John Baptist, and C. Muyanja. 1994. Homecoming in the Luwero triangle: Experiences of the displaced population of central Uganda following the National Resistance Army victory in 1986. In *When refugees go home: African experiences*, edited by Tim Allen and Hubert Morsink. Geneva: UNRISD/James Currey; Trenton: Africa World Press.

Kabwegyere, Tarsis B. 2000a. Civil society and the democratic transition in Uganda since 1986. In *No-party democracy in Uganda: Myths and realities*, edited by Justus Mugaju and J. Oloka-Onyango. Kampala: Fountain Publishers.

———. 2000b. *People's choice, people's power: Challenges and prospects of democracy in Uganda.* Kampala: Fountain Publishers.

Kaldor, Mary. 1999a. *New and old wars: Organized violence in a global era.* Cambridge: Polity Press.

———. 1999b. The structure of conflict. In *Common security and civil society in Africa*, edited by Lennart Wohlgemuth, Samantha Gibson, Stephen Klasen, and Emma Rothschild. Uppsala: Nordic Africa Institute.

Kapferer, Bruce. 1988. *Legends of people, myths of state: Violence, intolerance, and political culture in Sri Lanka and Australia.* Washington: Smithsonian Institution Press.

Kapferer, Bruce. 2002. Introduction: Outside all reason—magic, sorcery and epistemology in anthropology. In *Beyond rationalism: Rethinking magic, witchcraft and sorcery*, edited by Bruce Kapferer. New York: Berghahn Books.

Karlström, Mikael. 1996. Imagining democracy: Political culture and democratisation in Buganda. *Africa* 66 (4): 485–505.

———. 1999. Civil society and its presuppositions: Lessons from Uganda. In *Civil society and the political imagination in Africa*, edited by John L. Comaroff and Jean Comaroff. Chicago: University of Chicago Press.

———. 2004. Modernity and its aspirants: Moral community and developmental eutopianism in Buganda. *Current Anthropology* 45 (5): 595–619.

Karugire, Samwiri Rubaraza. 1980. *A political history of Uganda.* Nairobi: Heinemann Educational Books.

———. 1996. *Roots of instability in Uganda.* Kampala: Fountain Publishers.

Kasozi, A. B. K. 1999. *The social origins of violence in Uganda, 1964–1985.* Kampala: Fountain Publishers.

Kayunga, Sallie Simba. 2000. The impact of armed opposition on the Movement system in Uganda. In *No-party democracy in Uganda: Myths and realities*, edited by Justus Mugaju and J. Oloka-Onyango. Kampala: Fountain Publishers.

Keitetsi, China. 2003. *Child soldier: Fighting for my life.* Bellevue, South Africa: Jacana.

Kiplagat, Bethuel. 2002. Reaching the 1985 Nairobi agreement. In *Protracted conflict, elusive peace: Initiatives to end the violence in northern Uganda*, edited by Okello Lucima. London: Conciliation Resources and Kacoke Madit.

Kirsch, Stuart. 2002. Rumour and other narratives of political violence in west Papua. *Critique of Anthropology* 22 (1): 53–79.

Kitgum Deanery Catholic Commission for Justice and Peace. 1998. Children killed in UPDF-rebels skirmish. Kitgum (unpublished document).

Kleinman, Arthur. 2000. The violences of everyday life: The multiple forms and dynamics of social violence. In *Violence and subjectivity*, edited by Veena Das, Arthur Kleinman, Mamphela Ramphele, and Pamela Reynolds. Berkeley: University of California Press.

Koch, Klaus Friedrich, Soraya Altorki, Andrew Arno, and Letitia Hickson. 1977. Ritual reconciliation and the obviation of grievances: A comparative study in the ethnography of law. *Ethnology* 16 (3): 269–283.

Kony, Jane Lanyero. 1997. Evaluation of market performance in the war-ravaged north: A case study of sesame marketing in Gulu. BA thesis. Makerere University, Kampala.

Kopytoff, Igor. 1987. The internal African frontier: The making of African political culture. In *The African frontier: The reproduction of traditional African societies*, edited by Igor Kopytoff. Bloomington: Indiana University Press.

Kuper, Adam. 1999. *Culture: The anthropologists' account.* Cambridge, Mass.: Harvard University Press.

Kurkiala, Mikael. 2002. Objectifying the past: Lakota responses to Western historiography. *Critique of Anthropology* 22 (4): 445–460.

Kyemba, Henry. 1977. *A state of blood: The inside story of Idi Amin.* Fountain edition 1997. Kampala: Fountain Publishers.

Laclau, Ernesto, and Chantal Mouffe. 1985. *Hegemony and socialist strategy: Towards a radical democratic politics.* London: Verso.

Lamwaka, Caroline. 1998. Civil war and the peace process in Uganda, 1986–1997. *East African Journal of Peace and Human Rights* 4 (2): 139–169.

——. 2002. The peace process in northern Uganda, 1896–1990. In *Protracted conflict, elusive peace: Initiatives to end the violence in northern Uganda*, edited by Lucima Okello. London: Conciliation Resources and Kacoke Madit.

Landmine Monitor. 2006. Landmine Monitor Report 2006: Toward a mine-free world. Uganda. Downloaded November 2, 2006, from http://www.icbl.org.

Leopold, Mark. 1999. "The war in the north": Ethnicity in Ugandan press explanations of conflict, 1996–97. In *The media of conflict: War reporting and representations of ethnic violence*, edited by Tim Allen and Jean Seaton. London: Zed Books.

——. 2005. *Inside West Nile: Violence, history and representation on an African frontier.* Oxford: James Currey; Santa Fe, N.M.: School of American Research Press; Kampala: Fountain Publishers.

——. 2006. Legacies of slavery in north-west Uganda: The story of the "One-Elevens." *Africa* 76 (2): 180–199.

Leys, Colin. 1967. *Politicians and policies: An essay on politics in Acholi, Uganda, 1962–65.* Nairobi: East African Publishing House.

Lienhardt, R. Godfrey. 1961. *Divinity and experience: The religion of the Dinka.* Oxford: Clarendon Press.

Lindqvist, Sven. 1996. *Exterminate all the brutes.* New York: New Press.

——. 1997. *The skull measurer's mistake and other portraits of men and women who spoke out against racism.* New York: New Press.

Liyong, Taban lo. 1970. *Eating chiefs.* London: Heinemann Educational Books.

Lloyd, Albert B. 1907. *Uganda to Khartoum: Life and adventure on the Upper Nile.* London: Collins' Clear-Type Press.

——. 1948. Extracts from "Mengo notes," part 5: Acholi country 1 and Acholi country 2. *Uganda Journal* 12 (1): 82–92.

Lonsdale, John. 1994. Moral ethnicity and political tribalism. In *Inventions and boundaries: Historical and anthropological approaches to the study of ethnicity and nationalism*, edited by Preben Kaarsholm and Jan Hultin. Roskilde: International Development Studies, Roskilde University.

Lord's Resistance Army/Movement. 1996a. From Lord's Resistance Movement/Army (LRM/A) to all Ugandans. Unpublished document in possession of the author.

——. 1996b. LRA policy definitions and explanations. Unpublished document.

——. 1997a. A brief out look of the struggle, May 1997. Unpublished document.

——. 1997b. An alternative programme for a new Uganda. The Lord's Resistance Movement/Army Manifesto 1997. Unpublished document.

——. 1997c. A case for national reconciliation, peace, democracy and economic prosperity for all Ugandans: The official presentation of the Lord's Resistance Movement/Army (LRM/A), by Dr. James Alfred Obita, secretary for external affairs and mobilisation, and leader of delegation. PDF version downloaded April 15, 2003, from http://www.c-r.org/km.

——. 2001. Unicef determined to finish the people of northern Uganda. Press release May 2001.

——. 2006. Opening statement of the LRA peace delegation Juba—Southern Sudan, 16th July 2006 (unpublished document).

——. N.d. *Lord's Resistance Movement/Army (LRM/A) Manifesto*. Printed pamphlet.

Lowie, Robert H. 1937. *The history of ethnological theory*. New York: Holt, Rinehart and Winston.

Lucima, Okello, ed. 2002. *Protracted conflict, elusive peace: Initiatives to end the violence in northern Uganda*. London: Conciliation Resources and Kacoke Madit.

Malandra, A. 1939. The ancestral shrine of the Acholi. *Uganda Journal* 7 (1): 27–43.

Malinowski, Bronislaw. 1948. *Magic, science and religion, and other essays*. Garden City, N.Y.: Doubleday Anchor Books.

Malkki, Liisa H. 1995. *Purity and exile: Violence, memory, and national cosmology among Hutu refugees in Tanzania*. Chicago: University of Chicago Press.

——. 1996. Speechless emissaries: Refugees, humanitarianism, and dehistoricization. *Cultural Anthropology* 11 (3): 377–404.

Mamdani, Mahmood. 1976. *Politics and class formation in Uganda*. London: Heinemann.

——. 1984. *Imperialism and fascism in Uganda*. Trenton, N.J.: Africa World Press of the Africa Research and Publications Project.

——. 1995a. *And fire does not always beget ash: Critical reflections on the NRM*. Kampala: Monitor.

——. 1995b. Indirect rule, civil society and ethnicity: The African dilemma. In *From post-traditional to post-modern? Interpreting the meaning of modernity in third world urban societies*, edited by Preben Kaarsholm. Roskilde, Denmark: International Development Studies, Roskilde University.

——. 1996. *Citizen and subject: Contemporary Africa and the legacy of late colonialism.* Princeton, N.J.: Princeton University Press.

——. 2001. *When victims become killers: Colonialism, nativism, and the genocide in Rwanda.* Princeton, N.J.: Princeton University Press.

Marchetti, Mario. 1999. *Too long in the dark: The story of the two martyrs of Paimol and their relevance to Uganda today.* Gulu, Uganda: Archdiocese of Gulu.

Markakis, John. 1987. *National and class conflict in the Horn of Africa.* Cambridge: Cambridge University Press.

Matthews, Eric. 2002. *The philosophy of Merleau-Ponty.* Chesham, England: Acumen.

Mazrui, Ali. 1975. *Soldiers and kinsmen in Uganda: The making of a military ethnocracy.* Beverly Hills, Calif.: Sage Publications.

——. 1976. Soldiers as traditionalizers: Military rule and the re-Africanization of Africa. *World Politics* 28 (2): 246–272.

Mbembe, Achille. 1992a. The banality of power and the aesthetics of vulgarity in the postcolony. *Public Culture* 4 (2): 1–30.

——. 1992b. Provisional notes on the postcolony. *Africa* 62 (1): 3–37.

——. 2001. *On the postcolony.* Berkeley, Calif.: University of California Press.

McCleary, Richard C. 1964. Translator's preface to Maurice Merleau-Ponty's *Signs.* Evanston, Ill.: Northwestern University Press.

Merleau-Ponty, Maurice. 1962. *Phenomenology of perception.* London: Routledge and Kegan Paul.

——. 1964a. *The primacy of perception and other essays on phenomenological psychology, the philosophy of art, history and politics.* Evanston, Ill.: Northwestern University Press.

——. 1964b. *Signs.* Evanston, Ill.: Northwestern University Press.

Moorehead, Alan. 1960. *The White Nile.* London: H. Hamilton.

Mounteney-Jephson, A. J. 1890. *Emin Pasha and the rebellion at the equator: A story of nine months' experience in the last of the Soudan provinces.* London: Sampson Low Marston Searle and Rivington.

——. 1891. *Emin Pascha och de upproriske i Sudan.* Stockholm: P. A. Norstedt and Sons.

Movement Secretariat. 1999. *Movement fifteen point programme 1999.* Kampala: Directorate of Information and Public Relations, Movement Secretariat.

Mudoola, Dan M. 1993. *Religion, ethnicity, and politics in Uganda.* Kampala: Fountain Publishers.

Mugaju, Justus and J. Oloka-Onyango, eds. 2000. *No-party democracy in Uganda: Myths and realities.* Kampala: Fountain Publishers.

Munck, Ronaldo. 2000. Deconstructing terror: Insurgency, repression and peace. In *Postmodern insurgencies: Political violence, identity formation, and peacemaking in comparative perspective*, edited by Ronaldo Munck and Purnaka L. de Silva. London: Macmillan Press; New York: St. Martin's Press.

Munck, Ronaldo and Purnaka L. de Silva, eds. 2000. *Postmodern insurgencies: Political violence, identity formation, and peacemaking in comparative perspective*. London: Macmillan Press; New York: St. Martin's Press.

Murdock, George Peter. 1959. *Africa: Its peoples and their culture history*. New York: McGraw-Hill.

Museveni, Yoweri K. 1992. *What is Africa's problem?* Kampala: NRM Publications.

——. 2006. Statement by his Excellency Yoweri Kaguta Museveni, on the false negative headlines by the English newspapers, *New Vision* and *Monitor* about prospects of durable peace in Uganda, October 28, 2006. Uganda Media Centre, Office of the President. Downloaded October 31, 2006from www.mediacentre.go.ug.

Museveni, Yoweri K., with Elizabeth Kanyogonya and Kevin Shillington. 1997. *Sowing the mustard seed: The struggle for freedom and democracy in Uganda*. London: Macmillan.

Mutibwa, Phares Mukasa. 1992. *Uganda since independence: A story of unfulfilled hopes*. London: Hurst.

Ngoga, Pascal. 1998. Uganda: The National Resistance Army. In *African guerrillas*, edited by Christopher Clapham. Oxford: James Currey; Kampala: Fountain Press; and Bloomington: Indiana University Press.

Nordstrom, Carolyn. 1992. The backyard front. In *The paths to domination, resistance and terror*, edited by Carolyn Nordstrom and JoAnn Martin. Berkeley: University of California Press.

——. 1997. *A different kind of war story*. Philadelphia: University of Pennsylvania Press.

——. 1999. Requiem for the rational war. In *Deadly developments: Capitalism, states and war*, edited by Stephen Renya. Amsterdam: Gordon and Bearch.

——. 2001. Out of the shadows. In *Intervention and transnationalism in Africa: Global-local networks of power*, edited by Thomas Callaghy, Ronald Kassimir and Robert Latham. Cambridge: Cambridge University Press.

——. 2002. Terror warfare and the medicine of peace. In *Violence: A reader*, edited by Catherine Besteman. New York: Palgrave/Macmillan.

——. 2004. *Shadows of war: Violence, power, and international profiteering in the twenty-first century*. Berkeley: University of California Press.

Nyeko, Balam, and Okello Lucima. 2002. Profiles of the parties to the conflict. In *Protracted conflict, elusive peace: Initiatives to end the violence in northern Uganda*, edited by Okello Lucima. London: Conciliation Resources and Kacoke Madit.

OCHA/IRIN. 2004. *"When the sun sets, we start to worry . . .": An account of life in northern Uganda*. Nairobi: OCHA/IRIN. PDF version downloaded February 5, 2004, from htpp://www.irinnews.org.

Ocheng, D. O. 1955. Land tenure in Acholi. *Uganda Journal* 19(1): 57–61.

Odoki, Sabino Ocan. 1997. *Death rituals among the Lwos of Uganda: Their significance for the theology of death.* Gulu, Uganda: Gulu Catholic Press.

Ofcansky, Thomas P. 2000. Warfare and instability along the Sudan-Uganda border: A look at the 20th century. In *White Nile, black blood: War, leadership, and ethnicity from Khartoum to Kampala,* edited by Jay Spaulding and Stephanie Beswick. Asmara: Red Sea Press.

O'Kadameri, Billie. 2002. LRA/Government negotiations, 1993–94. In *Protracted conflict, elusive peace: Initiatives to end the violence in northern Uganda,* edited by Okello Lucima. London: Conciliation Resources and Kacoke Madit.

Okech, Lacito. 1953. *Tekwaro ki ker lobo Acholi (The cultural history of Acholiland).* Kampala: Eagle Press.

Okuku, Juma. 2002. Ethnicity, state power and the democratisation process in Uganda. *Discussion Paper no. 17.* Uppsala: Nordic Africa Institute.

Olaa, Ambrose. 2001. Uganda: The resilience of tradition: Displaced Acholi in Kitgum. In *Caught between borders: Response strategies of the internally displaced,* edited by Mark Vincent and Birgitte Refslund Sorensen. London: Pluto Press, in association with Norwegian Refugee Council.

Oloka-Onyango, J. 2000. New wine or new bottles? Movement politics and one-partyism in Uganda. In *No-party democracy in Uganda: Myths and realities,* edited by Justus Mugaju and J. Oloka-Onyango. Kampala: Fountain Publishers.

Omara-Otunnu, Amii. 1987. *Politics and the military in Uganda, 1890–1985.* London: MacMillan.

——. 1992. The struggle for democracy in Uganda. *Journal of Modern African Studies* 30 (3): 443–463.

——. 1995. The dynamics of conflict in Uganda. In *Conflict in Africa,* edited by Oliver Furley. London: I. B. Tauris Publishers.

Omona, George. 2005. Retreat for Acholi leaders: Together making a difference for peace (Acholi Leaders' Retreat, Paraa, 23rd–26th June 2005). Gulu, Uganda: ACORD Uganda.

Onyango-Obbo, Charles. 1997. *Uganda's poorly kept secrets.* Kampala: Fountain Publishers.

Onyango-Odongo, Jamal Mikla. 1976. The early history of the central Lwo. In *The central Lwo during the Aconya,* edited by J. M. Onyango-Odongo and J. B. Webster. Nairobi: East African Literature Bureau.

——. 1993. *Why Uganda's constitution failed.* Gulu, Uganda: Lapare General Agency.

——. 1998. The rebel war in northern Uganda. Unpublished book MS. Gulu: The Forum.

Onyango-Odongo, Jamal Mikla, and J. B. Webster, eds. 1976a. *The central Lwo during the Aconya.* Nairobi: East African Literature Bureau.

Onyango-Odongo, Jamal Mikla, and J. B. Webster. 1976b. A chronology for the Lwo-speaking peoples: Introduction. In *The central Lwo during the Aconya,* edited by J. M. Onyango-Odongo and J. B. Webster. Nairobi: East African Literature Bureau.

Orford, Anne. 2003. *Reading humanitarian intervention: Human rights and the use of force in international law.* Cambridge: Cambridge University Press.

Ortner, Sherry B. 1974. Is female to male as nature is to culture? In *Woman, culture and society,* edited by Michelle Zimbalist Rosaldo and Louise Lamphere. Stanford: Stanford University Press.

Oruni, Pilipo O. 1994. *What is right for Uganda.* London: Local Government Publication.

Oryema-Lalobo, Christine. 1999. *No hearts at home.* Kampala: FEMRITE Publications.

Ottemoeller, Dan. 1998. Popular perceptions of democracy: Elections and attitudes in Uganda. *Comparative political studies* 31 (1): 98–124.

Otunnu, Ogenga 1999a. Rwandese refugees and immigrants in Uganda. In *The path of a genocide: The Rwanda crisis from Uganda to Zaire,* edited by Howard Adelman and Astri Suhrke. Uppsala: Nordic Africa Institute.

——. 1999b. A historical analysis of the invasion by the Rwanda Patriotic Army (PRA). In *The path of a genocide: The Rwanda crisis from Uganda to Zaire,* edited by Howard Adelman and Astri Suhrke. Uppsala: Nordic Africa Institute.

——. 2002. Causes and consequences of the war in Acholiland. In *Protracted conflict, elusive peace: Initiatives to end the violence in northern Uganda,* edited by Okello Lucima. London: Conciliation Resources and Kacoke Madit.

Otunnu, Olara A. 2006. The Secret Genocide. *Foreign Policy* (July/August): 44–46.

Oywa, Rosalba. 1995. Uganda. In *Arms to fight, arms to protect: Women speak out about conflict,* edited by Olivia Bennett, Jo Bexley, and Kitty Warnock. London: Panos.

Pain, Dennis. 1997. *"Bending the spears": Producing consensus for peace and development in northern Uganda.* London: International Alert.

p'Anywar, Opoka J. M., and Anywar D. Rubben. 1999. Acholi traditional/cultural rituals, ceremonies and practices as a means of trauma healing of formerly abducted children. A paper prepared and dedicated to the authorities of World Vision children of war rehabilitation section. Gulu, Uganda: World Vision.

Parkin, David. 1985. Introduction. In *The anthropology of evil,* edited by David Parkin. Oxford: Basil Blackwell.

Parliament of Uganda. 1997. Report of the committee on defence and internal affairs on the war in northern Uganda. Kampala: The Parliament of Uganda.

p'Bitek, Okot. 1962. Acholi folk tales. *Transition* (6/7): 21–24.

——. 1966. *Song of Lawino.* Nairobi: East African Pub. House.

——. 1970a. *African religions in Western scholarship.* Kampala: East African Literature Bureau.

——. 1970b. *Song of Ocol.* Nairobi: East African Publishing House.

——. 1971. *Religion of the central Luo.* Nairobi: East African Literature Bureau.

——. 1973. *Africa's cultural revolution.* Nairobi: MacMillan Books for Africa.

——. 1974. *Horn of my love.* Nairobi: East African Educational Publishers.

——. 1986. *Artist, the ruler: Essays on art, culture, and values.* Nairobi: Heinemann Kenya.

People's Voice for Peace et al. 1999. Women's experiences of armed conflict, Gulu district, 1986–1999. Draft report. Gulu: People's Voice for Peace in cooperation with Isis-WICCE (Women's International Cross-Cultural Exchange), ACORD, PANOS, and UNICEF.

Pido, J. P. Odoch. 2000. Personhood and art: Social change and commentary among the Acoli. In *African philosophy as cultural inquiry*, edited by Ivan Karp and D. A. Masolo. Bloomington: Indiana University Press.

Pirouet, M. L. 1991. Human rights issues in Museveni's Uganda. In *Changing Uganda: The dilemmas of structural adjustment and revolutionary change*, edited by Holger Bernt Hansen and Michael Twaddle. London: James Currey; Kampala: Fountain Press; Athens: Ohio University Press; Nairobi: Heinemann Kenya.

Postlethwaite, J. R. P. 1947. *I look back.* London: T. V. Boardman.

Pratt, Mary Louise. 1992. *Imperial eyes: Travel writing and transculturation.* London: Routledge.

Prunier, Gérard. 2004. Rebel movements and proxy warfare: Uganda, Sudan and the Congo (1986–99). *African Affairs* 103 (412): 359–383.

Quinn, Joanna. 2004. Constraints: The Un-doing of the Ugandan Truth Commission. *Human Rights Quarterly* 26 (2): 401–427.

Radcliffe-Brown, A. R. 1952. *Structure and function in primitive society: Essays and addresses.* London: Cohen and West.

Ranger, Terence. 1994. The invention of tradition revisited. In *Inventions and boundaries: Historical and anthropological approaches to the study of ethnicity and nationalism*, edited by Preben Kaarsholm and Jan Hultin. Roskilde, Denmark: International Development Studies, Roskilde University.

Reid, Richard. 2002. *Political power in pre-colonial Buganda: Economy, society and warfare in the nineteenth century.* Oxford: James Currey; Kampala: Fountain Publishers; Athens: Ohio University Press.

Republic of Uganda. 1995. *Constitution of the Republic of Uganda.* Kampala: The Republic of Uganda.

——. 2000. *The Amnesty Act, 2000.* Kampala: The Republic of Uganda.

Richards, Audrey Isabel. 1939. *Land, labour and diet in northern Rhodesia: An economic study of the Bemba tribe.* Oxford: Oxford University Press.

Richards, Paul. 1996. *Fighting for the rain forest: War, youth and resources in Sierra Leone.* Oxford: International African Institute and James Currey; Portsmouth, N.H.: Heinemann.

——. 1998. Postscript to the 1998 printing of *Fighting for the rain forest: War, youth & resources in Sierra Leone.* Oxford: International African Institute and James Currey; Portsmouth, N.H.: Heinemann.

———. 2000. Rain-forest resource conflicts: Would stakeholder analysis help pacify labouring casuals in Sierra Leone? In *Tropical forest resource dynamics and conservation: From local to global issues*, edited by K. F. Wiersum. Wageningen, The Netherlands: Wageningen University.

Ricoeur, Paul. 1991. *From text to action: Essays in hermeneutics, II.* Evanston, Ill.: Northwestern University Press.

Robben, Antonius C. G. M. 2000. State terror in the Netherworld: Disappearance and reburial in Argentina. In *Death squad: The anthropology of state terror*, edited by Jeffrey A. Sluka. Philadelphia: University of Pennsylvania Press.

Rusch, Walter. 1975. *Klassen und Staat in Buganda vor der Kolonialzeit: Über die Entwicklung der Produktionsverhältnisse in Buganda bis zum Ende des 19. Jahrhunderts und die Herausbildung eines Staates, seinen Aufbau und seine Funktionen.* Berlin: Akademie-Verlag.

Rwabwoogo, Musisha Odrek. 2002. *Uganda districts information handbook.* 5th ed. Kampala: Fountain Publishers.

Säfholm, Per. 1973. *The River-Lakes Nilotes: Politics of an African tribal group.* Uppsala: Acta Universitatis Upsaliensis/Studia Sociologica Upsaliensia.

Sahlins, Marshall David. 1999. Two or three things that I know about culture. *Journal of the Royal Anthropological Institute Incorporating Man* 5 (3): 399–421.

SAPRIN. 2001. Uganda country report: A synthesis of the four SAPRI studies. Washington: SAPRIN (Structural Adjustment Participatory Review Initiative Network). PDF version downloaded April 22, 2003, from http://www.saprin.org.

Savage, G. A. R. 1955. *A short Acoli-English and English-Acoli vocabulary.* Kampala, Nairobi: Eagle Press.

Schoenbrun, David L. 1993. A past whose time has come: Historical context and history in eastern Africa's Great Lakes. In *History making in Africa*, edited by V. Y. Mudimbe and B. Jewsiewicki. Middletown, Conn.: Wesleyan University Press.

Seaton, Jean. 1999. The new ethnic wars and the media. In *The media of conflict: war reporting and representations of ethnic violence*, edited by Tim Allen and Jean Seaton. London: Zed Books.

Seligman, C. G., and Brenda Z. Salaman Seligman. 1932. *Pagan tribes of the Nilotic Sudan.* London: Routledge and Sons.

Sichone, Owen. 2001. Pure anthropology in a highly indebted poor country. *Journal of Southern African Studies* 27 (2): 369–379.

Sida. 2001. Country strategy Sverige Uganda 2001–2005, January 2001. Stockholm: Sida (Swedish International Development Co-operation Agency). PDF version downloaded August 4, 2003, from http://www.sida.se.

———. 2006. Sida country report 2005: Uganda. Stockholm: Sida (Swedish International Development Co-operation Agency). PDF version downloaded November 9, 2006, from http://www.sida.se.

Simons, Anna. 1999. War: Back to the future. *Annual Review of Anthropology* 28: 73–108.

Sluka, Jeffrey A. 2000. Introduction: State terror and anthropology. In *Death squad: The anthropology of state terror*, edited by Jeffrey A. Sluka. Philadelphia: University of Pennsylvania Press.

Southall, Aidan. 1998. Isolation and underdevelopment: Periphery and centre. In *Developing Uganda*, edited by Holger Bernt Hansen and Michael Twaddle. Oxford: James Currey; Kampala: Fountain Publishers; Athens: Ohio University Press; Nairobi: EAEP

Soyinka, Wole. 2004. *Climate of fear.* London: Profile Books.

Speke, John Hanning. 1863. *Journal of the discovery of the source of the Nile.* Edinburgh: W. Blackwood and Sons.

———. 1864. *What led to the discovery of the source of the Nile.* London: W. Blackwood and Sons.

———. 1865. *Upptäckten af Nilens källor. Resa genom förut okända trakter af Afrika.* Stockholm: E. T. Bergegren.

Stanley, Henry. 1878a. *Through the Dark Continent or the sources of the Nile around the great lakes of equatorial Africa and down the Livingstone River to the Atlantic Ocean.* London.

———. 1878b. *Genom de svartes verldsdel eller Nilens källor; kring de stora sjöarne och utför Livingstone-floden till atlantiska hafvet.* Stockholm: Albert Bonniers Förlag.

———. 1890a. *In darkest Africa or the quest, rescue and retreat of Emin, governor of Equatoria.* London: Sampson Low.

———. 1890b. *I det mörkaste Afrika: Emin Paschas uppsökande, befrielse och återtåg.* Stockholm: Norstedts.

Suárez-Orozco, Marcelo M., and Antonius C. G. M. Robben. 2000. Interdisciplinary perspectives on violence and trauma. In *Cultures under siege: Collective violence and trauma*, edited by Antonius C. G. M. Robben and Marcelo M. Suárez-Orozco. Cambridge: Cambridge University Press.

Tambiah, Stanley Jeyaraja. 1989. Ethnic conflict in the world today. *American Ethnologist* 16 (2): 225–349.

———. 1990. *Magic, science, religion, and the scope of rationality.* Cambridge: Cambridge University Press.

Tangri, Robert, and Andrew Mwenda. 2001. Corruption and cronyism in Uganda's privatization in the 1990s. *African Affairs* 100 (398): 117–133.

Taussig, Michael. 1984. Culture of terror, space of death: Roger Casement's Putumayo report and the explanation of torture. *Comparative Studies in Society and History* 26 (3): 467–497.

Taylor, Christopher C. 1999a. A gendered genocide: Tutsi women and Hutu extremists in the 1994 Rwanda genocide. *Polar* 22 (1): 42–54.

———. 1999b. *Sacrifice as terror: The Rwandan genocide of 1994.* Oxford: Berg.

Turshen, Meredith. 2001. An analysis of systematic rape and sexual abuse of women during armed conflict in Africa. In *Victims, perpetrators or actors? Gender, armed conflict and political violence*, edited by Caroline O. N. Moser and Fiona C. Clark. London: Zed Books.

Turton, David. 1997. Introduction: War and ethnicity. In *War and ethnicity: Global connections and local violence*, edited by David Turton: Rochester, N.Y.: Rochester University of Rochester Press.

Twaddle, Michael, and Holger Bernt Hansen. 1998. The changing state of Uganda. In *Developing Uganda*, edited by Holger Bernt Hansen and Michael Twaddle. Oxford: James Currey; Kampala: Fountain Publishers; Athens: Ohio University Press; Nairobi: EAEP

Uganda Human Rights Commission. 2003. *Annual Report January 2001–September 2002*. Kampala: Uganda Human Rights Commission. PDF version downloaded April 21, 2003, from http://www.uhrc.org.

UNICEF/World Vision. 1997. *Shattered innocence: Testimonies of children abducted in northern Uganda*. Kampala: UNICEF Uganda Country Office/World Vision Uganda.

United Democratic Christian Movement/Army. N.d. [untitled manifesto]. Unpublished document in possession of the author.

U.S. Department of State. 2001. Statement on the designation of 39 organizations on the USA Patriot Act's "Terrorist exclusion list" as of December 5, 2001. Downloaded March 4, 2002, from http://www.state.gov.

Usher-Wilson, L. C. 1947. An Acholi hunt. *Uganda Journal* 11 (1): 30–37.

Vincent, Joan. 1999. War in Uganda: North and south. In *Deadly developments: Capitalism, states and war*, edited by S. P. Reyna and R. E. Downs. Amsterdam: Gordon and Breach Publishers.

Wallensteen, Peter, and Margareta Sollenberg. 2001. Armed conflict, 1989–2000. *Journal of Peace Research* 38 (5): 629–644.

Wallerstein, Immanuel Maurice. 1974. *The modern world-system*. New York: Academic Press.

Ward, Kevin. 1995. The Church of Uganda amidst conflict: The interplay between church and politics in Uganda since 1962. In *Religion and politics in East Africa: The period since independence*, edited by Holger Bernt Hansen and Michael Twaddle. London: James Currey; Nairobi: EAEP; Kampala: Fountain Publishers; Athens: Ohio University Press.

———. 2001. "The armies of the Lord": Christianity, rebels and the state in northern Uganda, 1986–1999. *Journal of Religion in Africa* 31 (2): 187–221.

Weeks, Willet. 2002. *Pushing the envelope: Moving beyond "protected villages" in northern Uganda*. New York: Report submitted to the United Nations office for the coordination of humanitarian affairs. PDF version downloaded September 6, 2002, from http://www.idpproject.org.

Werbner, Richard. 1998a. Beyond oblivion: Confronting memory crisis. In *Memory and the postcolony: African anthropology and the critique of power*, edited by Richard Werbner. London: Zed Books.

——. 1998b. Smoke from the barrel of the gun: Postwars of the dead, memory and reinscription in Zimbabwe. In *Memory and the postcolony: African anthropology and the critique of power*, edited by Richard Werbner. London: Zed Books.

White, Luise. 2000. *Speaking with vampires: Rumor and history in colonial Africa.* Berkeley: University of California Press.

Whitehead, Neil L. 2004. On the poetics of violence. In *Violence*, edited by Neil Whitehead. Santa Fe, N.M.: School of American Research Press; Oxford: James Currey.

Whyte, Susan Reynolds. 1997. *Questioning misfortune: The pragmatics of uncertainty in eastern Uganda.* Cambridge: Cambridge University Press.

Wild, J. V. 1954. *Early travellers in Acholi.* Edinburgh: Thomas Nelson and Sons/East African Literature Bureau.

Willis, Roy G., and Signe Howell, eds. 1989. *Societies at peace: Anthropological perspectives.* London: Routledge.

Wilson, Richard A. 2001. *The politics of truth and reconciliation in South Africa: Legitimizing the post-apartheid state.* Cambridge: Cambridge University Press.

Winans, Edgar. 1992. Hyenas on the border. In *The paths to domination, resistance and terror*, edited by Carolyn Nordstrom and JoAnn Martin. Berkeley: University of California Press.

Women's Commission for Refugee Women and Children. 2001. *Against all odds: Surviving the war on adolescents. Promoting the protection and capacity of Ugandan and Sudanese adolescents in northern Uganda. Participatory research study with adolescents in northern Uganda May—July 2001.* PDF version downloaded September 10, 2002, from http://www.womenscommission.org.

Woodward, Peter. 1991. Uganda and southern Sudan, 1986–9: New regimes and peripheral politics. In *Changing Uganda: The dilemmas of structural adjustment and revolutionary change*, edited by Holger Bernt Hansen and Michael Twaddle. London: James Currey; Kampala: Fountain Press; Athens: Ohio University Press; Nairobi: Heinemann Kenya.

World Health Organization. 2001. Outbreak of Ebola haemorrhagic fever, Uganda, August 2000—January 2001. *Weekly epidemiological record* 76 (6): 41–46.

——. 2002. *Report on the Global HIV/AIDS Epidemic 2002.* Geneva: World Health Organization/UNAIDS. Downloaded November 2, 2006, from http://www.who.int/en.

World Health Organization et al. 2005. *Health and mortality survey among internally displaced persons in Gulu, Kitgum and Pader districts, northern Uganda.* PDF version downloaded November 2, 2006, from http://www.who.int/en.

Young, Allan. 1995. *The harmony of illusions: Inventing post-traumatic stress disorder.* Princeton, N.J.: Princeton University Press.

atre, 155; importance of, in social life, 146

Conflict: in Africa, 115

Contact zone. *See* Frontier

Control and balance: existential, 10, 14, 190. *See also* Jackson, Michael

Controller: rebel ritual functionary, 5, 221

Co pee camp, 150–151

Corner Kilak: battles of, 217–218

Corruption, 126, 205

Cosmology: definition of, 7, 26, 198; of terror, 189; war and cosmological imbalance, 217

Counterinsurgency strategies, 71–74, 84, 89, 106, 154; civilians taking part in, 91; helicopter gunships and, 90, 137, 233; mass-arrests (*panda gari*) and, 175–176; rape in, 90, 181–182; treason charges and, 9, 90, 93, 105, 110, 121, 229

Crazzolara, J. Pascale, 47, 53, 192, 211

Critical events, 216

Culture: in becoming, 32, 46, 61; definition of, 7; essentialism and, 109; as ontology, 189; personality and, 170; roots of, 199, 205–206

Curse, 51, 213; blessing and, as sides of same coin, 213, 217, 230; embedded in social life, 217; from God, 217; and power of magic words, 216

Daloz, Jean-Pascal. *See* Chabal, Patrick

Das, Veena, 7, 25, 157, 182, 216, 223

De Boeck, Filip, 146, 187

de Certeau, Michel, 50

Democracy, 11, 116, 218

Democratic Party, 66

De Temmerman, Els, 61, 76, 111, 178

Detention centers, 121

Development schemes, 134; aid dependency, 36, 113; corruption and, 126; jargon of, 116; lack of, 104; New World

Order, 126; spiritual violence and, 204; world-wide restratification, 126

Diaspora, 120, 219; big meeting (*kacoke madit*) of, 197

Diawara, Manthia, 126

Division: Christian and Muslim, 65; along educational lines, 77; ethnic, 68, north and south, 74; 81, 83, 94, 95, 194; of Pentecostalism and ancestral beliefs, 162, 207–208; along primordial lines, 80–81; youth against, 35, 194, 238, 244

Dolan, Chris, 79, 91, 113, 134, 185; on social torture, 135–136

Doom, Ruddy, and Koen Vlassenroot, 61, 71, 80, 118, 144; on peace as absence of violence, 200

Douglas, Mary, 180–181, 183

Dwyer, John Orr, 38, 42, 44, 52, 220

Ebola hemorrhagic fever, 169, 180, 187–190, 251 n.4, 252 n.5

Education, 82

Egeland, Jan, 128, 141

Ehrenreich, Rosa, 109, 115, 120

Elders: as government agents, 212–213; as partial, 218–219; "veranda" elders, 215, 218. *See also* Patrilineage

Emergency: chronic, 134; temporary, 135

Enemy: in dirty war, 86; to kill an, 210; traditional, 210. *See also* War

Englund, Harri, 116, 117, 129, 157

Equatorial province, 56

Escape: from the LRA/M, 221–222

Ethnicity: boundaries and, 46–47; deconstruction of ethnic categories, 82–83; as the explanation for conflict, 8, 64, 108–109; stereotypes and, 7, 35, 41, 60, 64, 75, 78–80, 94, 181–182, 238; as stigma, 26–27, 61, 78–79, 106, 219, 238. *See also* Division

Mudoola, Dan M., 42

Muno. See Foreigner

Museveni, Yoweri, 4, 63, 67–68, 73, 74, 82–84, 89, 92, 105–107, 113–114, 122–123, 127–128, 141, 194–197, 223, 227–230, 237, 242

Mutibwa, Phares Mukasa, 67, 141, 225

Mwenda, Andrew, and Roger Tangri, 125, 126

Myth: biblical, 49; of the spear and the bead, 47–52; storytelling and, 49–51

National Army for the Liberation of Uganda (NALU), 70

National Resistance Movement/Army (NRM/A), 67, 71, 72, 76, 82–84, 105, 182, 194

Negative peace. *See* Peace

New Moral Order, 5, 202

Ngoga, Pascal, 68–69

Nilo-Hamites, 36

Nilotes, 36; decentralized sociopolitical organization of, 34, 40, 66; nationalism of, 66, 94

Ninth October Movement (NOM), 70

No hearts at home (Oryema-Lalobo), 140

Nordstrom, Carolyn, 13, 89, 132, 152–153, 155, 239

Obote, Milton Apollo, 45, 65–68, 71, 74, 75, 82, 94, 215, 225

Ochora, Walter, 93, 95

Odhiambo, E. S. Atieno, 4

Odoki, Sabino Ocan, 159, 189, 236

Okello, Tito Lutwa, 67–68, 71, 74, 75, 94, 214, 215, 225

Okuku, Juma, 31, 42, 54, 75, 94, 95, 102, 110, 238

Old Homestead, The (Lamwaka), 222–223, 241

Oloka-Onyango, J., 68, 95

Olum olum: insurgents, 71, 75. *See also* Uganda People's Democratic Movement/Army

Omara-Otunnu, Amii, 76, 78, 83, 101, 107

Onen Acana II. *See* Payira

Ontological: security, 5, 51, 246 n. 10; stress and uncertainty, 189; terror, 189

Onyango-Odongo, Jamal Mikla, 45, 51, 52, 74, 82, 172

Operation Iron Fist, 112, 113, 197, 226, 229, 233

Orford, Anne, 134, 240

Oryema-Lalobo, Christine, 140, 164, 165

Ottemoeller, Dan, 94

Otti, Vincent, 85, 108, 136, 238

Otunnu Ogenga, 71, 75, 112

Otunnu Olara, 169, 195, 227

Outsiders: researchers as, 16, 22–23; Western diplomats as, 26

Oywa, Rosalba, 71, 182–183

Pabo camp, 157–158, 172, 175

Padibe: Acholi chiefdom, 44, 45

Pagak camp, 1–4, 11, 15, 137

Paicho: Acholi chiefdom, 44

Palaro camp, 131–132, 135, 139, 144–145, 240

Paluo, 36, 53

Pan-Africanism, 37, 40

Parkin, David, 225

Participant observation, 19

Patiko: Acholi chiefdom, 32, 56

Patrilineage: clan ancestors and, 207–208; clan elders and, 201; exogamous groupings and, 34, 185, 192; praisenames of, 192

Patrilocality, 184

Payira: Acholi chiefdom, 32, 43–45, 212, 217, 225; Chief Awich of, 44, Chief Onen Acana II of, 45, 212; Chief Yona Odiya of, 217–218

Vincent, Joan, 31, 40, 66, 69, 101

Violence: against civilians, 1–3, 154, 213; as a logic of its own, 100; entering the private sphere, 96–97, 189, 205; everyday routines and, 6–7, 238; extreme mutilations, 91, 156; historical conditions of, 117, 232; -proneness, 25, 223; retraction of killed enemies, 210. *See also* Structural violence

Vlassenroot, Koen. *See* Doom, Ruddy, and Koen Vlassenroot

Wallensteen, Peter, and Margareta Sollenberg, 200

Wallerstein, Immanuel Maurice, 242

War: on the Acholi, 107–108, 194; of annexation, 59; blessing of, 83, 211–219; as business, 140, 142, 152–155; colonial imagination of, 61; dirty, 11–12, 86, 89, 136, 200; government, 210; initiator of, 214–215; interclan, 210; of the past, 208–209; postmodern insurgencies and, 13; proxy, 85; quantitative definitions of, 199–200; regional, 88; re-politicizing, 121, women and children in, 208–209, 222. *See also* Terrorism

Ward, Kevin, 78

Weeks, Willet, 34, 73, 105, 115, 141

Werbner, Richard, 195, 241

West Nile Bank Front (WNBF), 70

White, Luise, 173, 193

Whitehead, Neil L., 223

Whyte, Susan Reynolds, 104

Wild, J. V., 49

Wilson, Richard A., 232

Winans, Edgar, 114

Witch (*lajok*), 203; witchdoctor, 205

Women's Commission for Refugee Women and Children, 8, 111, 115, 190

Woodward, Peter, 69, 76, 96

Young, Allan, 161

Youth, 194, 238, 243–244; definition of, 25–26, 245 n.4

Sverker Finnström is a researcher and lecturer in the Department of Social Anthropology at Stockholm University, Sweden.

Library of Congress Cataloging-in-Publication Data
Finnström, Sverker.
Living with bad surroundings : war, history, and everyday moments in northern Uganda / Sverker Finnström.
p. cm. — (Cultures and practice of violence series)
Includes bibliographical references and index.
ISBN 978-0-8223-4174-1 (cloth : alk. paper)
ISBN 978-0-8223-4191-8 (pbk. : alk. paper)
1. Acoli (African people)—Social life and customs. 2. War and society—Uganda—Northern Province. I. Title.
DT433.245.A35F54 2008
303.6'60996761—dc22   2007033637